Neither Dies nor Surrenders
A History of the Republican Party in Florida, 1867–1970

Peter D. Klingman

Neither Dies nor Surrenders
A History of the Republican Party in Florida, 1867–1970

Foreword by
Samuel Proctor

University Presses of Florida

University of Florida Press
Gainesville

Library of Congress Cataloging in Publication Data

Klingman, Peter D., 1945–
 Neither dies nor surrenders.

 Bibliography: p.
 Includes index.
 1. Republican Party (Fla.)—History. I. Title.
 JK2358.F5K55 1984   324.2759'04   84-7253
 ISBN 0-8130-0754-2 (alk. paper)

Copyright © 1984 by Peter D. Klingman
All rights reserved.
Printed in the U.S.A. on acid-free paper.

UNIVERSITY PRESSES OF FLORIDA is the central agency for scholarly publishing of the State of Florida's university system, producing books selected for publication by the faculty editorial committees of Florida's nine public universities: Florida A&M University (Tallahassee), Florida Atlantic University (Boca Raton), Florida International University (Miami), Florida State University (Tallahassee), University of Central Florida (Orlando), University of Florida (Gainesville), University of North Florida (Jacksonville), University of South Florida (Tampa), University of West Florida (Pensacola).

   Orders for books published by all member presses of University Presses of Florida should be addressed to University Presses of Florida, 15 NW 15th Street, Gainesville, FL 32603.

Contents

Foreword, by Samuel Proctor, vii
Preface, xi

Part One. Participation
    1. Ripon to Reconstruction — 3
    2. Advent of Florida Republicanism — 11
    3. Republican Factions and Reconstruction Politics — 26
    4. Politics of Reconstruction: The Record of the Republican Party — 49

Part Two. Isolation
    5. Southern Strategy Begins — 65
    6. Shaping Dissent and the Search for Order — 76
    7. Republicanism in the Solid South — 94
    8. Presidential Republicanism in Florida — 112
    9. Two-Party Vision, One-Party Reality — 130
    10. Primaries and Patronage, 1932–1952 — 141

Part Three. Reformation
    11. The New Breed and the Old Problem — 155
    12. The Kirk Years — 168
    13. Epilogue as Prologue — 190

Notes, 197
References, 217
Index, 225

For Pat Dodson,
Republican, Florida historian, and friend

and for Teresa

Foreword

THE PERIOD OF Reconstruction has produced more stereotyped ideas in the South than any other era of American history. The southern view that the Republican party was an evil influence in the South developed after the Civil War and persisted well into the twentieth century. Many Americans, particularly southerners, believed that Republicans had come to power only because so many whites had been disenfranchised and blacks had been given the right to vote by federal troops. Republicans, according to this view, were merely carpetbaggers, supported in their attempt to exploit and control the South by a few traitorous scalawags. Black voters were lured into the Republican party by the promise of material improvement (40 acres and a mule), education, political power, and a better way of life, but the party did not deliver on its promises. Instead, many believed that Republican opportunists bled the South dry and, after home rule was established in 1876, left it a legacy of high taxes, debts, and a history of corruption and malfeasance.

The South was redeemed, southerners believed, by the Bourbon Democrats, and the Republican party disappeared from the scene for nearly a century. When it looked as though the party might revive—during the Populist revolt of the 1890s and when Al Smith ran as the Democratic nominee for president in 1928—there were enough sensible white southerners to ensure that the Democratic party retained its majority status.

After World War II, when the South was no longer so dependent on agriculture and its industries and population were growing, there came to the South a revived, or perhaps new, Republican party—conservative, business-oriented, attracting an ever growing number of young, educated, energetic people who were on their way up socially and economically. These people needed the reassurance offered by the Republican party that their money and status would be secure and unthreatened.

Peter Klingman has set out to recount the full history of the Republican party in Florida from Reconstruction to the 1970s. While he shows that there is some validity to the stereotypic beliefs we encounter, Klingman challenges the "traditional idea that Negroes, carpetbaggers, and scalawags 'ruled' in Florida during Reconstruction." In drawing a complete picture of the party and the times, he has delved into the records, sparse as they are, read the newspapers, and talked with people who have played an important role in the state's Republican party since mid-century, and, in what he calls "Epilogue as Prologue," he hints at the direction he believes the party will take in the future.

The person who had the idea for this study was the antithesis of any stereotypical southern Republican. Mayhew Wilson (Pat) Dodson III, a native Floridian and a student of history, saw the need for a history of the party's activities in Florida that would put to rest the inaccuracies, misconceptions, and distortions that were based more on hearsay than on fact. He insisted that it was a job for a trained historian who could make good use of primary source material. Fortunately, before Pat's death he was able to work with the author.

Pat Dodson was born in Pensacola on October 7, 1929. He received a bachelor's degree from Vanderbilt University and a Master of Arts in English and history from the University of Florida. The University of West Florida conferred an honorary degree on him in 1974 in recognition of his many contributions to his community, the state, and the South.

While Pat was active in many civic and church organizations, his special loves were history and historical preservation. He served as chairman of the Pensacola Historical Commission and was a major force in establishing the Historic Pensacola Preservation Board. As chairman of the Florida Bicentennial Commission, he insisted that its emphasis be placed on publications, the research and writing of county histories, historic architectural inventories, the establishment and support of museums and parks, and the setting up of historic sites and properties.

Pat played an active role in government, serving as director of administration in the state's Department of Transportation and as a member of the Board of Regents. A recognized leader of Florida's Republican party, he was prominently involved in the presidential, gubernatorial, and senatorial campaigns of the 1960s and 1970s. A builder and developer, he was also a successful businessman in advertising and public relations. His honors were many—he is listed in *Who's Who in the South and Southwest*, and he received recognition from the American Association for State and Local History and many civic organizations.

Pat was also a published writer, poet, and editor. His wife, Peggy, and his children, David and Deborah Ann, are continuing the family tradition of active involvement in government, education, and civic affairs in Pensacola and West Florida.

Samuel Proctor

Preface

WHEN PAT DODSON and I first began discussing my writing a history of the Republican party in Florida, I volunteered two caveats: one, I was not then (or now) a registered Republican, and two, I doubted that I had much in common with conservative Republicanism found in the South. Pat's reply is what made this book possible. He wanted a nonpartisan, scholarly, and readable history that no Florida Republican personally involved could produce. As he himself wisely pointed out, one had only to read William Cash's partisan history of the Democratic party in Florida to appreciate the value of a more objective approach.

Most prefaces suggest to the reader what can be expected in the pages that follow; I think it more appropriate here to tell at the outset what the reader may *not* expect. *Neither Dies nor Surrenders* is not a political history of Florida. Rather, it is a narrative of a single political party, one which played only a minor role for much of the time between the Civil War and the present. Little or no effort is made to describe what Florida Democrats were doing, although I have attempted to set each chapter in a national or regional context. On the other hand, detailed accounts of how, when, and why Florida Republicans tried to work their way up to a status of parity with the Democratic party, and why for the most part they fell short, are the recurring motifs. Nor does this study seek to be encyclopedic, to encompass all Florida GOP activity, county by county or precinct by precinct. Even principal Florida Republicans are treated from the point of view of their relationship with the party generally rather than from a focus upon their contributions to Florida government. Such a perspective doubtless will not please everyone, but it seems most reasonable to me.

The narrative is divided into three parts. In the era immediately following the Civil War, Florida Republicans were active in state government—the politics of participation. Despite the traditionally unwholesome image of how Republicans acted in that era, I have found evidence to reinforce modern scholarship's view that Reconstruction was much less radical and unruly, at least in Florida, than modern Floridians like to think.

Following the end of Reconstruction, the Florida Republican party fell into a long and steep decline—the politics of isolation—which lasted until the middle of the twentieth century. Politically moribund for almost a century after 1876, the Florida GOP played only an occasional role in state and national politics. In discussing this era of Florida GOP history, I have attempted to draw out the few key personalities and elections that were of special interest. Republican factionalism in this second and quieter phase was every bit as bitter, and in some respects even more so, than in the periods preceding and succeeding it.

The final era of party development traced in this study is that which followed the defeat of Barry Goldwater in 1964—the politics of reformation. I have detailed the overthrow of the old patronage leadership in Florida's GOP and what motivated that upheaval, and I have sketched an outline of the major political issues and controversies of Claude R. Kirk's venture into Florida politics. This outline is not a full-scale judgment of Republican state politics in Florida from 1966 to 1970, nor should it be so interpreted. Such a survey awaits the passage of time, to gain perspective, and the desire to write a second volume. I do hint at the direction of the party for the future, however, in the last chapter, "Epilogue as Prologue."

Acknowledgments

Several people have contributed so significantly to whatever success this book may enjoy that I cannot thank them enough. Pat Dodson, shortly before his death following a protracted battle with cancer, asked me to write a history of his political party. Without his personal interest and enthusiasm, his keen insight into Florida GOP politics, his contacts with other politicians, as well as his generous financial grant to the author, this project could not have been completed. Bill and Bobbie James, with great faith and trust, graciously allowed me to borrow their official party records and correspondence for two years longer than either they or I had originally planned. Professor Sam Proctor, director of the University of Florida oral history program, furnished me tapes and transcripts for my oral history interviews. Staff members of each of the libraries and repositories in which I researched were generous with assistance. The late Professor Bertrand Heflin of Daytona Beach Community College, a former promotion manager of *Collier's* magazine, and Professor Philip A. Drimmel, also of Daytona Beach Community College, patiently and carefully read and criticized my drafts.

To all of these persons go my grateful thanks.

Part One. Participation

1

Ripon to Reconstruction

AMERICANS PRESENT at the birth of the Republican party more than a century ago could hardly have foreseen its flourishing survival in our modern era. It was, after all, a party formed around a narrow political issue, and it comprised reluctant joiners from other political affiliations, none of whom had much in common. The original Republican party centered primarily in the Midwest and Northwest, giving it sectional identification. Yet the protesters of the Kansas-Nebraska Act in 1854 united under the banner of the new Republican party, rapidly added to their numbers, and grew into a national organization. Six years later, a Republican entered the White House.

More than anything else, it was the Kansas-Nebraska Act, sponsored by Stephen A. Douglas, which sparked the rise of the Republican party. Like other mid-nineteenth-century visionaries, the Illinois senator foresaw the benefits of a transcontinental railroad. He wanted a route from Chicago to California, but others advocated more southerly routes. To win southern support for his proposal and for his probable presidential campaign in 1860, Douglas wrote the controversial Kansas-Nebraska Act, which provoked the creation of the Republican party, touched off anew the sectional conflict over slavery, inflamed Kansas in a bloody preview of the Civil War, and ended all hope of compromise between North and South.

The Kansas-Nebraska Act rested upon the theory of popular sovereignty. By allowing residents of any territory in the United States to decide for themselves whether to permit slavery, Douglas's bill overturned the cornerstone of sectional compromise, the 36°30′ line established by the Missouri Compromise in 1820. Under the new law it was possible (if economically impractical) for slavery to be extended north of that line—an important psychological victory for the South. Many northerners—both abolitionists, who abhorred slavery on moral grounds, and nonabolitionists, who feared slaves' competition with free labor—opposed expanding "the peculiar institution."

One such northerner was Alvin Bovay, an obscure Wisconsin politician. His disgust with the Kansas-Nebraska Act and with persons in Wisconsin who supported it led him to call a meeting of other dissenters for 28 February 1854 in Ripon's Congregational Church. A second, more formal convention was held in July in Madison, where a new slate of candidates for local, state, and national offices, all opposed to the Kansas-Nebraska Act, was fielded for the November elections. "Republican" was selected as the official name, and the new party was under way.

Nobody celebrated the birth of the Republican party. In most of the political contests that climaxed in the outbreak of the Civil War, there was little comfort. It was an era during which traditional politics broke down.[1] Whig and Democratic partisanship independent of section was eliminated by the deep fissures that appeared in the ideology of each party. Though the Kansas-Nebraska Act appeared to have caused the advent of the Republican party, the party grew in response to the fundamental polarization of North and South. Each section came to see the other as the opposite of a well-ordered society—politically, economically, and socially. While southerners insisted that slavery was the bedrock of civilized society, northerners perceived in slavery a threat to free labor, free soil, and free men.[2] At the very least slavery was not to be allowed to expand. The existing political framework could not reconcile these differences, and the traditional party organizations broke apart.

Against this political background, the Republican party was formed in 1854. At the outset, people seemed more inclined to agree with its principles than to join its ranks. Even as the party grew in stature and numbers outside Wisconsin, few professional politicians participated in its early activities; most wanted to preserve the status quo of the Whig and Democratic parties despite their increasing ineffectiveness. There was little evidence that the fledgling Republican party would fare better than had the many third-party movements preceding it.

For some politicians the chief problem with Republicanism was its identification with abolitionism. Ignored or overlooked was the fact that in 1854 many Republicans wanted only to contain slavery in the southern states. Even the man who first led the party into the White House was reluctant in 1854 to become a Republican. Abraham Lincoln did not yet openly support abolition, though he personally abhorred slavery. While he encouraged his fellow Illinois Whigs to cooperate with Illinois Republicans, he at first refused to join the party.[3] Eventually, millions voted for Republicans, and the party led the nation through the Civil War and its aftermath. This fact affected Republicans' political fortunes not only in the late nineteenth century but in much of the twentieth century as well, especially in the South and certainly in Florida. Until recently, the post–Civil War history of the party in the South was one of trying to redeem its reputation. In no other southern state was this more difficult than in Florida.

From the vantage point of the late twentieth century, it is clear that Florida escaped the worst effects of the Civil War. The state was of material and strategic importance to the Confederate cause and provided its full share of men for the fight. Florida served as the primary food basket of the South. Beef, grain, and other foodstuffs were produced on farms and plantations in the interior, and most of the salt consumed in the South during the war years was manufactured in works scattered along Florida's coasts. Florida's numerous harbors and inlets were useful as entrepôts for commerce that became the Confederacy's lifeline to Europe despite the Union blockade.[4]

Floridians suffered materially and economically: of 16,000 men in uniform, more than 6,000 were wounded or killed, and assessed value in real and personal property, excluding losses by emancipation, fell from $47 million in 1860 to $25 million in 1865. Emancipation resulted in another $22 million loss.[5] There was, however, little actual destruction of property in Florida, and there were no major military engagements, Olustee being the principal battleground. While costly in human lives, the battle did not approximate the carnage of Shiloh, Cold Harbor, or Gettysburg. Only a fanatic would find comparisons between Truman Seymour's attempt to march across northern Florida in late 1864 and William T. Sherman's march across Georgia.

The fiscal and economic policies of the Confederate government were chiefly responsible for Florida's severe property losses. Cotton had been the state's cash crop, but Richmond prohibited its production or sale to foreign markets in 1862, intending thereby to encourage outside mediation, especially from England, of the disputes between the Union and the Confederacy. The plan failed, even though England's fiber stocks were drastically reduced by the time Egyptian cotton arrived to replenish her flagging textile industry. Meanwhile, many Florida plantations fell into disuse as a result of the government's restrictions, and their value declined.

Property losses in the state were aggravated also by sporadic northern invasions and evacuations, particularly in Jacksonville. Each time Union forces stationed there prepared to withdraw or redeploy, local Union sympathizers also departed. Forced to evacuate hurriedly, loyalists managed to take little more than their personal belongings, abandoning all else. Yet when peace arrived, Florida was better off than her sister states. One pro-Confederate newspaper reported that, compared to the losses of the rest of the South, Florida's losses amounted to "a mere cipher." [6]

The end of the war brought new conditions and a strong wish for peace and stability. The antebellum leaders, those few wealthy planters who had taken the state out of the Union, seemed genuinely relieved that the war was over. In May 1865, Gov. Abraham K. Allison (who had replaced John Milton as chief executive following the latter's suicide in April) reported to Edward McCook, the Union commander who had received the surrender at Tallahassee, that Floridians accepted the supremacy of the Constitution and were willing to "resume the duties and privileges created by that instrument in a spirit of perfect good faith, with the purpose to abide therein." Former U.S. Sen. David Levy Yulee, who had been placed under arrest in May and confined in Fort Pulaski prison near Savannah, reflected the sentiments of many prominent Floridians when he wrote in December to a friend: "The conflict of arms is ended—ended by the unconditional surrender of the South; and thereby, as practical facts, Slave labor is abolished, and State Sovereignty is a Phantom. It is bootless to look back." He urged a postwar policy of "pacification," with both combatants practicing "generous forgetfulness and forgiveness of the past." [7]

Not all Floridians shared Yulee's feelings about the outcome of the war. Several observers noted that bitterness was common. One resident of the state hoped to leave the country rather than live under "yankee rule." [8] A northern visitor to Jacksonville in 1866 found southerners still "universally very bitter" about the war's outcome. Testimony before the congressional committee on Reconstruction provided further proof that some Floridians remained defiantly opposed to the North in spite of their resigned acceptance of defeat. [9]

Despite some changes as a result of emancipation and the end of secessionism, the war in Florida produced more surface scars than deep wounds. Neither bloodshed nor shattered dreams of southern nationalism, not even a hurtful consciousness of a lost way of life, could alter a fundamental reality: in 1865 as in 1565, Florida was still a frontier region of little significance to outsiders.

There were few Floridians to be concerned about, however. During the antebellum era many Americans were moving about in search of prosperity; mostly they followed Horace Greeley's advice and went west. Florida, on the other hand, offered only heat, swamps, insects, Seminoles, and a significant distance from flourishing centers of American society. Some settlers had come, but more had not; by the time of the Civil War, Florida had fewer than 150,000 residents, including slaves.[10] These residents were living in 1865 as they had been for generations, most of them in the upland region across the northern tier of the peninsula. Interior and southern Florida, excluding a few coastal settlements such as Tampa and Key West, were sparsely inhabited. Large distances between settled areas precluded close cooperation and encouraged instead a sort of provincialism. The north-south flow of the rivers restricted the natural east-west movement in the state, resulting in an urban population that was coastal and isolated—Key West at the peninsula's tip, Jacksonville on the ocean, Tampa and Pensacola on the Gulf.

These conditions greatly influenced post–Civil War politics. During and following Reconstruction, local issues in Florida dominated national or even statewide concerns. Republican and Democratic party development reflected and manifested this localism, hindering efforts to establish statewide party unity. Intraparty factionalism became the accepted situation, helping to produce the "political atomization" and the personality politics that became typical of the South.[11] Permanent party machines with politicians who could create and sustain a statewide political reputation were virtually impossible to find in Florida, a fact that burdened Republicans even more than Democrats. During Reconstruction and immediately after, the national Republican party ignored its state organizations in the South. Party stability and party unity suffered as a result, creating critical weaknesses for administrations responsible for imposing Reconstruction on the citizens of Florida, who hated their government.[12]

An enduring cliché of Florida politics is that the Republicans ruined any chance for a quick return to peace and prosperity. Rather, the story has it, a malicious gang of corrupt carpetbaggers, contemptible scalawags, and ignorant Negroes "ruled" Florida until the state was redeemed in 1876.[13] This belief caused Florida—especially North Florida—to turn solidly Democratic in post-Reconstruction state elections. The same mistrust of the Republican party exists in the 1980s. The great depth of this sentiment, even among some Florida Republicans, explains why GOP development in the twentieth century has been mostly of recent origin. Despite the modest effects of Republican administrations in the post–Civil War era, many Floridians have continued to believe that they had been deeply wounded by the political events of Reconstruction.

Reconstructing the ex-Confederacy was burdensome for the national Republican party. Following the elections of 1866, radical Republicans in Congress took control of Reconstruction. Overthrowing both President Andrew Johnson's conciliatory policy toward the defeated South and the conservative state governments created by this policy, radical Republicans proceeded to dictate the terms of the South's restoration under the provisions of the Military Reconstruction Acts, beginning in March 1867 and including the administration of Florida's Gov. David S. Walker, who replaced Union provisional Gov. William Marvin on 18 January 1866.[14]

An antebellum Whig and reluctant secessionist, Walker had won the governorship in an uncontested election on 29 November 1865. Less than half of the state's registered voters turned out, and the new legislature was composed of ex-slaveowners and war veterans.[15] A newly written state constitution was clearly a conservative document, containing little that benefited or protected freedmen, and it promised that antebellum Democrats would remain in power. Slavery was abolished and the secession ordinance was annulled, but there were few other significant changes. Freedmen could not vote or testify in court against whites; they were not permitted to bear arms, to join the Florida militia, or to run for public office. A strict vagrancy law replaced the slave code, severely limiting freedmen's rights to travel. As one political observer commented: "It is not proposed to invest [the Negro] with any more privileges. He would be too cruelly encumbered thereby. *When* his *nature* and *habits* are *thoroughly* changed, he may *possibly* be allowed the 'inalienable' right of suffrage."[16]

Northern Republicans witnessing these and similar events throughout the South were troubled. Practically all were convinced that white southerners would have to participate actively in the postwar restoration process. Without southern whites' acquiescence, Republican leaders in Congress believed, no Reconstruction program could succeed. Some radicals in the party did not share this view and would have preferred to impose harsh measures upon the defeated South, but they were few in number and did not reflect a majority opinion, disagreeing among themselves over vital issues. Writing in the *Atlantic Monthly* in December 1865, radical Massachusetts Sen. Charles Sumner cautioned against a too facile reunion. Sumner pointed out that it had been the original calls for compromise and concessions to the South that had propelled the country into the Civil War. He rejected completely the argument posed by other Republicans that the federal government had no constitutional authority to dictate the terms of southern restoration, arguing that the national government had already interfered in southern politics and had produced a de facto realignment, the results of the outcome of the war and emancipation. He warned Republicans against placing trust and confidence in the white South: "In trusting them [the Confederates] we give them political power, including the license to oppress loyal persons, whether black or white." [17]

More moderate Republicans perceived the goals of Reconstruction in other terms. There was a desire to heed Lincoln's plea "to bind up the nation's wounds." It can be debated whether this sentiment arose from charity toward the South or from sheer exhaustion, but it fell upon Andrew Johnson to carry out what he conceived to be the program of Reconstruction envisioned by the martyred president. Shortly after Lincoln's death, Johnson issued a "Proclamation of Pardon and Amnesty," restoring to the bulk of southern people their property and political power. Johnson's too-conservative aims shattered the Republican solidarity behind him, and the result was the advent of the Republican party's crisis in Reconstruction, not its domination.

While many Republicans disapproved of Johnson's posturing toward the South, few disagreed out of concern for the freedmen. Unfortunately, many historians of the post–Civil War period have tended to consider radical Republicanism by focusing on black-white relations. In reality, only a small number of Republicans cared about Negro equality; only the antebellum abolitionists were committed to it. Not all radical Republicans supported Negro equality, even though all who did were radical. Most simply favored Negro freedom and turned toward other considerations once emancipation had been achieved. GOP policy toward the freedmen of the South centered on a single theme—to devise and institute measures that would enable the ex-slaves to remain in the South and stay out of the predominantly white North. This was the critical reason why the conservative governments in the ex-Confederate states, including the Walker government in Florida, angered Republicans and why Andrew Johnson's program for Reconstruction in 1865–66 was overturned by a radical Republican Congress in the spring of 1867. The black codes that the South had instituted to control Negroes in ways akin to slavery would have encouraged the freedmen to seek relief in the North. The military administrations that began in March 1867 were created to prevent a mass exodus from occurring. As New York's Sen. Roscoe Conkling suggested during the 1866 congressional debates on civil rights, Republican approval of laws protecting Negro rights did not equate with concern for the Negro himself: "Four years ago mobs were raised, passions were aroused, votes were given, upon the false idea that emancipated negroes were to burst in hordes upon the North. We said then, give them liberty and rights in the South, and they will stay there and never come into a cold climate to die. We say so still, and we want them let alone."[18]

Other Reconstruction Republicans were primarily concerned that their party retain control of the national government. Southern Democrats had controlled the national government for three decades before the Civil War, and it seemed irrational to many Republicans to turn back that control now that the war was over. Their fears that such would happen were based upon the fact that abolition of slavery could substantially increase the number of southern votes in Congress. The original three-fifths count of slaves for congressional representation would be replaced by a full census; southern representation in Congress could increase as much as 20 percent. Thus the Republican party faced the task of somehow reducing the South's power in order to retain control. Either Republicans would have to benefit from the expected increase, a result possible through black suffrage and a southern Republican party, or Democratic leaders from the South would have to be excluded.[19]

These issues confronted the Republican party and the nation at the conclusion of the Civil War. Clearly the party lacked a single purpose or policy for reconstructing the ex-Confederacy. Given the narrow base of the Republican party, its divided membership exacerbated the tendency for factionalism. What is surprising is that so many southerners, historical and contemporary conservatives alike, should have expected Republican unity. As Republicans moved into the South, including Florida, to establish party organizations, their factional problems grew much worse. Republican disunity in Reconstruction Florida should have been predicted.

2

Advent of Florida Republicanism

POLITICAL CONFLICTS among Florida Republicans during Reconstruction had causes other than divisive national issues. Political events within Confederate Florida also contributed to the Republican party's problems. Former U.S. Senator David Yulee's observation of Civil War Floridians—"we are no more Whigs and Democrats, but Confederates all"—glossed over Confederate political disputes during the war.

Although most of the political disagreements in Confederate Florida concerned Gov. John Milton's conduct of the war, some centered directly on the role of Florida's unionists. Two groups of Floridians opposed secession yet remained within the state when the war came, and one group suffered measurably more than the other.

The successful businessmen who had migrated to Florida during the antebellum period and had established themselves in coastal cities—Tampa, Jacksonville, St. Augustine, Key West—were unwilling to abandon their investments, so they remained quietly in the background. Only when northern troops occupied the state did they step forward to declare their pro-Union sentiment, and only when federal forces made unscheduled evacuations did they suffer materially.

In the predominantly white, rural, northern counties were concentrated the poor, nonslaveholding farmers who also had opposed secession.[1] The war added overwhelming hardship to their already marginal living conditions. These unionists attempted to avoid the war as much as possible and were often persecuted for failing to support the Confederate cause. In the strictest sense they were more anti-Confederate than pro-Union, tending to desert when conscripted into the Confederate army and to form quasi-guerrilla bands which hid out in the piney woods and raided nearby plantations for food. The Milton government called them outlaws. When Reconstruction began, many were quick to become Republicans and support radical policies because of their disaffection with wealthier southern whites.

The Republican party's initial organizing strategy in Florida stemmed from the circumstances surrounding the presidential campaign of 1864. An increasing number of northern Republicans had become disenchanted with Abraham Lincoln, believing that he could not win a second term, especially against his popular Democratic opponent, George McClellan. The president was plagued by inconclusiveness on the battlefield, war-weariness on the home front, and ambitious rivals in his own party. His own secretary of the treasury and soon-to-be chief justice of the United States, Salmon P. Chase, was his most serious Republican opponent. More radical than Lincoln and more noticeably ambitious, Chase had begun in 1862 to bid for the GOP nomination for president. Florida proved to be an important focal point in this political struggle.

The Lincoln-Chase division was reflected in the proceedings of Florida's direct tax commission. Under a law passed by Congress in 1862, tax commissioners were appointed in each state in rebellion for the purpose of selling captured Confederate property to pay back taxes to the United States. Florida's commission was headed by Lyman Stickney, an army officer stationed at St. Augustine and a follower of Salmon Chase. Other members of the commission were John Sammis of Jacksonville, a unionist who backed neither Lincoln nor Chase, and Harrison Reed, an ex-Wisconsin newspaper journalist loyal to the president.

While Stickney and Reed were aware that control of the direct tax commission would produce political leverage in Florida, their dispute did not surface until the spring of 1863. In June, as Stickney was in Washington conferring with Chase, Reed and Sammis authorized a tax sale of unredeemed rebel property in Fernandina. Stickney had opposed such a sale, preferring to wait until more land could be made available and "more people present to secure homes." Besides this disagreement over timing of the sale, Reed and Sammis complicated matters by purchasing lots in Fernandina for themselves. Sensing an opportunity to garner support for Chase and to reduce Reed's influence in Florida, Stickney claimed that the sale was illegal. He demanded not only that the commissioner of revenue in Washington void the transactions but also that he remove Reed and Sammis as tax commissioners.[2]

The implications of this controversy for the Republican party soon became clear. The national press, opposing Lincoln's second-term nomination, used this issue to rally Republicans behind Chase, pilloring Reed and Sammis for personal graft. The pro-Chase Chicago *Tribune* argued, "It was notorious that the commissioners of taxes for Florida have sold vast tracts of land to themselves for a song. . . . But we have not heard that the guilty parties have been removed from office." Appealing to the anti-Lincoln forces in Congress, the *Tribune* urged that "adequate penalties" should be administered to punish this type of corruption.[3]

Harrison Reed attempted to justify the sale. In an effort to turn radicals away from Chase, Reed tried to show how the Fernandina sale was beneficial to Florida's freedmen. Thirty black families had purchased land in Fernandina during the sale, and the ex-slaves had been assured that homes would be built for them that could be paid for in long-term installments. Reed noted that the freedmen were "essential to the future prosperity of the South, and as free laborers if properly protected and directed, will cause the wilderness of the Slave States to 'blossom as a rose,' and 'the desert waste to smile with abundance.' "[4] Reed and Sammis lost their appeal; in September 1863 the sale was voided, and both men eventually resigned.

Even though Stickney won this encounter, Chase failed to wrest the Republican presidential nomination from Lincoln. The disclosure of the Pomeroy Circular (a public declaration for Chase that rejected Lincoln's second-term election chances) and other politically embarrassing revelations ended Chase's presidential "boom" early in 1864, but Florida's electoral votes still were of concern to the Republican incumbent in the White House. John Hay, Lincoln's private secretary, arrived in the state in 1864 to aid in organizing Florida's unionists into a state government loyal to Lincoln. Under the so-called 10 percent plan authorized by the president, any southern state that contained enough unionists in 1864 to equal 10 percent of the vote in the 1860 election could form a government and participate in the November campaign.[5] Hay characterized Florida's emerging Republicans for the president:

> I have found among the leading men I have met a most gratifying unanimity of sentiment. Those who have been formerly classified as Conservative are willing to accept readily the accomplished events of the war . . . while those of more radical views . . . are readily in favor of your plan. . . . There is no opposition to be apprehended from either native Unionists or [Chase's] Treasury Agents. The people are ignorant and apa-

thetic. They seem to know nothing and care about nothing. They have vague objections to being shot and having their houses burned. . . . They will be very glad to see a government strong enough to protect them. . . . I have the best assurances that we will get the tenth required; although so large a portion of the rebel population is in the army & so many of the loyal people refugees in the North, that the state is well-nigh depopulated.[6]

Despite Hay's efforts, this earliest attempt to reconstruct Florida and initiate Republican party politics was halted by the defeat of Union troops at the battle of Olustee in February 1864. After suffering heavy losses in an effort to cross the northern peninsula, Gen. Truman Seymour's army returned to Jacksonville. Lincoln's opponents charged that the expedition had been politically inspired, an attempt to secure a sufficient number of voters to implement his 10 percent plan in Florida. The congressional joint committee on the conduct of the war exonerated the president, concluding that the Olustee campaign had been indeed a military venture intended to cut off Florida's foodstuffs from the rest of the Confederacy.[7]

Once the actual fighting ceased and the era of Reconstruction began, differences among Republicans changed drastically. National Republican party officials adopted a laissez-faire approach toward the South, especially those states with few electoral votes. National party matters had almost no effect in shaping state party activities, and the National Republican executive committee, in turn, was unconcerned about state party organizations, political campaigns, and local politics. Washington offered little policy guidance, few experienced campaign speakers, and almost no money from national party headquarters.[8] Left isolated and alone to work out the problems of governing a war-weary state, the Republican party in Florida, as elsewhere throughout the South, had difficulty in handling the critical problems of Reconstruction. This indifference on the part of the national party leadership toward state politics, except in elections to federal offices, contributed as much to Florida GOP factionalism as did the social, economic, and political consequences of the Civil War.

On 2 March 1867, Congress overturned the independence of the southern states that President Andrew Johnson had been fostering since 1865. The civil governments that had been established differed little from those of the antebellum era. None of the ex-Confederate states voluntarily would ratify the Fourteenth Amendment, thus angering many northern Republicans. Slavery had been abolished, but it had been replaced by strict black codes that ordered the lives of freedmen as though they were still slaves. Though secessionist ordinances were repealed in most southern states, they were not annulled. By so distinguishing, the South conceded its inability to enforce secession against the North's superior strength but not its belief in secession as a valid political theory. The war might have ended, but the feelings that had created it ran as deep as ever.

Northern Republicans also were disturbed by Andrew Johnson. The president's mild and conciliatory posture concerning the South and his increasingly strident criticism of Congress wore away his Republican support. When Congress was turned over to a Republican majority following the 1866 fall elections, the second phase of Reconstruction began. All the conservative state governments in the South, including David S. Walker's administration in Florida, were voided by the new Reconstruction laws passed in March 1867. In effect, Congress declared that no legal civil governments existed anywhere in the ex-Confederacy, and the military was given temporary command of the South. New state constitutions were to be drawn up, and freedmen were to be given better protection. The new laws gave a fresh start to Reconstruction, now under the direction of Congress, not the president. The changes also cleared the way for the formation of Republican party organizations in each of the ex-Confederate states.

Florida unionists were only one component of the Republican party that was to direct the events of congressional Reconstruction. There were also many ex-Union soldiers who chose to remain in Florida when the war ended, and freedmen also played an integral role in Republican affairs during Reconstruction. Reconstruction historians have traditionally portrayed these various groups of Republicans in vivid, ugly terms. For example, William Watson Davis, author of *Civil War and Reconstruction in Florida* (1913), described carpetbag Republicans in Florida as corrupt and contemptible men whose single motivation was greed. To Davis, the freedmen were little more than puppets, illiterate and ill-prepared, manipulated by white Republican masters.

This portrait of Florida's Republican party in Reconstruction is the one still perceived by many modern-day Floridians of all political persuasions. It obscures a more accurate picture of the men and events of the postwar era that modern scholarship has produced. Unencumbered by a need to justify white racism or to defend the illegal tactics of anti-Republican violence employed by Reconstruction conservatives, a more objective examination leads to a different set of conclusions.

Not all carpetbaggers who came to Florida were white, nor were they all venal and corrupt. Josiah T. Walls, for example, Florida's three-time black Congressman from 1870 to 1875, illustrates the carpetbagger's experience. An ex-slave who had enlisted in the Union army in Pennsylvania and later settled in Florida, Walls not only managed to win three terms in Congress but also held seats in the Florida assembly and senate, served one term as mayor of Gainesville, was appointed to the Alachua County Commission, and served as brigadier-general in the Florida militia commanding black and white troops. He was a member of the Florida bar with his own law firm. He owned and published two East Florida newspapers, employed forty laborers in his own lumber mill, and was by 1884 the state's largest truck farmer with more than 3,000 acres under cultivation. Although a freedman, Walls was no Republican dupe; what differentiated him from other political leaders in the Florida GOP was only his skin color.[9]

The Florida unionist who became a Republican—the scalawag of Reconstruction imagery—has also suffered historical distortion. The two groups of unionists in Florida—poor whites and businessmen—joined the Republican party for different reasons. Poor white Floridians who suffered through the Civil War became Republicans because of their wartime hardships, especially those caused by high taxes, impressment, and conscription.[10] Conscription especially led to the formation of guerrilla bands in various parts of Florida, including Taylor, Lafayette, and Levy counties. Angered by the conscription law's "substitution clause," which enabled a wealthier white to buy his way out of the conflict, by the exemptions granted to slaveowners, and by having to fight outside the state away from their homes and families, many poor Floridians evaded military service. Both the Confederate military and the Milton government expressed concern to Jefferson Davis about the high rate of desertion among Floridians, and measures were taken to punish deserters. Nevertheless, some managed to receive aid from Union troops, and many received sympathy from Floridians. In all, more than 2,000 conscripted Floridians deserted during the Civil War.[11] When the Republican party was forming in the wake of the 1867 Reconstruction acts, four such men were present at the 1868 constitutional convention, all aligned with the radical faction.[12]

Jacksonville businessmen led by Ossian B. Hart were the other important group of unionists in Florida. It was primarily through their organizing efforts that the Republican party of Reconstruction was begun. The party dates from Hart's founding of the Union-Republican Club in Jacksonville in 1867. The membership of this first formal organization of Republicans refutes the traditional image of the scalawag. Most were like modern Republican businessmen—educated, energetic, and deeply conservative.[13]

The traditional view of the ex-slave also stands in need of revision. Florida's freedmen were woefully unprepared for freedom, lacking the skills and experience necessary for living as free men. They also lacked the political astuteness and sophistication needed to challenge their former masters for a share of the post–Civil War South. Often gullible, the freedmen were easily manipulated by whites, both Republican and Democrat. Their lack of education was a serious obstacle to economic, social, and political advancement under Reconstruction.

But by 1867, Florida freedmen had begun to make some progress. In March 1865 the Bureau of Refugees, Freedmen, and Abandoned Lands had been created to aid the ex-slaves, and the post of assistant commissioner for Florida was filled in September by Col. Thomas Osborn, a former Union army officer. The bureau's early tasks were essentially nonpolitical: The agents were there to help feed, clothe, educate, and prepare the freedmen for their changed status resulting from emancipation. Because bureau agents required ex-slaves to continue working the plantation fields of their former masters in order to hasten economic recovery, they met little opposition from the ex-slaveowners. Schools were established on many plantations; blacks as well as whites taught in them. Private philanthropic societies in the North also sent aid to the South.[14]

Ex-slaves also made progress in less visible ways. Though they lacked political experience, the freedmen possessed certain economic advantages. Slaves had farmed the land for generations, and if they were to receive land for themselves, as rumored, they would at least be able to feed themselves. In every southern city slaves had performed skilled tasks as artisans, wheelwrights, shipbuilders, masons, and blacksmiths. Freedmen, too, had great potential for economic development in the postwar free South.[15] Politics could be learned, and there arose quickly a small cadre of Negro leaders willing and able to articulate the political needs of blacks during Reconstruction.[16]

Soon after the Reconstruction acts were passed by Congress, Florida's Republican party began to organize formally. Three different factions appeared, although they soon collapsed into two. Each reflected the particular mixture of personalities, interests, and experiences that marked the state's postwar situation. In Jacksonville, the Union-Republican Club met in the offices of Ossian B. Hart, and on 14 April 1867 a formal constitution was ratified by its members. This event was the initial meeting of Florida's Republican party, and a declaration of political principles was included in the constitution:

>   Sec. 1st—The Sovereignty of the States is subordinate to that of the United States.
>   Sec. 2nd—All persons born or naturalized to the United States, and subject to the jurisdiction thereof, are citizens of the United States and of the States wherein they reside.
>   Sec. 3rd—No distinction founded on race or color ought to abridge or in any way interfere with the civil or political rights and privileges of any citizen of the United States.
>   Sec. 4th—The States lately in rebellion against the United States, renounced and lost their rights and privileges as States of the Union: they can claim to be restored thereto only upon compliance with such conditions as may be prescribed by the Government of the United States.
>   Sec. 5th—The leaders of the late rebellion should forever be excluded from the exercise of political power.
>   Sec. 6th—The Congress of the United States has full jurisdiction over the whole subject of "reconstruction."
>   Sec. 7th—Freedom of discussion is a birthright of every American citizen.
>   Sec. 8th—The education of the masses is absolutely necessary to the continued existence of a free government.[17]

The Union-Republican Club of Jacksonville was essentially a faction of moderate Republicans, white and black. Among the future leaders in Florida's Reconstruction era who signed the declaration of principles were two governors, Harrison Reed and Ossian Hart; one congressman, Horatio Bisbee, Jr.; one state comptroller, Clayton Cowgill; one secretary of state and the most able Negro Republican in the state, Jonathan Gibbs; an editor of two pro-Republican newspapers and state party chairman, Edwin Cheney; one candidate for lieutenant governor, Jonathan Greeley; and other prominent Jacksonville businessmen. The club members publicly endorsed a statewide meeting of all Florida Republicans to establish party machinery in advance of the constitutional convention. A platform convention was scheduled for July 1867 in Tallahassee.

By the time the platform convention opened on 11 July, the Union-Republican Club had been joined by two other factions. One was the result of political activity among the freedmen by agents of the Freedmen's Bureau. Under the aegis of Thomas Osborn, ex-slaves had been enrolled in the Lincoln Brotherhood, a secret Union society. There had been secret societies of Unionists in the Confederate South as early as 1862, but not until Reconstruction were Negroes allowed to join. By the time of the platform convention, the Florida Lincoln Brotherhood had emerged as an important Republican faction. Its chief characteristic was that while its rank-and-file members were black, its leadership was white and moderate.[18]

Competing with the two moderate factions was the radical group, also composed mainly of ex-slaves, known formally as the Loyal League of America and popularly as the "mule team." The radicals were led by two whites, Daniel Richards of Illinois and Liberty Billings of New Hampshire, and a Negro ex-barber from Maryland, William U. Saunders. Richards had been a member of the Florida tax commission, and he and Saunders claimed to represent the national Republican committee in Florida. Billings, an officer in a Negro regiment, had settled in Fernandina after the war. Even though the mule team began to organize later than either of the moderate factions, having started only in the spring of 1867, they managed to ready a sizable political force in time for the platform convention. Traveling across the black-belt counties in a wagon drawn by mules, Richards, Billings, and Saunders informed Florida freedmen that unless they joined the Loyal League, blacks would not be recognized as Republicans. Richards's boast that he and his friends "literally created the Republican party in Florida" was extreme, however.[19]

The July platform meeting was notable in that it eventually caused the two moderate factions to combine, thereby eliminating the radicals from further influence in Florida's Reconstruction. At this first gathering of Florida Republicans, the Union-Republicans lost some of their political leverage when Ossian Hart was defeated by Thomas Osborn for chairman of the convention. The radicals had swung their support to Osborn. Had they been able to maintain that kind of influence throughout Reconstruction, Florida's post–Civil War era might well have been different. That possibility was removed at the constitutional convention six months later when the two moderate factions merged to quash the radicals completely.

Despite the factional differences, some unanimity at the Republican platform meeting was achieved. A series of resolutions was adopted reaffirming Republican devotion to the Union and denouncing the lack of cooperation among Florida's conservatives. The platform also called upon Congress to protect the freedmen from "gross injustice" and to remove the poll tax, which conservatives had imposed upon ex-slaves in the constitution of 1865. Limits to white Republican commitment to Negro equality were evident as well. On the convention floor, segregated seating was strictly observed by the delegates despite the objections of Liberty Billings, and there was little mixing of blacks and whites outside the convention.[20]

While liberal Republicans were thus engaged, conservatives in 1867 were torn by indecision. Following the Reconstruction acts, conservative Floridians faced a limited number of political options, none of which seemed satisfactory. A few still believed that all Negroes, unable to survive in freedom, would soon perish. Some of the old slave-owning class wanted the national government to colonize Negroes in three or four states set aside for that purpose. As one ex-Confederate bitterly noted, "It makes a rebel almost insane with rage to speak of a negro government in Fla. and all the Southern States."[21] Some northern Republicans partially agreed; Massachusetts Congressman George Boutwell's plan for separating whites and blacks, however, included settling the latter in the three southeastern states of Georgia, South Carolina, and Florida.[22]

Conservatives decided to respond to the new constitutional convention by manipulating the referendum requirements to their advantage. Under the provisions of the Reconstruction acts, a November referendum on any new constitutional convention was necessary in each of the southern states. Although Republicans had met already in their platform meeting and had assumed that there would be public approval for a new constitution, conservatives had difficulty in agreeing on the proper course of action in opposition. A general boycott was first proposed to indicate to the state and nation that conservatives in Florida would not cooperate with any new Republican party program. But as November approached, conservatives switched to a strategy based upon the fact that a majority of the registered voters had to approve a constitutional convention. They turned toward a mass registration of conservatives. If conservatives registered in sufficient numbers and *then did not vote at all,* the proposed convention could be prevented and Florida would continue to be governed under the 1865 constitution.

The election was held over a three-day period, 14–16 November 1867. Approximately 26,000 voters registered and some 14,000 cast ballots. The results overwhelmingly supported a constitutional convention. Delegates were chosen around the state: 43 of 46 were Republicans, and 18 were black. Republican participation in the politics of Reconstruction Florida had arrived.[23]

Accounts of the convention that opened in Tallahassee on 20 January 1868 have been influenced by the traditional images of Reconstruction. More than anything else, it was Negro participation in the writing of Florida's new constitution that generated controversial accounts of what actually happened. To John Wallace, a Negro page on the convention floor in 1868, most delegates, black and white alike, proved to be either ignorant or foolish. William Watson Davis described the convention as an instance in history in which "enlightenment and honesty were more than balanced by stupidity and dishonesty." Solon Robinson, reporter for the New York *Tribune* who was sympathetic toward the radical Republicans, commented favorably on the conduct and decorum of the Negro delegates. Robinson was impressed by their parliamentary skills, especially as he contrasted them with the bulk of white delegates whom he criticized as self-aggrandizing. He was removed from the convention when moderate Republicans gained control of the convention hall.[24] From a more recent perspective, Jerrell Shofner has observed that the 1868 convention was the product of behind-the-scene compromises and concessions between moderate white Republicans from both Osborn's and Hart's factions and conservatives aligned against radicals who lost out "because they asked too much and could not accept less."[25]

Locating the convention in Tallahassee initially favored the radical faction of Richards, Billings, and Saunders. The mule team was composed primarily of freedmen from surrounding plantations, and they managed to arrive, caucus, and plan their strategy before most of the other delegates could reach Tallahassee. On Saturday, 18 January, they met to select a slate of convention officials, and opening day the following Monday bore out Daniel Richards's boast that "we have secured a majority of friends in the Constitutional Convention. . . ."[26] Only 29 of the 46 elected delegates were present that first day, and the radicals were firmly in charge.

Meanwhile, both moderate factions led by Osborn and Hart had begun their merger in an effort to eliminate the mule team. Osborn's black support had diminished in the wake of the organizing tactics of the radicals, and he joined with Hart and the other white-dominated moderate factions. As a result, by the time the convention split into two camps and the moderates quit Tallahassee in early February to write their own constitution, Republicans in Florida were reduced from three factions to two—radicals, almost all of them black (excepting a few poor white farmers and carpetbaggers), and moderates, almost all of them white.

Frustrated by the radicals' early planning, the moderates left Tallahassee midway through the convention and reorganized, along with some conservative whites, in nearby Monticello to draft their own constitution. The moderate-conservative combine returned to Tallahassee during the night of 10 February, capturing control of the convention hall. The next few days were marked by political turmoil. Liberty Billings walked the city's streets making speeches in an effort to keep his delegates in line. The moderates worried that he was inciting violence, but only one man, a black radical, was shot during this period.[27] Both factions continued to claim to represent the lawful constitutional convention, although the moderates actually retained possession of the hall and the radicals were forced to hold their meetings either in the local Negro church or outside in the public square. Finally, Gen. George Gordon Meade, commander of the military district including Florida under the Reconstruction acts, agreed to intervene and restore order.

When Meade arrived in Tallahassee, he accepted the resignations of the chairmen of both factions, Richards and Horatio Jenkins, a moderate white from Alachua County. He then ordered all the delegates back to the convention hall for a roll of all eligible delegates. At this juncture the moderates gained firm control: Horatio Jenkins was reappointed as permanent chairman, Daniel Richards and other radicals were ousted, and the constitutional document prepared by the moderates at Monticello became the guideline for the proposed constitution. On 14 April 1868, the congressional Joint Committee on Reconstruction approved the moderate Republican constitution for Florida after comparing it with the radicals' draft. It was then offered to the electorate of Florida for ratification.[28]

Despite the bitter divisions of the convention, there were few significant differences between the drafts. Each reflected the contributions of the conservatives at Monticello. First, the radicals would have had most of the county and state offices filled by election, opening up political opportunity for the state's large Negro majority. The moderate version had most of these offices filled by appointment by the governor, ensuring that Negroes would not be able to control state government. Second, the radicals included in their draft much stronger prohibitions against ex-Confederates participating in Reconstruction. The moderates' document omitted any reference to the rebellion and required only a simple loyalty oath to take office.

The most significant difference between the documents was on the issue of apportioning representative districts in the legislature. Because the radicals wished to ensure as much black control as possible, they wanted representation on the basis of population, which would favor the black-belt counties. The moderate, and final version, favored the smaller, predominately white counties through more restrictive representation. Each county was apportioned at least one representative, and no county could have more than four. The net effect was to ensure that Reconstruction Florida under Republicans remained in white hands. The traditional idea that Negroes, carpetbaggers, and scalawags "ruled" in Florida during Reconstruction stands in defiance of the facts.

The 1868 Republican constitution was a progressive document nonetheless. Its declaration of rights stated that "All men are by nature free and equal." [29] Subsequent events show that the principle was hardly practiced, but in other ways the constitution was a sound statement of American political ideals. The executive branch was organized so that the governor was elected for a four-year term and could succeed himself. He was granted veto powers and the right to call special sessions of the legislature. He had the right to appoint, with the consent of the state senate, his official cabinet, including the secretary of state, attorney general, comptroller, treasurer, surveyor-general, superintendent of public instruction, adjutant general, and commissioner of immigration. The governor was empowered to appoint in each county a tax assessor, collector of revenue, treasurer, surveyor, superintendent of common schools, and county commissioners. In those counties with large or majority black populations, Republican governors often appointed Negroes to fill these offices.

The 1868 constitution also expanded the capacity of the courts to provide better justice for Floridians by increasing the number of judges and justices of the peace. The governor had the power to appoint circuit judges, three of the supreme court justices, all county judges, county sheriffs, and county clerks. In addition he could appoint as many justices of the peace as he felt conditions warranted, and Republican Governors Harrison Reed, Ossian Hart, and Marcellus Stearns used this office as a means of rewarding loyal blacks.

To some, it seemed that Republicans intended to tighten their control on state government through the appointive power of their chief executive. Actually the intention was to limit the impact of Negro voting. One negative effect of the governor's authority to appoint was that it produced factionalism in Republican circles, especially during the administration of Harrison Reed. A politically ambitious man but a maverick in his own party, Reed often faced more difficulties when dealing with Republicans than with conservatives. His potential use of patronage to build an independent political base threatened many Republicans, putting him continually at odds with his party, another factor that added to the tarnished Republican image during Reconstruction.

The authors of the 1868 constitution also recognized the need to educate more of Florida's children. They provided for a common school system for all children, regardless of color, and a tuition-free university. The Republican party created a common school fund with revenue from several sources, including the sales of public land and a state property tax. Special state institutions for the deaf, blind, and insane were set up; a state prison was authorized; homestead exemptions were allowed; taxes on all citizens were made at uniform rates; and no tax money could be used to develop private companies chartered in Florida. While the poll tax was not repealed, it was reduced.

The constitution's progressive clauses established a bicameral legislature designed to meet in annual sessions, its representation based upon the state census. Traditional counting of the Negro population as only three-fifths of the white population was abolished, and suffrage was granted to every male over twenty-one without regard to race or previous condition of servitude. An important restriction prohibited laws establishing educational qualifications for eligible voters until 1880. This provision gave the uneducated freedmen an opportunity to participate at the polls, and even after 1880 no previously registered voter could be denied this franchise for lack of education.

Despite all the political turmoil over the 1868 constitution, Florida was promptly readmitted to the Union.[30] The constitution itself and the processes by which it was created compared favorably with events elsewhere in the South. In Mississippi, for example, radicals had unsuccessfully tried to include such unpalatable provisions as loyalty oaths and exclusion of ex-Confederates that, when put to a vote for ratification, were defeated. The same voters elected a Democratic governor, congressmen, and majority in the state legislature. Radicals charged fraud, causing Congress to step in. Mississippi was not readmitted to the Union until 1870. Conservative opposition in Virginia was even more successful in preventing radical Reconstruction than in Florida. While Florida's Republican Congressman William Purman could claim later that he had prevented the state from being "niggerized,"[31] Virginia voters could reject or ratify specific provisions of their constitution with the permission of Congress. When Virginia eventually was readmitted in 1870, state officials were not required to take a loyalty oath, nor were ex-Confederates excluded from political participation in any way. In a general sense Virginia escaped Reconstruction completely, and Georgia and Texas also faced delays in gaining readmission to the Union because of congressional opposition to their constitutions.[32]

Perhaps the most telling indication of how well Florida's 1868 constitution worked was that it remained in effect until 1885, well beyond the end of Republican domination and longer than the constitution of any other southern state. Led by moderate and conservative whites, Reconstruction Florida was never plunged into an era of radicalism or "Negro rule." The political impact of the freedmen had been neutralized effectively, although clearly Republicans were more concerned with the welfare of blacks than had been Gov. David Walker's conservative administration or subsequent Democratic administrations. It was certainly a less radical and more progressive state constitution and period of Florida history than most interpretations have suggested.

3

Republican Factions and Reconstruction Politics

THE MODERATE-CONSERVATIVE COALITION that achieved success at Florida's 1868 constitutional convention fell apart when Harrison Reed won election as the state's first Republican governor. The factions that arose from that meeting plagued Republicanism until the close of Reconstruction in 1876. Despite temporary shifts and sundry alliances to meet political challenges, especially during election campaigns, Florida Republicans found it impossible to forge a stable organization. They were wrenched apart by differing special interests and sometimes by personal clashes—radicals opposed moderates, blacks opposed whites, northerners opposed native-born Floridians, state officials opposed federal appointees. V. O. Key's description of Florida as a politically atomized, "no-party state" was a fitting one before the era of the solid South.[1]

Much of the party's turmoil in Florida related to the decentralized posture of the national party organization. The Republican party barely existed on the national level during the early years of Reconstruction. It was a congeries of state and local affiliates, each concerned with its own normal political affairs: naming candidates, fund-raising, conducting campaigns, distributing patronage and favors to deserving supporters, and fighting off Democratic attacks. Although the Republican National Committee had come into existence in February 1856 to oversee presidential canvasses, it was little more than a servant to a few powerful Republican state organizations in the North and Midwest. Aside from routine tasks of raising money, hiring speakers, and disseminating campaign literature, the national committee restricted itself to helping states where critical elections were in doubt. Between campaigns the committee served no purposeful function until called together the December preceding a presidential election to prepare for the Republican national convention.[2]

Because of this decentralization, southern party organizations were left alone to work out their problems. Across the South, intra-Republican factionalism weakened the party's hold on state governments. Although the political infighting in Florida grew worse after Harrison Reed became governor, Republican control lasted longer there than in any other southern state. Reed's political style annoyed his fellow Republicans, as did his insistence on cooperation with conservatives. Reed's conflicts with Sen. Thomas Osborn over control of the Republican party's machinery and patronage were both personally and politically inspired, but they stemmed from factional divisions that became known as "ring" and "anti-ring," which persisted after both men had bowed out of Reconstruction Republican politics.

The special burden of using Negro support to maintain Republican hegemony in Florida also fueled party divisions. The small cadre of blacks who represented Florida's freedmen, including Jonathan Gibbs, Josiah Walls, and Charles Pearce, realized that the constitutional convention had cut them off from the fountainhead of power. Walls especially grew disenchanted with his party, though he was the only Florida Negro raised to political prominence by it, and even he eventually attempted to work independently of it.[3]

In some measure the deepest party fissures stemmed from the character and personality of Harrison Reed. He had been a Wisconsin newspaper editor before his appointment to Florida's direct tax commission during the Civil War. As mentioned in chapter 2, Reed's entry into Florida Republican politics was marred by the controversy with Lyman Stickney over the Fernandina land sale scandal. Though he redeemed himself long enough to win election as governor, his penchant for disputes remained an irritating source of internal Republican factionalism.

Reed's political legacy echoed that of another major contributor to Republican factionalism, President Andrew Johnson, whom Reed admired and supported. Johnson was always a political "outsider," a trait that widened his differences with Republicans in the Congress.[4] In spite of his well-demonstrated affection for the Union (Johnson had remained fixedly loyal even as his native Tennessee defected to the Confederacy), the president was either unable or unwilling to inflict sufficient retribution upon the defeated South to satisfy most Republicans. In practice, Johnson was not a true Republican; rather, he was a Democrat who had joined Abraham Lincoln's second-term Union party ticket in a coequal display of patriotism and nonpartisan politics. Historical circumstance in the person of John Wilkes Booth made Andrew Johnson president of the United States and leader of the Republican party with which he had little in common: he had been a southerner, a Democrat, and a conservative. Mainstream Republicans who favored his impeachment in 1866, on the other hand, were northerners who had been moderate in their demands concerning readmitting the ex-Confederate states to the Union. Harrison Reed could have been poured from the same mold. Like Johnson, he was not perceived by his contemporaries as a neutral figure or as a dedicated party man. Headstrong, dedicated to certain principles and to a maverick political style, Reed often found it difficult to reconcile his role in Reconstruction Florida with the outlook of his party colleagues.

"I am exceedingly anxious that the political programme should be harmonized on the basis of the material interests of the state," Governor Reed wrote David Yulee, Florida's leading Democrat, a year before he took office. Reed's goal thrust him into a difficult political situation, however.[5] He rejected both radical and conservative extremes during his tenure as governor and satisfied no one. Eventually he suffered through four impeachment attempts, each directed by a coalition of disaffected Republicans and Democrats. Although Reed tried to soften the impact of Reconstruction on his more partisan opponents in an attempt to move Florida forward economically, by and large his efforts were unprofitable and unpopular. Using the power granted him by the state constitution and satisfying his personal predilections, Reed sought to establish a state administration composed equally of Democrats and Republicans. He appointed clerks and judges from both parties in each Florida county. Two former slaveowners and firm Confederates, Robert Gamble and James Westcott, joined his cabinet as comptroller and attorney general, respectively. By August 1868, Reed had filled more than two hundred vacancies at the local, county, and state levels, the bulk with white southerners of both parties.[6]

Reed's campaign for cooperation failed to win over many Democrats and fostered increased Republican opposition. According to the chief pro-Republican newspaper in the state, the Tallahassee *Sentinel*, old-line secessionists were unalterably opposed to any Republican administration. The Democrats were accused of creating an image of Florida Republicanism as a "hateful tyranny established for their oppression and destruction." A few Democrats accepted appointments; nevertheless, some campaigned against Reed, while others joined the Republican opposition which was trying to bring him down.[7]

The center of the governor's Republican opposition lay in the fragmented remnants of the moderate-conservative coalition. Apart from the radical faction, Republicans prior to the constitutional convention had been organized by either the Union-Republican Club of Jacksonville, to which Reed belonged, or by the Freedmen's Bureau political organizing unit headed by Thomas Osborn. Prominent members from both groups voiced their opposition to the politics and policies of Reed's administration: Edward Cheney, publisher of the *Florida Union* and chairman of the Republican state executive committee; William Purman, bureau agent elected to Congress from West Florida; Sherman Conant, U.S. marshal; Horatio Bisbee, U.S. attorney elected to Congress from East Florida; Ossian B. Hart, state supreme court justice and eventual successor to Reed as Republican governor of Florida; and Marcellus Stearns, third and last Republican governor during Reconstruction.

Sen. Thomas Osborn, long considered Reed's chief opponent, and Edward Cheney, chairman of the state party, were Reed's staunchest critics, differing with him over the role of the party in Florida. Cheney wanted to increase the strength and impact of the state committee by appointing special agents in each county to regulate local political activity, a proposal viewed by the governor and his supporters as an attempt to centralize power in the hands of the anti-Reed forces, the so-called ring of Florida Republicanism.

In October 1869, Republicans held a state convention to consider several proposals, including Cheney's, for better organization of their party. Seventy Republicans from fifteen counties assembled in Tallahassee. In an effort to placate growing Negro discontent with party leaders, Josiah Walls, already gaining power among black Floridians, was elected chairman of the convention. The state executive committee was empowered by the delegates to appoint county executive committees in each Florida district. Laws were urged that would enable all citizens, regardless of color, to enjoy "equal and exact" rights to public transportation facilities. A month after this meeting Cheney's state executive committee again convened, requesting that mass meetings be held across the state on 20 December to consider further means of strengthening the party.[8]

The most common source of friction between Harrison Reed and the ring, however, was not the issue of party control but the appointment of federal officeholders. The source of most of Florida's patronage was Senator Osborn. Senator Abijah Gilbert, who had been elected to replace Adonijah Welch, was an old, wealthy Republican who exercised little independent judgment. Both he and Charles Hamilton, congressman-at-large from 1868 to 1870, preferred to accept Osborn's recommendations without reservation.

At first, Governor Reed also acquiesced. Together, Reed, Hamilton, Gilbert, and Osborn supported the nomination of Horatio Bisbee as attorney general in 1869. But in 1872, when Reed's differences with Republicans were most acute, he requested that President Grant remove Bisbee and Sherman Conant from their respective posts as district attorney and marshal. At stake was control of Florida patronage. A storm of protest arose from anti-Reed Republicans around the state, although J. S. Adams, member of the Internal Improvement Fund's Board of Trustees and a pro-Reed Republican, wrote confidently that the governor's action would take the power away from the ring faction and restore a balance to Republicanism in the state: "We . . . expect to secure the election of a Republican Senator in place of Mr. Osborn and two Republican Congressmen; and I will add this . . . I express the feeling and wishes of all the Federal officers of the state outside the . . . ring of Senator Osborn's special friends."[9]

President Grant complied, then reversed himself and reinstated both Bisbee and Conant. The removals appeared to have threatened Grant's chances of carrying the state in the 1872 national election. "The removal of Conant and Bisbee will ruin our party and defeat our ticket," wired David Montgomery, a Republican presidential elector, to the president. "Have these officers restored or most of our workers will withdraw from the canvass." Both Ossian B. Hart and Marcellus Stearns, Republican candidates for governor and lieutenant governor to succeed Reed, also wired Grant in support of Bisbee and Conant, as did Josiah Walls, who even traveled to Washington to protest the removal personally.[10]

Compounding these frictions was Reed's conflict with his party over state policy. During the initial legislative session in 1869, the state legislature authorized the sale of $100,000 in revenue bonds to replenish the empty treasury. Reed went north to arrange for their sale, believing that he had received the required permission for the journey from state comptroller Robert Gamble. Gamble, however, proceeded to arrange for the bonds' disposition with Senator Osborn and William Gleason, the Republican lieutenant governor. Osborn had agreed to take the bonds from Gamble for seventy cents on the dollar. Reed, in the meantime, was offered seventy-five cents by J. Cooke and Company in New York City, and he was angered by Gamble's interference as well as by Osborn's. "Your arrangements will be ruinous to me," the governor wrote to Gamble, "and compel my resignation if carried out. . . . The negotiation by Osborn gives him entire control of political affairs; if sanctioned, my honor is gone."[11] Although Reed was defeated, Osborn failed to dispose of the bonds, thereby aggravating their personal conflict. Reed also refused to allow Osborn to purchase a large tract of valuable timberland in West Florida from the state at less than market value.[12]

Reed's difficulties with both Democrats and Republicans led inevitably to attempts to remove him from office. The initial move against him came when he vetoed the salary bill that the legislature passed during the November 1868 special session. Although the lower house committee empowered to draw up articles of impeachment failed to do so prior to adjournment, Horatio Jenkins of Alachua County presented a memorial outlining the charges against Reed. The governor was guilty of "falsehood and lying while transacting business with the members of the legislature and other officers of the State . . . [guilty of] incompetency in as much as he has filled commissions to officers in blank . . . [guilty of] embezzlement, having taken from the State Treasury securities and money, and sold such securities, and then failed to return a portion or all of the proceeds." Jenkins also charged that Reed had engaged in corruption, bribery, and selling of public offices and had nominated unqualified people.[13]

On 3 November 1868, the day Reed was formally impeached, Lt. Gov. William Gleason issued a proclamation declaring himself the lawful governor of Florida pending the outcome of the investigation and trial. Reed appealed to the state supreme court on 9 November for a ruling as to whether legally he had been impeached. Members of the administration and the Republican party began to take sides. Secretary of State George Alden sided with the ring. He removed the seal of Florida from his office and relocated across the street from the capitol in a hotel where Gleason had established himself. In his turn, Reed removed Alden from office and, in a shrewd maneuver to garner Negro support, appointed Jonathan Gibbs as Alden's replacement.[14]

When the supreme court declared Reed to be the lawful governor of Florida, on 24 November 1868, he retaliated against Republicans who had opposed him. Jenkins, whom Reed earlier had appointed to a judgeship in Alachua County, was summarily removed, prompting young Garth James, brother of famed novelist Henry and philosopher

William and Jenkins's neighbor in Alachua County, to remark: "He is a poor broken-down adventurer now, and a warning to all men who do not make some attempt to serve something higher [than] themselves." On 14 December, Gleason was removed from office.[15]

The second effort to oust Reed was dispatched with far less controversy. When the state legislature convened for its first session on 4 January 1869 (with William Gleason still serving as president *pro tempore* until January 10 in defiance of the supreme court's ruling against him), Samuel Walker of Leon County joined with the Democrats to attempt another impeachment. Walker had been Reed's opponent in the governor's race the year before, representing the radical Republicans, and doubtless he was still smarting from the defeat. Reed again was accused of taking bribes, specifically $500 for appointing a clerk in Leon County, and for illegally spending state revenue.[16]

The assembly voted for a new impeachment investigation, and an inquiry into the governor's conduct began. The impeachment committee submitted two reports. The majority report, signed by white Republican John Varnum, black Republicans Henry Harmon and Emanuel Fortune, and two Democrats, made no specific recommendations either for or against impeachment. The minority report, however, written by black Republicans Auburn Irwin and E. J. Harris, exonerated Reed. Although Thomas Osborn was in Tallahassee to bolster the attack on his Republican archrival, a final vote on 26 January 1869 not to impeach overwhelmingly favored the governor.[17]

As much as any other factor, the loyalty of black Republicans in the legislature saved Reed. By the time the actual vote occurred, these legislators had established a basic political posture for the immediate future as anti-ring Republicans. Since the constitutional convention had ensured that blacks' civil and political rights would continue to be secondary to the rights of whites, blacks responded by refusing to support Osborn's plans to oust Reed each time impeachment proceedings were undertaken in the lower house.

Although most blacks were disappointed by their failure to win power as Republicans, they lacked any enthusiasm for campaigning as independents or for forming coalitions with the Democrats. William Saunders, a member of the original radical faction, undertook an independent race for Charles Hamilton's congressional seat in 1868. Backed by Republican party moderates, including Reed and Osborn, Hamilton claimed that Democrats had persuaded Saunders to enter the race to split votes, thereby allowing William Barnes, the Democratic nominee, to win. Whether Saunders had in fact been bribed, he failed to siphon enough votes from Hamilton to alter the outcome. Hamilton polled 3,000 more votes than Barnes and Saunders combined. Saunders netted fewer than 1,000 votes, carrying only Alachua County.[18]

The issue of how blacks were to share in Republican activity was brought to the surface as a by-product of the Saunders-Hamilton contest. Since the constitutional convention, white moderates in the party had been busily engaged in fence-mending with discontented black radicals. As time passed, it became obvious that the blacks' increasing demands for offices would have to be met, at least in limited fashion.

More important, however, Saunders's attempted independent campaign suggested to black politicians their most painful conundrum: although excluded from the exercise of real power by the Republican party, no independent race by a Negro candidate could generate sufficient support among Florida freedmen. To accomplish racial advances, blacks were forced to use only regular Republican channels. Thus, Saunders lost heavily while Josiah Walls held his seat on the Alachua County Republican executive committee for twenty years, giving him a powerful voice in Alachua County and making him a spokesman for his black followers within the party.

Reed also benefited from the Saunders debacle. Forced by political circumstance to choose between Reed and the ring that had defeated radical hopes in 1868, black Republicans remained loyal to their governor. Nor had Reed diminished his reputation among black Floridians by appointing Jonathan Gibbs to his cabinet. Charles Pearce, Leon County senator and a bishop in the Florida A. M. E. Church, reportedly threatened to hand his black voters to the Democrats if Reed were impeached.[19] Eventually moderate ring Republicans appealed to Negroes by acquiescing to the nomination of Josiah Walls to replace Charles Hamilton in Congress in 1870.

The third attempt to impeach Reed came in early 1870. The governor was accused of having accepted a $7,500 bribe from George Swepson in connection with the scandal involving the Jacksonville, Pensacola, and Mobile Railroad. Reed had called the legislature into special session in June 1869 to push for railroad development in Florida. Even as a Wisconsin newspaperman, he had ardently supported internal improvements. Florida's lack of adequate rail service in the post–Civil War era limited the state's material advancement. During the decade following the Civil War, Florida's railroads were "the fewest, the weakest, and the poorest" of all the southern states'.[20] In his message to the

1869 special session, Governor Reed urged that "the railroad system of the state should be prosecuted to completion as early as possible in order that the business of Florida may not be absorbed by the superior energy and capital" of other states. He felt that as much state credit and state aid as was consistent with the "public interest" should be invested in railroad development.[21]

The majority of legislators, both Democratic and Republican, agreed with Reed, and a bill incorporating the Jacksonville, Pensacola, and Mobile Railroad Company was passed during that special session. State aid to the company amounted to $14,000 a mile in the form of state bonds to be issued to the company as new track was completed and of the right of bondholders to exchange company bonds for state bonds of greater value. The state held a statutory lien on all rights, property, and franchises of the J. P. & M. as security.[22]

Although on the surface it appeared legitimate, the deal turned into Florida's largest scandal of the Reconstruction era. The major figures involved were the principal investors—George Swepson, a North Carolina financier who had already bilked Florida in another railroad venture; Milton Littlefield, Swepson's agent in Florida; and J. P. Sanderson, a Florida Democrat who aided Swepson and Littlefield in convincing the legislature and Governor Reed that their plans were legal and sound. Reed issued the J. P. & M. some $4 million in state bonds, of which less than one-third went toward the intended construction. The remainder was misappropriated by Swepson and Littlefield for expenses and debts, interest payments, a European tour by Littlefield, and other sundry expenses. The state government was held liable for the losses.[23]

On 4 February 1870, a lower house committee charged Reed with bribery and embezzlement. This time the governor escaped impeachment by only a narrow margin since all the Democrats and a few Republicans voted for his removal. Reed was convinced that a conspiracy existed between Republicans and Democrats, centering on his successor, George Wentworth of Pensacola, who had been elected to replace William Gleason as president *pro tempore* in the senate in case of impeachment. A supporter of Thomas Osborn, Wentworth had been elected by a coalition of Democrats and Republicans, according to the Tallahassee *Sentinel,* and was rumored to have offered to call for new elections within sixty days of taking office from Reed. Once again the governor was sustained by black Republican legislators still angry with the moderate group of ring Republicans.[24]

The fourth and final impeachment encounter in 1872 climaxed the stormy relations between Harrison Reed and his enemies. The crisis began on 2 January 1872, the opening day of the sixteenth legislative session. The key issue was the bond sale to the J. P. & M., but several other political factors were operating. In his remarks to the legislature, Reed threw caution aside and openly challenged his political opponents. He accused the Democrats of encouraging and spearheading violence aimed at reducing black and white Republican activity that had ripped apart several of Florida's black-belt counties, especially Jackson County. The governor charged that Democrats were behind the many acts of "disturbances, breaches of the peace, infractions of the law, and scenes of fatal and disgraceful violence . . . in many localities within our borders." Under pressure for his role in the Swepson-Littlefield fraud, Reed also attacked the Democratic opposition for its role in supporting measures to increase state expenditures and then campaigning as though Republicans were responsible for them. Past Democratic administrations, Reed pointedly observed, were adept at "saving at the spigot and losing at the bunghole." He admonished his fellow Republicans for being economically "reckless" in the face of Democratic attacks on Republican spending. Pointing out that between 1848 and 1861 Democratic administrations were not required to maintain accurate fiscal accounts, for which they could be held liable, Reed commented sarcastically, "This was during the halcyon days of peace, prosperity and harmony 'before the war.' There were no 'scalawags,' 'carpetbaggers,' nor 'freedmen' to disturb the political sea—all were 'honest' men in those days." He concluded, "The 'honest' men who controlled the old government . . . are not the proper persons to assail the character of the present administration, nor to charge it with fraud and corruption, as they have been doing for the past three years." [25]

In attacking previous administrations, including the postwar conservative administration of David Shelby Walker, Reed ruptured his tenuous relations with the Democrats, a tie that had proved unrewarding in spite of his assiduous efforts to foster bipartisan cooperation. Serious political repercussions resulted. The senate in 1872 was "controlled" by a slim Republican margin of one vote; in fact it was totally useless because of rampant factionalism. Furthermore, the contested election in 1870 between Republican Samuel Day and Democrat William Bloxham for lieutenant governor had yet to be resolved in the courts. As the moves against Reed got under way in the initial session in 1872, Bloxham renewed his case in the supreme court to reverse the narrow election outcome that had awarded Day the seat. According to Democratic strategy, if Reed could be impeached and thereby suspended or removed from office, Reconstruction itself could be overturned. With Reed out and Bloxham in, first as lieutenant governor and then as acting governor, the Democrats would control not only the governorship but also the senate and county appointments. Thus, the 1872 impeachment attempt was the most critical of the Reconstruction series.

Impeachment was equally crucial from the Republican point of view. With the Florida Supreme Court undecided about the Day-Bloxham contest, Samuel Day continued as acting lieutenant governor. To offset the disaster that would come about if Bloxham won, ring Republicans worked out a strategy to impeach Reed without bringing him to trial. If it appeared that Bloxham would win his court case, Day, acting in place of the suspended Reed, would simply call the legislature into special session to hold a trial. Reed could then be acquitted of the charges, and the Republican party would maintain its hold on the governor's office and state appointments. At best, the Democrats would win only the lieutenant governor's office and a slim margin of control in the senate; a sweeping end to Republican participation in the politics of Reconstruction would be averted. Ultimately, that is what occurred.

Backed by twenty-four Republicans in the lower house, Marcellus Stearns, a member of the ring faction and successor to Reed and Hart as Republican governor, approached ex-Gov. David Shelby Walker with a proposal: If Walker could convince his Democratic supporters to vote with several Republicans for impeachment, Reed would be suspended without delay. Angered by Reed's attack on his own administration, Walker persuaded a Democratic caucus of legislators to vote for articles of impeachment.[26]

Not all Democrats supported the move. One observer commented that many of his party's members who were not in the legislature were confused: "So far as I can tell, the Democrats made no terms. . . . I am informed that Governor Walker thinks Day a better man than Reed and, consequently, the change may do some good. . . . Others of us were very much astonished to hear it had been accomplished and, like almost everyone, considered the party agreed to the opposite policy." Former Sen. David Yulee, no longer visibly active in Florida politics, regarded impeachment as an internal Republican affair, one that would not substantially alter Democratic strength in the state: "The fact is, the Reed impeachment was a movement in the Republican Party in the struggle of 'rings' for control of the party machinery and has no important significance."[27]

Reed's impeachment resulted from a *unanimous* vote in the assembly. Day was sworn in as lieutenant governor and Liberty Billings, the ex-radical organizer turned moderate Republican senator from Fernandina, was elected president *pro tempore* of the senate. Formal articles against Reed were presented in the senate on 10 February 1872.[28]

Trial was scheduled to begin on 14 February, but it was the nineteenth before Reed entered a plea of not guilty before Justice Randall and the senate members of the impeachment jury. The proceedings provoked dissimilar reactions in the Tallahassee press. The pro-Reed, pro-Republican *Sentinel* characterized the impeachment as a "conspiracy which had been concocted to destroy the Republican party by the joint action of certain depraved members of this party and a number of inconsiderate and reckless spirits among the Old Hunker Democrats." On the other hand, the principal pro-Democratic newspaper in Tallahassee, the *Weekly Floridian,* withheld wholehearted support for impeachment. The newspaper noted instead that many of the charges were difficult to substantiate and others clearly untenable: "Until the testimony is in some way accessible, we shall not indulge in comment."[29] Once Reed had pleaded not guilty and his attorney had filed a motion requesting no delay in the trial, the Republican plan was carried into action. George Wentworth moved that, since the assembly and the senate had agreed to an adjournment, the senate sitting as an impeachment jury should also be required to adjourn. Justice Randall approved, the legislature adjourned, and Reed was suspended indefinitely.

Suspended from office only a few months before completing his term, Reed refused to cooperate with his party's plan, even though it would possibly have ensured future Republican control. The day after the court and legislature acted, Charles Dyke, Democratic editor and publisher of the *Weekly Floridian,* supplied Reed with the necessary ammunition to incite even greater turmoil. On 20 February 1872, Dyke's editorial appeared: "The respondent having been arraigned and pleaded not guilty to the charges, and the court having adjourned . . . *sine die* . . . under the circumstances, *does not* [this] *operate as an acquittal of the accused?* We believe that some of our best lawyers take the ground that such is the case."[30]

Reed apparently concurred with Dyke's thinking. On 8 April, while Acting Governor Day was attending a Republican campaign-planning session in Gainesville, Reed returned to Tallahassee from his home in Jacksonville to assume once more the office of governor. He issued a proclamation declaring his legal right to be governor, removed two of Day's appointees, and appointed several county officials. The governor then requested a supreme court ruling clarifying the confusion of two men claiming the same office. The supreme court ruled on 29 April that Reed was governor of Florida both de facto and de jure but that he was under suspension until the senate formally acquitted him. The court refused to rule on Dyke's contention that a *sine die* adjournment constituted a legal acquittal.[31]

On 4 May, Harrison Reed was formally declared innocent of all charges against him by a senate vote of ten to seven. Six Democrats and four Republicans voted in his favor. It is difficult to identify the final determinants in the vote. The long-standing view is that Reed's impeachment victory came as a result of the collapse of the Osborn faction. Others have argued that Reed, Day, and Osborn came to terms.[32] While Democrats were not unanimously in support of a single policy, William Bloxham's eventual court win over Samuel Day in the 1870 lieutenant governor's race bore out the soundness of the ring Republican's strategy. What is clear is that neither faction could establish a firm political program. Politics remained a mixture of personal clashes, alignment shifts for temporary interests, and confused expectations. Unfortunately, Reed's relationship with his party only sharpened the focus on these considerations instead of resolving the opposed political forces or the deeper problems of Reconstruction.

During Reconstruction, Florida's Republican party suffered as Democrats worked to divide it, alternately supporting and opposing Reed as expediency dictated, but in general Democrats opposed the ring faction of the Republican party more staunchly than they did Reed. During the impeachment fights, for example, the pro-Democratic press interspersed its editorial attacks on Reed's administration with even greater vituperation about the ring. Summing up Harrison Reed's administration, which earlier had been labeled "villainous, corrupt, and imbecile," the pro-Democratic *Floridian* commented on the governor's final impeachment skirmish: "We believe that Harrison Reed would have made a better Governor, that he would have acted with more justice to the entire people but for the wicked and maligned influence of the federal officeholders."[33]

Not all faint Democratic praise of Reed was intended to foster Republican schisms. Reed's efforts to help maintain a white-supremacy government in the 1868 constitutional convention, his insistence on appointing Democrats to a number of state and local offices, his refusal to react fully against Democrat-inspired violence, as well as the participation of Democrats in many Republican state economic development programs, confirmed Democrats' suspicions that Harrison Reed was not the anti-Christ.

But Democrats never ceased to drive wedges into Republican unity whenever possible. In 1869, there occurred a movement in the legislature to unseat Republican Abijah Gilbert. Gilbert, who had bribed his way in 1868 into Adonijah Welch's seat, came under fire when he apparently refused to pay more money to legislators who had voted for him.[34] He was wealthy enough to sustain extortion but not inclined to perpetuate his tenure in office at exorbitant expense, and the legislators "elected" Ossian B. Hart to replace him, even though Gilbert's term had hardly begun. Sensing an opportunity to scuttle Republicanism, the Democrats supported Hart. When their political intent was revealed by Cheney's *Florida Union,* Dyke's *Floridian* seized the occasion to make Republicans even more sensitive to the pain of their own factionalism: "It is true that Judge Hart received the votes of Conservatives . . . but has the *Union* forgotten that a year ago one of Governor Reed's pet schemes was to bring on an election for senator and get rid of Gilbert; and can it now say it did not favor the movement then? Does it, or does it not, know that he made propositions to Democrats to the effect that if they would go for that 'other man' they should have certain offices?" As it turned out, Gilbert's right to remain in the U.S. Senate was upheld by that body; Hart settled for a seat on Florida's supreme court.[35]

An even more striking example of the Democrats' efforts to divide Republicans came in the 1873 election of Thomas Osborn's replacement as Florida's senator. There was a significant nexus between the end of Harrison Reed's power in Republican circles and the simultaneous close of Thomas Osborn's career. Each man had been instrumental in the formation of the Republican party in Florida, Reed through the direct tax commission and the Union-Republican Club and Osborn through the Freedmen's Bureau and the Lincoln Brotherhood. Each man claimed the loyalty of Negro Republicans, although Reed's impeachment proceedings seemed a good argument that practical Negro loyalties lay more on his side. More important, each controlled an equal share of Reconstruction power. Because of the decentralized nature of state and national politics in the nineteenth century, as well as the specific powers granted him under the 1868 constitution, Reed wielded enormous executive and political influence. Osborn, on the other hand, gained access to national Republican leaders more easily than Reed, but he more often encountered a disinclination by party chieftains to meddle in the affairs of a southern state. His political power stemmed from his control of federal patronage appointments. Osborn and Reed shared personal qualities that brought them into conflict: each was ambitious, strong-willed, and incapable of sharing power.

Reed's term ended in 1872; Osborn's term in the senate ended the following year. Osborn's influence over his faction of ring Republicans was badly shaken by his failures to oust his adversary through impeachment, and there was no evidence of support for his reelection. Instead, Simon B. Conover, a ring Republican who had been elected speaker of the house, provided Democrats with another opportunity to create unrest among Republicans. Conover was supported by Democrats in his bid to replace Osborn, purportedly having bribed his way into the office.[36] As a result, Florida Republicans entered into a new phase of factionalism. The old notions of ring and anti-ring were displaced. Intraparty factions quickly centered around two new personalities, Conover and the man who replaced him as speaker and who later would become governor, Marcellus Stearns. After Conover's election, the state witnessed a Republican ring senator defended by Democrats and attacked by Republicans. The pro-Republican Tallahassee *Sentinel* complained that Conover's election had been secured through "the alignment of the colored voters with the Democrats by means of professions of extraordinary good will, and by the distribution of a few offices to leading colored men." The pro-Democratic *Floridian,* on the other hand, praised Conover, commenting that his campaign speeches had been "happily conceived, well-expressed, clear and forcible."[37] Again Democrats managed to splinter Republican ties with relative ease.

Although the role of Democrats in provoking Republican factionalism between 1868 and 1872 cannot be overstressed, at key times Republicans alone destroyed their party unity. The fiercest intraparty conflict took place at the nominating convention in Gainesville in 1870. As early as May of that year, months before the convention was scheduled, Republican candidates were already splintered. In Leon County, there were two factions, one, headed by Bishop Charles Pearce, backing Reed, the other supporting Thomas Osborn. Another critical blackbelt area, Alachua County, also fielded two factions.[38]

The convention got under way in the Alachua County courthouse on 19 August. Some three hundred Republicans from across Florida met to select candidates for lieutenant governor and congressman-at-large. Because Negro Republicans were demanding more political input, moderate white party chiefs decided that Charles Hamilton's congressional seat should go to a black. When the balloting began, the depth of the factionalism was revealed. Despite his professions of party unity, Charles Hamilton retained a large bloc of delegates committed to his renomination and led by Sen. William Purman from West Florida. The ring group, under the direction of Senator Osborn, backed a Negro candidate, Robert Meacham of Tallahassee. Osborn hoped that Meacham would attract blacks away from Harrison Reed and thereby enhance his own control of state Republican patronage. Many black delegates in fact were committed to neither Purman's nor Osborn's group. At the conclusion of the first ballot, blacks Jonathan Gibbs, Henry Harmon, Charles Pearce, Josiah Walls, and Robert Meacham had all received support. During the next eight tallies, there was little shifting among the delegates. Pearce conceded that only a coalescence of Negro votes could force an independent Negro into the nomination. He renounced his own candidacy and came out in support of Josiah Walls, already the compromise choice for chairman of the convention. One by one, Harmon, Gibbs, and many of Hamilton's black supporters switched to Walls. Finally, Walls won on the eleventh try, after a riot nearly broke out when Osborn tried to cheat on the count and Purman tried to vote twice on the same ballot. As one newsman reported, "Walls was now the ascending luminary and his fortune was made."[39]

Selection of a candidate for lieutenant governor was equally strained by factionalism. Thomas Osborn's ring lined up behind Horatio Jenkins, a prominent anti-Reed Republican. The Purman-Reed ring, on the other hand, supported Samuel Day, an old Civil War unionist from Columbia County. The black delegates again remained loyal to Reed. Day won the nomination on the second ballot. Eventually, both Day and Walls were beaten in close elections, as much the result of continued Republican discord as of Democratic voting strength.[40]

However bitter the factionalism, there were occasions nevertheless when Republicans managed to achieve a measureable amount of harmony. One such case occurred during the election campaign in 1872.

A number of political considerations combined to produce a Republican victory at the polls at a time when many observers, Republicans and Democrats alike, were expecting a large-scale Republican defeat.

Early in 1872, the national party began to break up. Dissidents led by U.S. Sen. Carl Schurz declined to support Ulysses Grant for a second term. Upset by the continuing excesses of Grant's subordinates in office and by the corruption and scandals that marred his administration, a national Liberal-Republican party was organized in the spring at a meeting held in Nashville, Tennessee.[41]

In the South, the splinter movement inspired many Democrats to consider new political alignments. In Missouri, for example, B. Gratz Brown, a Liberal Republican, won the gubernatorial race against his usual Republican opponent. The Democratic party in Missouri offered no third candidate, choosing to support Brown. Moreover, a chief result was that the Missouri Democrats, who aligned with Liberal-Republicans, also captured control of the state legislature.[42]

Florida's Liberal-Republicans attracted few legitimate reformers from the old Republican party. Instead, the new party was engineered by Democrats led by William Bloxham, who had won against Day in the 1870 lieutenant governor's contest after the supreme court overturned Day's narrow edge. Bloxham believed that Florida Democrats could match the results in Missouri, and he even advertised publicly for Negroes to join the "reform" ticket.[43]

Compounding factionalism at the national level was the turmoil surrounding Harrison Reed. His last impeachment trial had occurred in April, and the Bloxham-Day contest was not resolved until early June. In October, Reed added to the party's disputes by requesting the removals from office of Horatio Bisbee and Sherman Conant. By mid-October, however, the Republican muddle began to clear, at least in Florida. The Liberal-Republicans chose Horace Greeley to oppose Grant. The crusty editor of the New York *Tribune* had been a faithful party member since before the Civil War, but unfortunately he was a weak campaigner. Bisbee and Conant were reinstated by Grant on 11 October, over Reed's objections, and the governor reluctantly decided to work for the state and national tickets alongside the ring. Meanwhile, Liberal-Republicans met in a convention in Jacksonville on 14 August, as did the Democrats. Republican dissidents discovered that the Democrats refused to cooperate as a coalition, nominating instead only their party's choices, with the result that most of the reformers returned to the Republican fold; the remainder joined the conservative

Democrats "in an absolute surrender." Even as early as July, Thomas Osborn was reporting that the Liberal-Republican movement lacked vitality. He commented that "the Greeley feeling is weaker here than in any other state."[44]

One harmonizing factor that aided Republicans was the nomination of Ossian B. Hart and Marcellus Stearns for governor and lieutenant governor. Hart, a native, was instrumental in the formation of Florida's party through the Union-Republican Club of Jacksonville. Although he and Reed had their differences, by and large they were friends. Stearns, on the other hand, was more clearly a ring Republican. He had maneuvered the last Reed impeachment proceeding as speaker of the house, and both he and Thomas Osborn had been agents of the Freedmen's Bureau. The Hart-Stearns ticket was a victory for Republican unity. Hart was already a sick man, however, and, it turned out, would not live out his full term.[45]

Another factor that turned Republicans toward victory in 1872 was the selection of William Purman as the congressman from West Florida. Under reapportionment, the state had been allotted two House seats. Walls claimed the East Florida seat, but delegates to the Republican state convention in Tallahassee, where the entire ticket was constructed on 22–24 August 1872, divided over the second nominee. At first the race was between Robert Meacham and William Gleason. But as both men were inextricably bound up with the worst examples of past factionalism, the delegates agreed to promote someone who could maintain a sectional balance and be cross-representative of Florida. William Purman was a logical choice. Hart, Stearns, and Walls represented the eastern, southern, and middle portions of Florida, and Purman of Pensacola, an early member of the party and the Freedmen's Bureau, won the nomination with relative ease.

Basking in their newly wrought unity, many Republicans by the fall of 1872 were predicting a successful campaign. Alva A. Knight, a party hack whom Reed had made circuit judge, reported that "Florida is safe for Grant and Wilson. Hon. O. B. Hart and Major M. L. Stearns are working the situation in South Florida and are meeting with great success."[46] So was Josiah Walls: he campaigned successfully for reelection to Congress in 1872, only to be unseated by Silas Niblack when the House of Representatives ruled against Walls in 1870. Walls had attempted to remove the shield of Liberal-Republicanism from the activities of Bloxham's movement. He also criticized local party activists for their persistent dissension when Florida Republicans were working hard to create a new unity. In Leon County, Walls accused blacks who promised to support Bloxham of being two-faced. "In doing so," he recounted to an enthusiastic audience in Tallahassee, "they put me in mind of the colored man up North who had promised to vote. On being asked what it meant he said: 'Massa John, that was talk the other day; this is business. . . .' And so I am confident that any promises Bloxham has received is only talk, and on the fifth of November, you will show him you mean business." A Bloxham victory would only mean at the very best a Florida governor with a "Republican head and a Democratic body."[47]

The Republican party swept Florida that November. Hart beat Bloxham by more than 1,500 votes; both Purman and Walls won their contest by wide margins; and, of course, Grant swept Greeley across the nation as well as in Florida, where he won by more than 2,000 votes. Dampening Republican elation, however, was the fact that in the state senate and house there still were only slim majorities.[48] John Wallace, a black, a Republican, and a witness of Reconstruction in Florida, attributed the party's widespread victories to three elements: Greeley's weak showing as a national candidate and his connection with Bloxham; the constant attempt by Democrats to separate blacks and whites in the Republican party along racial lines (which was unsuccessful during this particular campaign); and the great personal appeal of Grant.[49]

Although the 1872 election appeared to signal a new Republican unity, none developed. By 1874, the party was again seriously divided. The terms ring and anti-ring remained in constant use, but the alignments were now less clear than the labels indicated. Following Gov. Ossian Hart's death only a few months after assuming office, Gov. Marcellus Stearns emerged as the state's leading Republican. Once a member of the Osborn ring, Stearns carried through with Edward Cheney's earlier plans for centralizing state party committees. County committees, appointed by the state central committee, were established in opposition to locally constructed bodies.[50] Floridians elected to federal offices formed a new opposition faction led by Sen. Simon Conover and Congressmen Josiah Walls and William Purman. To illustrate the confusion, John Wallace referred to the Stearns group as the ring Republican faction while the pro-Republican Tallahassee *Sentinel* used the identical term to label the Conover faction.[51] Eventually this resplintering was to cost the party dearly. Walls lost his second district East Florida seat to Jesse J. Finley after the 1874 election was twice contested in the House of Representatives, and a Democrat from Pensacola, Charles W. Jones, replaced retiring Republican Sen. Abijah Gilbert. Purman of West Florida managed to win reelection but not without first enduring a Republican convention fracas with followers of Stearns that involved clubs and pistols.[52]

Factionalism during the Reconstruction period peaked with the elections of 1876. The precampaign phase was as divisive as before. This time not even the usual late mergings of factions could restore the party's strength by November, because of the problems of the national Republican party in choosing a successor to Grant, the deep internal fracturing between Stearns's and Conover's forces, and the determination of the Democrats to bring home a winner.

Republican successes in most southern states were tapering off by 1876, but in Florida the party had hopes of holding on. On the 1876 ticket with a dark-horse presidential candidate, Ohio's governor and ex–Civil War general, Rutherford B. Hayes, were Marcellus Stearns (serving out the unfinished term of Ossian Hart); William Purman (in the first congressional district, also an incumbent); and Horatio Bisbee (who had garnered the nomination in East Florida when Josiah Walls failed to win a fourth one). Bisbee, the former district attorney, was opposed by Finley, the Democratic incumbent.

Factionalism among Republicans in 1876 surfaced when Senator Conover decided to contest Stearns for the gubernatorial nomination against Democrat George Drew. The preconvention period proved to be an especially bitter time, as Conover and Stearns traded countercharges of bribery and corruption. Edward Cheney and the state Republican executive committee supported Stearns's incumbency, although Conover clearly gained strength in all areas of the state. When Stearns was nominated in early June, the Conover delegates bolted the regular Republican convention in Tallahassee and set up their own nominating convention. Not only was Conover chosen as nominee for governor, but a competing slate of delegates also was selected for the national convention. The split was felt in many Florida counties where competing campaign committees were established. By September, however, the schism had healed: Conover dropped from the race (though amid charges that Stearns had bought him out).[53]

After finally restoring some harmony, Florida Republicans launched a two-pronged anti-Democratic campaign. First, they attacked Drew and his party followers for being in favor of the rich man, commonly called Bourbon politics: "Born to command and reared with aristocratic instincts, there is no incense so sweet to Bourbon nostrils as the praise that willing, abject dependents offer to their boss." Second, they attacked Drew's Whig antecedents. The *Sentinel* itself complimented its Democratic foes for yielding "the lead to the live, progressive elements" under Drew, then reversed itself, inquiring whether Drew had won the Democratic nomination because of his "political versatility and success in boxing the compass." Not only had Drew been a Whig during the antebellum era; he had also opposed secession and had legitimately joined the Liberal-Republican movement in 1872. Unable to find clear issues to oppose Drew's candidacy, the pro-Stearns *Sentinel* decried Drew's "disloyalty to secession" and ridiculed his novel campaign technique of giving hats to supporters. A man with little sense of humor, Drew had written a somber letter about his hats describing them "as a sample of Florida production and home manufacture." The *Sentinel* could not resist a comeback: "Under proper culture, how many hats might be expected to the acre, and their value in the rough? What could Drew and Hull hat lands be bought for or pre-empted, and what kind of fertilizers are best? Is irrigation necessary? Do they grow on the stalk or vine, and when does the plant bloom, shoot, or tassel? . . . Tropical countries produce breadfruit and palmetto fans, and why not Drew and Hull hats?"[54]

Despite the lightheartedness, Republicans knew well that their survival in Florida was in jeopardy. Black voters suffered intense intimidation from both Republican and Democratic white politicians who traveled the state threatening Negroes who did not promise to support their party's candidates. There were new surges of violence and a record amount of fraud at the polls. The presidential contest between Rutherford B. Hayes and Samuel J. Tilden proved to be one of the closest and certainly the most disputed election in American history. When the results were disclosed, Hayes had garnered 185 electoral votes, Tilden 184. There were twenty votes, including four from Florida, that were doubtful.

With the Florida election suddenly of national significance, visiting Republican politicians spent considerable time in the state, especially Sen. William E. Chandler of New Hampshire, a member of the national party committee. He sought to influence the outcome of the presidential election, although the gubernatorial contest was also in doubt, promising local Republicans that "funds will be on hand to meet every requirement."[55] Democrats' actions were identical. Abram

Hewitt, Tilden's campaign manager, was notified by a Florida Democrat that the "Radicals intend fraud—We need material aid to check them. Can we get it?"[56]

Both parties claimed that a considerable amount of fraud had occurred. For example, Republicans charged that in Manatee County the absence of a county clerk, the lack of public notices and public registration lists, and improper counting had resulted in a return to the state canvassing board of 262 Democratic votes and 26 Republican votes against a population of 100 whites and 2,660 blacks. They also disputed the return from Jackson County where, in one precinct, the ballot box had been hidden after Republicans had voted. When the ballot box was restored so that Democrats could vote (under the rule that the parties would vote alternately), the final count produced no Republican votes at all. Similarly, Democrats contested the returns from Alachua and Duval counties, among others. In Alachua, they alleged that Republicans illegally added votes in the Archer precinct after the ballot box had been taken home for the night by Leonard Dennis, a local Republican leader. In Duval, the returns were not certified by the county judge, a Democrat, because the votes were incorrectly totaled at several precincts by Republican inspectors.[57]

On 6 December 1876, the Florida Board of Canvassers issued certificates of elections awarding Hayes a majority of 924 votes. More than 1,800 votes cast for both parties were thrown out in the process of reaching the final figure. That same day, Republican electors voted, and the duplicate sets of returns were forwarded to Washington.[58]

Because Louisiana and South Carolina followed the same procedure, Congress was thrust into a deadlock. Investigating committees were formed in the House and Senate. In Florida, a series of judicial actions awarded the governorship to George Drew, who was inaugurated on 2 January 1877. Although the contested presidential election eventually went to Hayes as the "compromise of 1877," Drew's installation as governor marked the end of any active Republican role for the remainder of the century. No Republican would win a statewide office again until 1928.

Details of Republican factionalism in Florida under Reconstruction can be understood in light of the three factors that have been identified with subsequent Democratic party politics: a multiplicity of state factions, a dispersion of leadership, and a discontinuity in the grouping of voters into factions.[59] Republicans during Reconstruction suffered a fundamental division between state and federal officeholders. Because governors were empowered to make so many appointments, their patronage powers equaled or exceeded those of congressmen or senators. Ring and anti-ring splits were neither illusory nor over principle; they involved the spoils of political office. Josiah Walls once remarked that while patriotism was "the love of office," politics was "the art of getting it."[60] Both factions were riddled with true politicians if not genuine patriots.

Among Florida's Reconstruction Republicans, a dispersion of political leadership occurred because of the state's frontier conditions. Vast distances made it almost impossible for any single person to become known and accepted throughout the state, and sectionalism resulted. Geography splintered Republican interests in frontier Florida as economics would a century later.

Just as Democratic voters in the twentieth century, Florida's Republican voters under Reconstruction often shifted from faction to faction. In Jacksonville, for example, county and state elections between 1870 and 1875 divided voters even at the precinct level into ring and anti-ring without regard to race; but municipal elections indicated a disregard for those divisions. Moreover, local leaders John Scott and Joseph Lee shifted from ring to anti-ring on two separate occasions.[61]

If Reconstruction Republicans had outnumbered Democrats by a larger margin, factionalism might not have been so disastrous. Eventually the party lost the November general elections because the factions were not able to reconcile their differences and combat Democratic fraud and voter intimidation. Officeholding and the power of patronage rather than principles divided Reconstruction Republicans. Disunited and distant from the national GOP, Florida's Republican party slumped after 1876 into a long period of isolation. The politics of participation had come to an end.

4

Politics of Reconstruction:
The Record of the Republican Party

"THE REPUBLICAN PARTY, neither North nor South, can be made out to be a congregation of saints unalloyed of earthly taint, nor are its leaders to be regarded with the reverence and homage which are claimed for the disciples of a higher gospel," observed a Jacksonville newspaper editor midway through Reconstruction.[1] Undoubtedly, sainthood was undeserved, but not all Republicans who shouldered Florida's postwar burdens were single-minded opportunists. Among them were men who accepted the immense responsibilities of Reconstruction with dedication and sincerity.

The problems encountered by state governments of the ex-Confederacy were profound and complex. Though Florida in fact had escaped the most damaging effects of the war, there was a lack of adequate roads, railroads, and canals, and too few schools to educate children of either race. There was an insufficient number of judges and courts to serve much more than a crude system of justice, and hospitals, asylums, and prisons were poorly equipped or nonexistent. Florida's fiscal condition resembled that of other southern states—depleted treasury, ruined credit, obsolete tax collection system, and almost no general operating revenue. In calmer times, these difficulties would have been severe; in the turmoil of emancipation, they were nearly unmanageable.

Reconstruction Republicans left a controversial legacy. In expanding state services, including a modern public school system, and in restoring Florida's financial credibility, they made lasting achievements. Developing Florida economically and commercially, building transportation networks, and establishing permanent civil and political rights for the freedmen were left to later generations.

The Republican party never "ruled" Reconstruction Florida, nor was it able to root its programs deeply enough to overcome the opposition. In the legislature, Republicans owned a working majority only through the initial term of Governor Reed's administration. In 1868, at the onset of Republicanism, there had been a party majority of thirty in the lower house; by 1871, that margin had been reduced to four; by 1875 (before Republican participation formally ended), the Democrats had become the majority party. Republicans in post–Civil War Florida were divided by background, experience, geography, education, and race. Negroes and carpetbaggers comprised only a minority of the party membership; the majority included southern unionists or scalawags.[2]

Erroneous beliefs that the Republican party in Florida was a unified organization opposed only by a token party of Democrats have promoted a variety of misimpressions about what Republican politicians did or failed to do in the wake of the Civil War. Chief among them has been the criticism of Governor Reed's administration for its reputed failure to suppress violence. Historians have excoriated Republican governments across the South for fostering the murders, shootings, lynchings, and burnings that marked life in the postwar era. William Watson Davis blamed Republicans for the terrorism, arguing that reactionary Ku Klux Klan violence was directly related to the Negro's becoming involved in politics. If Republicans had not insisted that Negroes receive civil, economic, and political rights equal to or greater than those enjoyed by their former masters, the reign of terror in Florida would never have taken place; nor would the frontier atmosphere, already tumultuous, have become lawless. Other factors added to the political pressures, including an excessive amount of drunkenness among rural Floridians and the presence of a few genuinely unlawful men.[3]

Terrorism in Florida coincided with a similar wave of lawlessness elsewhere in the South between 1868 and 1871. It was a period rife with political reprisals against Republicans by Democratic sympathizers attempting to achieve illegally what could not be accomplished at the ballot box—to overthrow southern Republicans and end Reconstruction. The Ku Klux Klan—called Young Men's Democratic Clubs in Florida—rode through the state's black belt intimidating, harassing, and even killing many black and white Republicans. Only federal legislation in 1871 was able to curb this lawlessness. But by the time Congress passed the Enforcement Acts, the Klan's contempt for law and order had become endemic. More than two hundred people were killed in Jackson, Madison, Columbia, Alachua, Suwannee, Hamilton, Taylor, and Lafayette counties.[4] The exact number of Floridians who were driven off their land or silenced by the Klan's threats or killed but never accounted for can never be determined.

Weapons for personal self-defense became a necessity. In Gainesville, for example, local residents walked the streets carrying shotguns, pistols, and knives. Stabbings, shootings, and brawls were almost routine. Nineteen citizens were killed in the county during this three-year period—all of them Republicans. One resident citizen testified before a congressional committee that at least six secret societies operated in Alachua County "to prevent certain parties from exerting too great an influence with the colored population."[5]

The worst of the Klan's campaigns took place in Jackson County, where more than 150 were killed in the so-called Jackson County War. The acknowledged leader was J. P. Coker, a bellicose ex-Confederate, who amused himself and his fellow Klansmen in front of Republican polling stations by threatening to kill any Negroes who tried to vote.[6] When the troubles began in Jackson County, Coker tried to blame Republicans, especially the former Freedmen's Bureau agents William Purman and Charles Hamilton (both of whom eventually served in Congress).

Purman was an early casualty in the Jackson County War; he was shot and seriously wounded in the neck while walking a deserted Marianna street in March 1869. The assault initiated a chain of violence against other Republicans in the county: Dr. John Finlayson was assassinated soon after Purman was wounded, and on 28 September, twenty-three Negro men, women, and children proceeding to a Sunday afternoon picnic near Marianna were attacked by hooded and armed assailants who killed one man and a small child. A white Jackson County farmer and his daughter were shot and killed as they sat on the front steps of their home on the evening of 1 October 1869. It was reported by some to have been an unfortunate accident, a mistaken attempt to kill Coker. Nonetheless, the next day "a carnival of deaths" swept through Jackson County and continued for several months thereafter. Murder became such a common occurrence that John Q. Dickinson, a white Republican county leader who dared to face the consequences, commented that "the frequency and cold blood which have characterized our murders has not been to me so fearful an act as the carelessness with which the public learns [of] a new outrage."[7] Soon after, Dickinson too fell victim to the Ku Klux Klan.

Despite the forgiving inclinations of many historians, there was never much doubt in Jackson County or in Florida generally about the ultimate purpose of the violence: to prevent participation by Negroes in the Republican party of Florida and in Reconstruction. As soon as any Negro in Jackson County would publicly renounce his interest in politics, stop voting, and remain quietly at home, Coker's men would stop molesting him. According to Emanuel Fortune, Jackson County's representative at the 1868 constitutional convention and father of New York editor Timothy Thomas Fortune, Coker planned to weed out all Republican influence in the county. Fortune himself left Jackson County and eventually moved out of the state.[8]

Governor Reed's administration was unable to cope successfully with the Ku Klux Klan, either in Jackson County or elsewhere in Florida. At first Reed believed that sending the state militia into Jackson County would only exacerbate conditions, since more than half of the militia were blacks and all were untrained and ill equipped to handle large-scale civil disobedience. He changed his mind when the situation rapidly grew worse, however. Once Reed decided that the state had to intervene, he purchased a shipment of arms. In late 1868, an entire trainload of military equipment arrived in Jacksonville from New York City and was immediately transferred to a special train for the state capital. The arms and supplies never reached their intended destination. Sympathetic railroad officials permitted the Klan to board the train near Lake City, and the entire shipment was seized and destroyed by Klansmen.[9]

A reduction in terrorism seemed to coincide with the passage of federal statutes aimed at suppressing the Ku Klux Klan. The first Enforcement Act was passed by Congress in May 1870, and though some historians have suggested that it and subsequent acts were of little importance in ending the violence, they were nonetheless an indication that Klan terror threatened Reconstruction and the existence of the Republican party in the South.[10]

The first Enforcement Act outlawed "force, bribery, threats, and intimidation." It prohibited election officials from discriminating against Negroes who wanted to vote and provided for sanctions against any disguised group traveling public highways who interfered with or attempted to proscribe the civil liberties of others.

The second act instituted a number of new election reforms and was passed after the Republicans suffered heavy losses in the off-year congressional elections of 1870. National Republican leaders were of the opinion, substantially correct, that their party's decline in Congress was due to the unequaled fraud and corruption, intimidation, and violence in the South. To stop these abuses, the new statute provided for supervisors at polling places to certify registration lists and returns. Republicans and Democrats accused each other's election workers of fraud tactics, including forging voter signatures, stuffing ballots, purging voter lists without cause, and giving the state and local canvassing boards obviously incorrect and altered returns.[11]

The third act, popularly known as the Ku Klux Klan Act, clearly proscribed any sort of conspiracy against the government of the United States, persons holding public office, juries, or the enforcers of federal equal protection laws. President Grant was empowered to order federal troops into the South and to suspend habeas corpus if necessary. Any criminal prosecution that might result from enforcing this statute would be undertaken in federal courts.[12]

Twenty-one indictments were handed down in Florida following the election of 1870. One was against former Gov. Abraham K. Allison, who was found guilty of preventing Negro Republicans from casting ballots in Gadsden County. On 12 February 1872, Allison was sentenced to serve six months in the Leon County jail and was fined $550. Apparently not believing that President Grant would allow a former state governor to serve time in prison, Allison petitioned for a full pardon, but Grant refused to review Allison's case and the ex-Confederate served his full sentence.[13] A number of other prominent Democrats were indicted for similar offenses, including Judge Pleasant Woodson White and state Senators John Crawford, Alexander McCaskill, and William Kendrick. Although none was successfully prosecuted, the threat from Washington did seem to lessen the terrorism.[14]

Despite the Enforcement Acts, the Ku Klux Klan accomplished its main goal: even with federal troops present, the violence in Jackson County continued until most Republicans were either dead or had moved away. Nationally, Republicans seemed to be losing interest in their southern organization. More critical issues pushed aside concern for Negro freedoms and the problems of a hostile South. The failure of federal attorneys to prosecute more cases under the Enforcement Acts—probably because southern Negroes were afraid to testify in open court against their aggressors—also dampened Republican enthusiasm, and many Republicans in Washington seemed resigned to the eventual victory of white supremacy in the South.

By 1873, economic depression was sweeping the nation and Europe, and congressional concerns turned to tariffs, currency, and fiscal policy. The panic of 1873 hurt every sector of the national economy:

banks were forced to close, currency payments were halted, many manufacturers shut down, railroad construction ceased, the stock market fell, and bankruptcies multiplied. Workingmen across the nation suffered too: wages declined, unemployment rose, farm prices fell, bread lines appeared in many cities, and labor strikes, crime, and even illness noticeably increased.[15] Amid social turmoil caused by the depression generally, the Ku Klux Klan became only one of many problems left unsolved by Republican Reconstruction administrations.

Public education was the Republican party's finest Reconstruction legacy. Following emancipation, the Reconstruction government in Florida, as in other southern states, not only provided an elementary education for many more children than ever before but also found new ways to fund an expanded school system. (A common school fund in Florida during the Civil War had been spent for military purposes by the Confederate government of John Milton.)

The constitutional convention recognized the need for public education, and the 1868 state constitution directed Florida's government to provide schooling for all children "residing within its borders, without distinction or preference." A new system of public schools was to be established and a free university as well. A superintendent of public instruction was added to the governor's cabinet, symbolizing the elevated importance of education. The constitution required the governor to recreate the state's common school fund and defined ways in which funds were to be acquired. Government grants, private donations, and direct legislative appropriations were to be sought. A portion of all fines levied and collected by the Florida courts and a percentage of Florida's per capita tax revenue were earmarked for the school fund; 25 percent of revenue derived from sales of public lands owned by the state and a special property tax for education completed the funding methods worked out by the Republicans.[16]

Republican leaders confronted political and social crises as the program to revitalize education unfolded. Over the strenuous objections of Charles Pearce, black Republican chairman of the assembly's education committee, the bill that finally passed the state legislature in 1869 permitted segregation of Florida's schools but required local school officials to establish "separate schools for the different classes in such manner as will secure the largest attendance of pupils, promote harmony and advancement of the school, when required by the patrons."[17] In fact, local schools were commonly segregated according to race.

Other provisions in the law were less controversial and even relatively modern by current standards. To oversee the whole state educational program, a state board of education was established, composed of the state superintendent of public instruction, the attorney general, and the secretary of state. Responsibilities were specified for counties and schools. Each county was required to maintain a school district under the direction of a county superintendent and a county school board. Trustees were appointed to guide education at each school and to employ teachers. The 1869 school law also prescribed a minimun three-month school term each year.[18]

The law took hold slowly. By 1871, two years after its passage, revenue for schools in the state continued to come not from the school fund but from other sources, chiefly the Freedmen's Bureau and private philanthropy. Bureau schools were predominant during the immediate post–Civil War period, serving to educate freedmen, however crudely, into their new status. Many adult ex-slaves as well as children attended the Freedmen's Bureau schools for the rudimentary education they offered. A number of private northern church groups and secular aid societies also opened new schools in the South. Most prominent in Florida were the schools established by the American Missionary Society.[19] Lacking major appropriations from the state legislature, Florida's communities often depended on these outside sources. For example, the Peabody fund was made available to Florida's schools in 1869. Two years later, contributions from the fund to Florida's public schools totaled more than $41,000 in actual monies and textbooks.[20]

According to a contemporaneous survey of Reconstruction Florida, 80 percent of the state's Negroes and 20 percent of the whites were illiterate. In most counties after the war, there were no school facilities at all. In others, the schools were barely adequate for teaching. Most Florida children did not attend school regularly, as plantings or harvests emptied the classrooms.

Before Republicanism ended in Reconstruction Florida, however, the administrations of Governors Harrison Reed, Ossian B. Hart, and Marcellus Stearns had begun to make some headway. By 1873, the state school system was virtually complete. Except in Dade, Brevard, and Holmes counties, school superintendents had been appointed and were at work. In August 1873, Superintendent of Public Instruction Jonathan Gibbs reported to a meeting of the National Education Association at Elmira, New York, that Florida had enrolled 18,000 students at a cost of slightly more than $100,000.[21] Three thousand more children were added to the school rolls in 1874, and almost $140,000 was spent on public education by the Republican administration. The next school year, 1874–75, witnessed the most dramatic increases, demonstrating the effectiveness of the Republican party's commitment to public education; 32,372 students were enrolled at a cost of more than $150,000, indicating that the school law passed in 1869 was taking hold. By this time, the party had also managed to right the state's weakened financial situation, and increased tax revenues were having an impact on the education budget. More than $188,000 in tax revenue was used to support Florida's new educational system in 1875.[22]

Republicans were concerned that members of both races should receive at least an elementary education. Because the Freedmen's Bureau and private philanthropies had been concentrating their efforts on Negro education, white Floridians benefited more from the work of the Republicans than did Negroes. By 1874, eleven secondary schools were open in Florida, eight for whites and three for blacks. The Florida legislature had passed a law on 18 February 1870 that authorized the establishment of Florida State Agricultural College for Negroes—three years after the state university for whites had been founded.[23]

Public education in Reconstruction Florida was successful because of the commitment of the Republican party. By 1890, long after Reconstruction had been overturned and Democratic control had been firmly established in Florida and throughout the South, the illiteracy rate among Florida's Negroes had dropped from its pre-Reconstruction 80 percent level to less than 50 percent. If subsequent Democratic administrations had maintained the same interest in biracial education, the success of the public educational system might have been even more dramatic. However, the Democrats drew back from educating Negro children, claiming that the Republicans had spent exorbitantly. Each year after 1876, Democratic governors and state legislators called for cuts in spending, especially for education. School tax millage rates after Reconstruction declined steadily, curtailing schooling for blacks much more than for whites. Yet because of the earlier efforts by the Florida Republican party, Florida claimed the lowest rate of illiteracy among the states of the Confederacy.[24]

Regarding the economic development of post–Civil War Florida, neither the Republicans nor the Democrats could claim much success. Both parties generally sacrificed economic welfare to politics, especially in two important aspects of southern postwar development, railroads and public land policy. The Swepson-Littlefield fraud case (outlined in chapter 3) stands as the extreme example of Republican corruption, but prominent Democratic politicians of that era were equally corrupt. Although Gov. Harrison Reed was tried twice for impeachment because of his involvement in the fraud, both Democrats and Republicans in the state legislature had joined in passing the original bill authorizing the bonds "as a most excellent measure . . . for developing the western section of the state." Even Milton Littlefield, one of the principal architects of the affair, remarked that at least one Democratic legislator had been bribed to produce "the legislative swag" for two other Democrats. Nor was Governor Reed the only chief executive involved in the fraud case. Former Gov. David S. Walker accepted a retainer from Littlefield and Swepson in return for influencing Florida's Democrats to support the scheme.[25]

Few Republicans worked more diligently for economic development than Congressman Josiah T. Walls of the second district of East Florida. Although Walls spent the bulk of his time in Congress arguing for more civil and political rights for Negroes, he was also Florida's greatest booster during Reconstruction. He concentrated his efforts on bringing Florida much-needed federal monies for internal improvements. In the last session of the Forty-third Congress, for example, Walls successfully sponsored legislation establishing new customshouses, post offices, and other government services for Jacksonville, Cedar Key, and Key West.[26] He introduced bills to improve navigation on the St. Johns and the Apalachicola rivers and to add harbor facilities at Pensacola and Key West.[27] Besides seeing that seven more postal routes were established for Floridians, Walls actively sought federal aid for railroads, canals, and steamship companies, winning praise for his efforts from Republicans and Democrats alike. Contrasting his legislative work with that of his Republican colleagues, Congressman William Purman and Sen. Simon Conover, a Jacksonville newspaper commented, "In all the play so far, except for the effort of Mr. Walls . . . [the Florida delegation] has been as dumb as lambs bound and corded for the slaughter pen."[28] Walls continuously urged new settlers to come to Florida, "my own sunny state." One historian has concluded that of all the Negro Republicans who served in Reconstruction congresses, Walls was the most dedicated to serving the needs of his constituents and his state.[29]

Although Republican efforts to guide Florida's postwar fortunes by expanding business opportunities prefigured the dynamism of the New South, the reactionary emphasis was against the plantation system and its Democratic supporters. Depicting Democratic planter aristocrats as the rear guard of the antebellum South, Republicans were fond of proclaiming themselves the vanguard of a postbellum "New South": "The old saws and antediluvian maxims, however proper in the days of Roman chariots and galleys, are barely applicable to an age in which the locomotive and steamship are notable and commanding features."[30]

Florida's Republicans took several steps during Reconstruction to bring about reform and modernization of commerce. Most party leaders thought that Florida's fiscal credibility would have to be restored before significant amounts of capital or skilled labor would be invested. Because Congress had passed more liberal homestead legislation, many Americans were again heading west. Prior to secession, Florida's population had dwindled, and it was feared that in the wake of the Civil War it would dwindle again. With rural blacks deserting the cotton fields for the urban centers, farm labor threatened to become desperately scarce. Furthermore, many white Floridians were convinced that southern freedmen could not meet Florida's needs for cheap and industrious agricultural labor. Republican officials in Governor Reed's administration saw the need for more settlers in their state, and a Bureau of Immigration was created to encourage people to move to Florida. By the mid-1870s, the concept of Negro extinction had died away, but the fear of Negro migration had not. In 1874, Florida's commissioner of immigration, J. S. Adams, was greatly alarmed by what he perceived as "a vast migration of colored labor leaving the state."[31]

These fears proved unfounded. Florida's population increased steadily throughout Reconstruction, and census returns show that between the Civil War and 1880 more Negroes migrated into Florida than out of it.[32] Both political parties expressed an interest in attracting new ethnic groups, and several newspapers advocated an influx of Italian and Chinese immigrants, who were thought somehow to be especially suited to tilling Florida's soil.[33] The white population in the state also rose dramatically in the same period, doubling to 142,000 by 1880.[34]

The increases in costs of government under Reconstruction made Republican administrations look bad, but Governors Reed, Hart, and Stearns actually helped restore Florida's financial strength. Following the Civil War, the conservative administration of Gov. David S. Walker paid all state expenses in scrip, which was often unredeemable for weeks at a time, then often discounted by as much as twenty-five cents on the dollar. As Governor Stearns left office a decade later in 1876, scrip was selling at ninety cents on the dollar and was widely accepted across the state.³⁵ Both Republicans and Democrats, however much they disagreed over politics and elections, acknowledged that the Republican party knew how to manage finances.

Claims by contemporaries and later by historians that Republicans during Reconstruction were extravagant spenders were untrue. While there were increases in expenditures, the services offered to Floridians were greatly expanded, particularly public education.

Despite financial aid to Florida's schools from the Freedmen's Bureau, private donations, and the Peabody Fund, the revamped educational system still cost the state more than $100,000 in 1874—twenty-five times the amount spent by the Conservatives in 1866.³⁶ Wholly new social services offered by the Republicans added to the costs of state government. Before Harrison Reed's term, for example, there was no state prison; by 1875, the prison system was costing more than $28,000 per year. Republicans opened new hospitals and asylums, and by 1874 they were spending seven times more than any previous Democratic administration had on care for the insane.³⁷ The need for more state officials to handle the new and larger social service programs increased goverment's costs. In addition, the governor's cabinet was increased from five to eight, and numerous new judges across the state added considerably to the payroll.³⁸ Even without the rapid growth in Florida's population during Reconstruction, enlargement of state government would have been justified. Former slaves, whose judicial, civil, social, economic, and political well-being had been beyond the concern of state government during the antebellum era, were now free citizens whose needs were the government's responsibility.

When the increase in expenditures for education is subtracted, the remaining increases are surprisingly small—further proof that the Republican party of Reconstruction Florida was not a collection of spendthrifts. Republicans reduced costs steadily to such a degree that the state was spending only about $1,000 more in 1876 than David S. Walker's administration spent in its last year. Republican George Wentworth's 1869 legislative proposal reduced salaries for all Florida officials. The governor's salary dipped from $5,000 to $3,500; the chief justice's from $4,500 to $4,000; salaries for associate justices were reduced by $450 yearly; and the lieutenant governor's pay dipped by $200. Wentworth's bill passed the house unanimously and the senate by a vote of thirty-eight to five.³⁹ Two additional amendments to the constitution sponsored by Republicans in the legislature further reduced the costs of government. Biennial rather than annual legislative sessions were introduced along with abolition of state-financed county courts;[40] but the Republicans were no longer in charge to claim credit for the amendments.

With state government forced by circumstances to provide more services to more people, additional revenues had to come from taxes. Property taxes rose rapidly. In 1860, the annual rate was 16-2/3 cents per $100 of valuation; it increased to $1.37 in 1872. Not all the added tax was levied by the state, however; county taxes accounted for most of the increase. Florida's tax law structure favored wealthy landowners. A plantation owner was permitted to pay his state taxes in scrip, which was normally valued under par, and was also allowed to appraise his own property for tax purposes. Although this system was established before the Civil War, the Republican party of Reconstruction was not inclined to reform it. County tax assessors rarely collected (or at least rarely reported to the state comptroller) the full or fair share of tax revenue owed to the state. Even Comptroller Robert Gamble, a Democrat, complained in 1871 that fourteen counties were collecting less revenue than the law mandated.[41]

Yet even if taxes had been collected aggressively and properties assessed at their full market value, Florida's tax burden under its Republican administrations would have been relatively light. Taxes on property were higher in twelve other states in 1870. Florida's per capita tax was less than similar tax burdens in twenty-nine other states. During the Republican party's tenure, the burden of taxation was spread much more equitably than under previous or subsequent Democratic administrations. Only during Reconstruction did poorer Negroes pay proportionately less of their income in taxes than did wealthier whites.[42]

Another fiscal issue blemished the Republicans' image—the reputed size of Florida's debt, supposedly run up through wasteful spending. In reality, Florida's debt was relatively small and certainly was necessary for redevelopment and expansion. Democrats charged that under Republican (Reconstruction) administration, the state debt increased to more than $5 million. That figure, however, includes the $4 million in bonds issued to the Jacksonville, Pensacola, and Mobile Railroad. Although Republicans were involved in the affair, adding the cost of the Swepson-Littlefield fraud to the state debt is unwarranted. Not only did Florida hold a statutory lien against the railroad, which was exercised to recoup some of the loss, but the railroad itself was eventually sold to settle with the original bondholders.[43] The balance of the debt, which increased less than $700,000 throughout Reconstruction, seems moderate enough in contrast with the expansion of population and services. Furthermore, Governor Stearns's administration was able to reduce the debt by $37,000 by 1876.[44]

Florida's record of fiscal responsibility should be compared with other states' administrations during Reconstruction. For example, South Carolina authorized a $1.5 million bond issue to redeem a $500,000 debt in bank notes. In North Carolina, the same Swepson-Littlefield partnership resulted in more than $17 million in worthless state-issued railroad bonds. Other railroad schemers bilked Arkansas of more than $9 million; Georgia lost $6 million; and Alabama lost between $17 million and $30 million. Democrats were involved in these and other schemes as they had been in Florida.

"Dunningite" charges of immense indebtedness were exaggerated grossly. While Florida Republicans were reducing their state's indebtedness, Republicans in Alabama added only $2.5 million not $30 million as Democrats claimed, and in Mississippi there was little difference in expenditures or tax rates between Democratic- and Republican-controlled counties.[45]

Against the backdrop of chaotic politics, fraud, corruption, violence, and terror that accompanied Reconstruction, it is sometimes difficult to accept the idea that the Republican party across the South achieved any successes or fostered significant and rewarding changes. But Florida did manage to overcome the dislocations of the Civil War, and in some crucial ways the state actually flourished during Reconstruction. The Republican party did not bring Florida to ruin, either deliberately or accidentally, as many historians have claimed. Reconstruction was a tragic era not because it failed completely but because it did not realize its promises of development and equality.

Part Two. Isolation

5

Southern Strategy Begins

CERTAIN EVENTS IN HISTORY seem to slice through time, dividing the immediate past into distinctive periods and making a particular event seem especially important. The election of Rutherford Hayes as president in 1876 was such an event for most southern Republicans and Democrats, including those in Florida. With the demise of the only remaining Republican governments in Louisiana, South Carolina, and Florida, the last traces of party stability and strength resting on black votes and white leadership were finally and totally excised.

Reconstruction had ended when Hayes's Republican supporters and southern Democrats of the Congress struck their bargain at the Wormley Hotel in Washington on 26 February 1877—the Democrats exchanging the White House for southern home rule.[1] No longer was the hue and cry against federal military intervention heard during electioneering, though both black and white Republicans still suffered intimidation. Even President Grant had grown weary of those "autumnal outbreaks" of violence that incessantly marked elections in the South. Indeed, incidents of violence had been fewer before the Ku Klux Klan terror, but the decline was a result of the general weakening of Republican political strength.

The will to intercede in the affairs of the ex-Confederate states had diminished considerably among national Republican party chiefs. The economic panic and the depression that followed it in 1873 were still present three years later, though conditions had begun to improve. Nonetheless, the gloomy economy did manage to sweep aside interest in the South's political reconstruction. With large numbers of northerners, westerners, and easterners out of work, concern for southerners simply faded.

In addition to their preoccupation with the panic of 1873, Republicans in Washington had accepted the political fact that the old-style party alignment of blacks and whites had not produced Republican hegemony in the South. President-elect Hayes and his close advisors wanted to lay the groundwork for a new political alignment in the South, one that would rejuvenate southern Republicanism. The key to their new southern strategy lay in what Horace Greeley and his Liberal-Republican movement had attempted to accomplish in 1872 when Greeley campaigned in the South against Grant and his administration's reputation for excesses and corruption. This campaign was the seedbed for a revision in the Republican party's strategy in the South. What Greeley advocated in 1872, Hayes attempted to institute in 1877—to divide southern whites politically along antebellum lines. By so doing, Hayes hoped to incorporate into the Republican party the "persistent Whigs" of the South.[2]

Prior to the Civil War, the South had experienced a vigorous and rather clearly defined two-party system of Whigs and Democrats. The southern Democrats eventually spearheaded the secession but only after a long period of defending slavery, state rights, and the honor of the South. Whigs, on the other hand, arose in opposition to the politics and policies of Andrew Jackson in the 1830s. The men who made up the Whig party in both the North and South often were characterized as "respectable." Whereas the basic composition of the Democratic party before the Civil War had included small farmers and city workers, the Whigs were merchants, bankers, and (in the South) plantation owners. There were even a few mountain dwellers, mostly in North Carolina, who had joined the Whig party to foster the building of roads and railroads. Generally, southern Whiggery supported Henry Clay's *American System*. The famed Kentucky compromiser had long advocated economic development that would bind the future of the South more securely to that of the nation as a whole. Clay argued persuasively in the Senate for high tariffs on foreign imports to encourage domestic production, for the creation of a national bank that would enable the United States to stabilize its currency and facilitate business transactions, and for internal improvements that would unite the entire country by a network of canals, roads, steamship routes, and railroads. President Andrew Jackson opposed most of these goals, especially the national bank, and so did the rank-and-file Democrats who supported him.

The Civil War divided northern and southern Whigs as well as Democrats. Northern Whigs, for the most part, had joined the newly formed Republican party in an effort to limit the extension of slavery and preserve the economics of free labor, but southern Whigs were hard pressed to find political alternatives to their party. At first, southern Whigs opposed secession, preferring instead to stand for sectional compromise, unionism, and peace. During the various secession conventions that followed Lincoln's election in 1860, Whigs worked unsuccessfully to prevent the South's withdrawal from the Union.[3] Once the matter had been resolved and the war actually had begun, southern Whigs turned to supporting the South's cause.

Reconstruction found southern Whigs independent again. During the first phase of Reconstruction under President Andrew Johnson, Whigs dominated the provisional state government administrations. Johnson's distaste for radical reconstruction measures and his moderate terms for reconciliation appealed to many southern Whigs. But as Reconstruction progressed and Johnson's impeachment trial in 1866 left the administration of Reconstruction to Congress, southern Whigs again were without any political alternatives. Most united with southern Democrats, calling themselves conservative and opponents of the newly formed Republican organizations. Only a few moderate Whigs chose to join the Republicans in an effort to ameliorate radical Reconstruction.

Southern Whigs and Democrats gradually discovered their traditional differences as the Republican party began to weaken. This process became more obvious after Greeley's campaign. Even though President Grant in 1872 won an overwhelming victory, receiving wide support from the South, Greeley's call for abandoning southern blacks and carpetbaggers in favor of reuniting moderate whites against the perennially divided secessionists and Negroes stimulated Hayes's new southern strategy four years later. President-elect Hayes argued that southern Republican state governments could no longer adequately protect Negroes. It made more sense, Hayes believed, to promote sectional peace and preserve the Republican party by abandoning the old Republican strategy and redividing southern whites along their traditional political lines. "The whites must be divided there before a better state of things will prevail," the new president wrote in his diary.[4]

The Wormley House bargain reflected this shift. In return for their support for his presidential aspirations, Hayes promised southern congressional leaders that he would appoint a southerner to his cabinet and withdraw federal troops still stationed in the South, thereby ensuring the demise of Republican governments in South Carolina and Louisiana. In addition, he pledged to support the South in its quest for more internal improvements.

No doubt both sides made the pact in good faith, but the results proved singularly unrewarding for the new Republican strategy. Hayes's appointment of David M. Key, a former Tennessee Whig, as postmaster general put practically all of the available federal patronage power in the hands of a southerner. By late April, the troops were withdrawn, as Hayes had promised, and the unstable Republican party state governments fell, as predicted, shortly thereafter. But the southern Democratic congressmen who had signed the Wormley House bargain reneged on supporting Republican James Garfield of Ohio as speaker of the House of Representatives in the 1877 congressional session. Republicans, in turn, withdrew their pledges of support for southern internal improvements.

Most injurious to the future of the Republican party in Florida and other southern states was the failure to redevelop the state party organizations. Not only did southern Whigs decline to join the Republican party in sufficient numbers to reward Hayes's new southern strategy, but Negro rights also slipped away along with their support. The compromise of 1877 cemented the pattern of race relations in the South for several generations and determined southern political alignments for almost another century. "The settlement was not ideal from any point of view, nor was it very logical either. But that is the way of compromises."[5]

These political maneuvers at the national level had a profound effect on Florida Republicans. In South Carolina and Louisiana, federal troops still buttressed Republican state governments, but Florida's Republicans seemed to be aware that Governor Stearns had little chance of staving off a Democratic victory in 1876. Stearns himself lost to George Drew by more than 500 votes. Their contest reflected a number of national issues, but the greatest concern revolved around Florida's affairs during Reconstruction.

Drew personally became a key issue in the gubernatorial campaign. After unsuccessfully trying to elect the antebellum Democrat William Bloxham, Democrats finally turned to moderate ex-Whig George Drew. Originally from New Hampshire, Drew had amassed a sizable fortune in the lumber business. By the time he became governor, he was a millionaire. As was true of most Whigs, Drew originally opposed secession, but he had also served for a brief period in the

Union army. That fact was well hidden by his supporters during his campaign against Stearns. The fact that they were successful demonstrates why, in Florida at least, Hayes's policy of attracting ex-Whigs into the Republican ranks was so difficult. It also explained why the southern strategy conceived by the national party leaders could not succeed. Whereas a Democrat in 1876 could still be tainted with secessionism, a Whig could generate broad-based support against almost any Republican. There was little incentive under those conditions for former Whigs to join with Republicans.

Drew's victory over Stearns also hinged on the extensive split-ticket voting in eastern Florida, where intra-Republican factionalism historically had been most extreme. There was growing disillusionment among Floridians over the Republicans in state government. Their incessant party feuds amid charges of ring corruption and abusive rhetoric had disaffected the voters. Though they chose to support a Republican presidency, many Floridians were ready to approve a change in state government. No matter how the precinct voting came out in the presidential race between Hayes and Tilden, Drew's victory over Stearns was unqualified.[6]

On 2 January 1877, almost three months before Hayes assumed the presidency and two months before the Wormley agreement, Drew took the oath of office before Chief Justice Edwin Randall. His simple inaugural speech belied the fact that much turmoil had preceded the event. Stearns at this time was undergoing pressure from many of Florida's most influential Republicans and from the federal men there to watch over Hayes's interests in the state. Both groups would protest Drew's victory in the courts. Some felt that if Stearns did not join them in the fight, Hayes's case against Tilden would be weakened immeasurably. Others believed that Stearns should pursue the matter for the sake of justice for his cause. As in past elections, incidents of fraud, intimidation, and violence hindered or prevented Republicans from turning out to vote in full force. Rumors of major troubles brought out federal troops to meet the threats in some areas. However, even while the tension was at its peak, the level of active violence was not uncommonly high.[7]

Florida was a pivotal state for Hayes and Tilden. Sen. William Eaton Chandler of New Hampshire managed Hayes's victorious campaign. Manton Marble of the New York *World* filled the same function for the national Democratic party.[8] Each side quickly became involved in the governor's race. The political atmosphere in Tallahassee was a nervous mixture of fear and uncertainty: "It is all a whisper and a wink. There is nothing frank or easy. The truth of the matter is that both parties are at sea. Neither knows exactly what to do and yet is bewildered by the fear that the other will do it first."[9]

Despite the pressure, Stearns resisted going to court for adjudication. On 14 December 1876, Chief Justice Randall issued an opinion, in which the other justices concurred, validating Drew's claim to victory. Upon hearing of the decision, Stearns remarked to his advisors, "This beats us in the state but we shall try to save Hayes. The opinion is a surprise to everyone here."[10]

Just how much the decision actually surprised Stearns is open to question. Edwin Randall had been one of the first appointees of Gov. Harrison Reed in 1868 when the state was reorganizing under the new constitution. Throughout Reed's intraparty conflicts and impeachment struggles, Randall remained one of his firm supporters. Stearns, on the other hand, spearheaded much of the Republican internal opposition, especially after Sen. Thomas Osborn retired from politics. It is clear that Stearns's active role against Reed during Reed's tenure as speaker of the Florida House of Representatives had much to do with Randall's refusal to support Stearns in 1876. Samuel McLin, one of the Republican members of Florida's board of canvassers who was trying desperately to save Stearns as well as Hayes, wrote of Randall that he "was only glad of an opportunity to sacrifice Stearns. The traitor would have destroyed the electoral vote if necessary to make his spite on Stearns and the others."[11]

But past Republican squabbling was not the sole reason for Stearns's refusal to press further against Drew. Stearns knew well the implications that would arise from the new southern strategy designed by Hayes and the national Republican party. With either Tilden or Hayes in the White House, the southern Republican parties, formed around blacks, unionists, and carpetbaggers, were doomed. Tilden, a Democrat, would be unsympathetic to preserving southern Reconstruction Republicans by the deployment of federal troops. With Hayes, the problem was exactly the same, since he would have to make compromises with southern Democrats in Congress to ensure his own victory. In either situation, Stearns predicted, "We may look for the warm loving embrace of southern whites by the next administration."[12] Despite his outward calm and apparent acceptance of the conditions that faced him, Stearns personally was bitter about his defeat. On the same day that Drew assumed the office of governor of Florida, Stearns hitched up a team of horses at a Tallahassee livery stable and drove off into the Leon County countryside to avoid making an official appearance. Eventually, President Hayes assuaged Stearns's bitterness by appointing him to a post in Arkansas.[13]

Florida's return to Democratically controlled state government was not accompanied by a total or immediate Republican eclipse. For one thing, Drew himself played down the significance of the transition. He promised during his inaugural address that Florida's Negro population would not suffer the loss of all their gains made under Republican party control during Reconstruction. Indeed, a number of Republicans around the state were cheered by the fact that Drew, an ex-Whig and not a confirmed southern Democrat, seemed to be a man of moderation. Several pro-Republican newspapers pointed out with relief that Drew made no cabinet appointments from the ranks of the Ku Klux Klan.[14] Harriet Beecher Stowe, whose novel *Uncle Tom's Cabin* once had caused Abraham Lincoln to describe her as "the little woman who wrote the book that made this great war," had been a resident of Florida since 1866. Stowe wrote to friends in the North that Drew's victory was received with approbation by most, if not all, prominent pro-Republican newspapers. It was a sign, she noted, that "the lion and the lamb . . . may yet lie down together."[15]

If some white Republicans were not taken aback by Drew's victory, the same feeling was noticeably lacking among Florida's Negroes. "Well, we niggers is done," was the summation of one wizened old man who watched Drew's inaugural ceremony in Tallahassee.[16] Despite the new governor's assurances, the demise of the Republican party in Florida was a major concern of blacks. Nor did many Republican blacks find solace in Hayes's far-off guarantees of "better protection" as part of the new strategy for the South. No one was asking the president from whom they needed protection. In an effort to alleviate Negro suspicions, President Hayes appointed Frederick Douglass as minister to Haiti. That did little to assuage the gloom felt by most thoughtful Negro leaders. Few Florida freedmen would have argued with the Rev. Alexander Crummell's remark to a friend in New York: "I have the most serious misgivings, for President Hayes putting one black man forward does not compensate for his putting four and a half million black men in the South back and giving supremacy . . . to the old power-holding body."[17]

On 4 July 1877, a meeting of Negroes was held in Tallahassee. From all over the state, delegates gathered to reflect on their future under Democratic rule. The tone of the meeting indicated how deeply the defeat of the Republicans and the end of Reconstruction was felt by the freedmen. A number of the most prominent Negro Republicans spoke to the state convention, among them Charles Pearce and John Wallace; but, in keeping with the new national strategy, only a handful of white Republicans was present. Outgoing Republican Sen. Simon Conover, whose factional political wars with Stearns had contributed greatly to the Republican defeat in 1876 and who had himself been defeated in the Senate by Democrat Wilkinson Call, spoke to the assembly, urging Negroes to remain quiet and uncritical of the new administration, at least publicly. Disavowing any connection with the new Republican desire to exempt Negroes, he hastened to add, "I do not meantime wish to be understood as advising that you altogether withdraw your interests in politics." [18]

The state's major pro-Democratic newspapers viewed the convention with suspicion. Some predicted that a "new departure" Republican movement would grow from it, a feeling aroused by the presence of the few white Republican party leaders. The Jacksonville *Daily Sun and Press* was especially critical of their attendance at the 4 July gathering, portraying them as men "who see the drift of sentiment among the colored people and deem it wise to seek its control rather than oppose it." [19]

Such feelings were generated unnecessarily. Although a few nationally important Negro leaders, among them Louisiana's former lieutenant governor P. B. S. Pinchback and Frederick Douglass, were calling for a new political strategy for Negroes, Florida freedmen as yet had little choice but to acquiesce in the shift away from Reconstruction. Well in advance of Booker T. Washington's plea that southern Negroes erase their interest in politics and concentrate instead on economic advancement, the convention delegates drafted an open letter to the citizens of the state stressing their economic needs and desires. Politics went untouched, prompting the Tallahassee *Floridian* to comment: "On the whole we are inclined to applaud . . . the Convention for [its] good sense. They make no foolish complainings and raise no groundless fears. They did not get much into politics and have fairly represented their material wants and needs." [20]

Some immediate changes were apparent once Drew took office. For the first time since the Civil War, federal troops were not stationed in Florida to preserve internal security, the last detachment having pulled out less than three weeks after his inauguration. When the legislature reconvened in January 1877, the Republican members for the first time found themselves on the minority side of the aisle. They comprised a truly isolated and impotent bloc. Even prior to the judicial decisions in a number of contested election races, the Democratic majority was guaranteed by overwhelming numbers.[21] After several contested elections were awarded to Democrats, the only Republicans remaining in the lower house were those from Alachua, Duval, Marion, Jefferson, and Leon counties. The Republican candidate in Escambia County had won by more than 100 votes over his Democratic opponent. The committee on privileges and elections upheld his election; but the committee's decision was subject to the vote of the entire body, and the majority voted to overturn the committee's recommendation. One committee member, a Democrat from Putnam County, voted for the Republican in committee but opposed him on the floor.[22] As might be expected, each of the standing committees in both houses was formed without a single Republican in a position of importance.[23]

Republicans who had survived the disastrous results of the elections of 1876 were reduced to adopting political styles similar to Democrats in the Republican legislatures of early Reconstruction days. Harassment, stalling, and efforts to create divisions and controversy characterized Republican activity as the minority party.

Simon Conover in 1879 is an example. Wilkinson Call, a leading Democrat and staunch Confederate, once before had been sent by a Florida legislature to Washington; shortly after Reconstruction commenced under President Andrew Johnson in 1866, Call was one of several conservative southerners elected but never seated as the Congress took control away from the president.[24] Conover was still the choice of most of the Republicans in office in 1879, even though his splintered political campaign against Gov. Marcellus Stearns probably cost the party the 1876 election. In fact, Conover had opposed Stearns primarily because he recognized that another term in the U.S. Senate for him was unlikely. Although most Republicans cast their ballots for Conover, a few were content to cast meaningless votes along the lines of past intraparty rivalries. Josiah Walls in the senate and Leonard Dennis in the house, for example, had been Republican combatants in Alachua County throughout Reconstruction, dividing local Republicans time and again. During the previous campaign, they had perpetuated the division. By the time they united their factions for party unity in late September 1876, it was too late.[25] Once Walls and Dennis became powerless, they renewed their political friendship, each voting for the other in several elections.²⁶ Had they worked together earlier, their party might have had a better chance of survival.

On 26 January 1877, the legislature voted to award to Samuel J. Tilden Florida's certificate of election for the presidency. Democratic legislators were responding to a Democratic state canvassing board's ruling that a recount indicated victory for Tilden. It is interesting to note how the Republican opposition responded. When the issue was debated in the house, Republicans A. B. Osgood and T. W. Long demanded another recount, calling it to a vote under a bill titled "showing the wisdom and ability of the Florida legislature."²⁷ Robert Meacham, a Negro Republican from Leon County, introduced a bill in the senate to display his displeasure with the results of both the governor's race and the national campaign. He demanded that the victories of Democrats Drew and Tilden and their running mates over Stearns and Hayes should be announced in his bill, calling it "an act to count four men into office without being elected."²⁸ These and similar proposals by Republicans were defeated with little effort, but Congress merely accepted the Florida certificate as one of many disputed returns.²⁹ That legislative decision, if it had been allowed to stand, would have ensured Tilden's election.

The parties' change of attitude toward the state constitution also indicates how different were conditions in 1876 compared to 1868. Earlier, the appointive powers of the governor had been a source of major controversy and concern; even some Republicans had worried about how Harrison Reed would use the power. Democrats opposed it instinctively as a provision that ensured Negro participation to a limited degree. With Democrat George Drew in the governor's office, however, Democratic party leaders found it a convenient device for removing Republicans from local and county offices. In county after county, Drew, acting upon the advice of his close advisors and also the county Democratic executive committees, systematically replaced Republican officials with Democrats. Drew's private secretary, Charles Dyke, Jr., openly defended the wholesale upheaval. It was not the governor's intention, he announced, to "reward those who were loudmouthed in the denunciation of those people who supported him."³⁰

Republicans attempted to thwart this Democratic housecleaning. Sen. J. T. Walls introduced a bill that directly opposed the law, which he had advocated as a member of the 1868 constitutional convention. In 1877, Walls understood that a home rule amendment would protect Negroes in their exercise of the franchise in areas where they were the majority of the population. Whereas in 1866 the appointments overturned Democratic control of the black-belt counties by guaranteeing the appointment of Negro officials, only direct local elections could accomplish the same goal in 1877. Drew appointed white Democrats to office in those areas where Negro Republicans comprised the majority, and Walls's bill was easily defeated.

The efforts by Hayes and the national Republican party to establish a new political relationship with the South failed in Florida as it did in other ex-Confederate states. Not until 1884 would the Florida Republican party attempt a merger with dissident Democrats to form an Independent party ticket. That effort to reacquire political power also proved to be a failure. Unfortunately for the Republican party in Florida, that attempt in 1884 plunged the party even further into political obscurity. By the beginning of the twentieth century, neither a Republican presidency nor any new southern strategy could rescue Florida's Republicans from their total political isolation.

6

Shaping Dissent and the Search for Order

THE 1876 ELECTION had barely ended when southern Republicans began an imperative search for a new political order. Even though the national compromise that had made Rutherford Hayes president had stilled fears of renewed civil war, and the smooth transition from a Republican governor to a Democrat had quieted the political crisis in Florida, critical problems remained. Three obstacles stood in the path of Republican resurgence in the South—how to rid the party of Negroes and carpetbaggers so that moderate whites and ex-Whigs might be encouraged to join, how to restructure a coalition of Republicans throughout the South to respond to the Democratic surge to power and control, and how to cope with the changing attitudes of the post-Reconstruction era. While very much interconnected, these issues were also separate and distinct.

The largest stumbling block was the removal of blacks. Negroes had formed the original wellspring of southern Republicanism during Reconstruction, but by 1877 it seemed to national Republican leaders that the blacks and their carpetbag chiefs were responsible for the party's failure to maintain control of the South. William E. Chandler, New Hampshire's senator and a principal patronage advisor to Presidents Hayes, Garfield, and Arthur, stated matter-of-factly, "Our straight Republican, carpetbag, negro governments, whether fairly or unfairly, have been destroyed and can not be revived."[1] The remainder of the nineteenth century witnessed various efforts to redefine the Republican party in the South along so-called Lily White lines. The other two issues—how to adjust to Democratic resurgence and changing attitudes—were more directly related. Nationally, the goal of pushing blacks, radicals, and carpetbaggers out while pulling in moderate whites and Whigs produced a return to the rhetoric and issues of the Civil War and early Reconstruction by both political parties. Republicans found it useful to wave the bloody shirt of Democratic secession, slavery, and war. Democrats during their post-Reconstruction campaigns filled their political rhetoric with the equally emotional issues created during Republican-controlled Reconstruction—corruption, radicalism, and, most important, Negro rule.

The Republican party was hard pressed to retain its identity in the South. In an attempt to appeal to the rise of agrarian discontent among Grangers, Alliancemen, and Populists, traditional Republicans searched in the last decades of the century for campaign issues that made sense. The Republicans nationally had become the habitual choice of the majority of voters. Republican Joseph Hawley of Connecticut is reported to have said in 1884 that his party "could nominate a wooden Indian cigar store sign for president, and elect it."[2] But in the South, the party was suffering virtual elimination. By 1896, there was "a big Republican monopoly in the North" and a "little Democratic monopoly in the South." In only a few states were the parties still competitive and differences clearly defined. In most areas a one-party system had evolved, and it was created "not by competing with the opposition party but by eliminating it."[3]

The condition of Florida's Republican party bordered on ineptitude. Contributing more than anything else to their woes was their inability to give up their personal feuds and factionalism from the time of Reconstruction. Former Gov. Marcellus Stearns and Sen. Simon B. Conover continued to clash with each other even though both men were defeated in their reelection efforts. Stearns left office in January 1877 and Conover's senate seat was taken by Wilkinson Call about a year later, but their differences and conflicts continued to divide the party.

John Tyler, editor of the *Florida Sentinel,* son of the former president, and supporter of Governor Stearns, condemned Conover. He accused the senator of being only a Democrat in Republican disguise, bent on disruption of the Florida Republican party. Tyler was also convinced, as were many other pro-Stearns Republicans, that Conover had been bribed to run against the governor in 1876 and later was counter-bribed by Stearns to pull out. He also believed that Conover had once recommended Democrat William Bloxham to President Grant for a federal appointment. Conover allegedly endorsed Florida's most powerful Bourbon politician for a position as surveyor general, describing him to the president as a Republican "good and true at heart." The nomination was withdrawn by Conover only when Sen. Abijah Gilbert protested vehemently against it. Gilbert succeeded in obtaining the position for his own son. Conover also aroused Tyler's ire by announcing his intentions to return to Florida politics and to run for office once again. Yet prior to leaving the Senate, Conover alienated Stearns's supporters by sponsoring a bill that removed salaries for members of the Arkansas Commission, to which the former Florida governor had been appointed, making the memberships honorary instead. To Tyler it demonstrated that the old ring feud of Reconstruction was far from over.[4]

Patronage in Florida, a concern of many Republicans in the post-Reconstruction era, caused some unhappiness and much uneasiness. F. E. Humphreys, collector of customs in Pensacola, recommended two Democrats to Chandler but promised that these appointments would be the only exceptions to his desire "to ensure the benefit and credit of the Republican Party." In fact, Humphreys's plan related to the long-standing schism between Senator Conover and Governor Stearns. When Humphreys was recommended for his post as customs collector, Senator Conover refused to endorse the nomination, claiming that it was supported by George Wentworth of Pensacola, Stearns's chief ally in West Florida. If Democratic Sen. Charles Jones had not backed Humphreys, he might have lost the appointment. Humphreys was also supporting the two Democrats as a favor to Jones. One post, an inspector's, was desired by Jones's brother-in-law; the other was a clerking position in Humphreys's customs office. Humphreys wrote to Chandler, "These are the only concessions I propose to make outside of the Republican Party, and in fact I don't consider [them] a concession to the Democracy, but to Senator Jones personally."[5]

Other patronage problems for Florida Republicans centered on past political activity. For example, Leonard Dennis was nominated for a federal appointment while under indictment for election fraud in the 1876 election. On the evening of 7 November 1876, Dennis had taken to his home a ballot box from a Gainesville precinct. The following morning when the votes were tallied, an extra 219 votes were allegedly counted.[6] Despite this, Dennis was enthusiastically endorsed by federal Judge Thomas Settle who saw Dennis as "a promising and uncompromising Republican . . . conspicuous in preventing fraud in Alachua County designed by the Democrats, upon which they claimed the state for Tilden." According to Settle, it was Dennis's "courage and vigilance [that] defeated them and they consequently hated him and have procured half a dozen indictments against him, all utterly

Shaping Dissent and the Search for Order

frivolous."[7] Dennis escaped prosecution, but he never received the appointment from Hayes. As a consequence, he was one of the driving forces behind an independent splinter campaign to elect Josiah Walls to Congress in 1884.

Bourbon Democratic Gov. William Bloxham did his best to harass Republicans seeking federal appointments in Florida. In 1879, Dennis Eagan of Madison was nominated by Congressman Horatio Bisbee for the position of federal tax collector for Florida. Bloxham opposed Eagan's nomination and tried to block his appointment. The incumbent, Alva A. Knight, was a Republican but was also engaged in defending a Democratic candidate for Congress, Noble Hull, who had run unsuccessfully against Bisbee in 1878. Former lieutenant governor under George Drew, Hull contested the outcome but eventually lost to Bisbee in the House of Representatives. Bloxham ordered his state comptroller to reject the bond posted in Eagan's behalf by several prominent Florida Republicans, then submitted a petition to Washington challenging their (and by inference Eagan's) fiscal integrity. Bloxham claimed that they had fraudulently undervalued their properties in previous tax assessments (although the law permitted undervaluations for citrus lands not yet profitably bearing fruit). Eagan successfully posted a second bond and eventually acquired the post. The fracas indicated, as Dennis suggested, that "no Republican could possibly give a bond that would meet the approval of our present delegation."[8]

Patronage tended to separate southern Republicans who were appointed to federal positions by the Hayes administration from those who were not. Senator Chandler received several warnings from members of the Florida Republican party who were concerned over the party's future. William G. Stewart, Negro postmaster in Tallahassee, wrote Chandler in March 1879 that Simon Conover's failure to win reelection to the U.S. Senate meant that Democrats in Florida "would take advantage of us. The Senator is our friend and as long as he can help us, he will certainly do so."[9] Stewart urged Chandler to use the power of patronage carefully.

In 1883 when Chandler was advising President Chester Arthur on Republican patronage matters, J. Willis Menard, a Key West Negro Republican newspaper editor, wrote to Chandler requesting that Republican appointments in Florida be used so that the party could "get in good fighting trim for 1884. We want to remove all obstacles." Menard was writing particularly to ask that the local customs collector in Key West be removed from office and to advise Senator Chandler that his local Republican executive committee was preparing a report to support that action. Menard earlier had warned Chandler, "If the Administration desires to carry this State in 1884, it will have to make certain changes, and place men in Federal positions who will work in harmony with the colored men in the State, and thereby present a united front to the Bourbon enemy in the next struggle." [10]

Negro Republicans like Menard were not the only Florida Republicans complaining about the unequal dispensing of patronage to carpetbaggers and blacks. Clayton Cowgill, who had been state comptroller during Reconstruction, also was upset. While Rutherford Hayes was still in the White House, Cowgill attacked his southern strategy of neglect: "I hope our next President, if Republican, will be a man of some nerve and may not entertain the opinion that all southern Republicans are necessarily rascals in some form." Cowgill indicated his personal regret for having contributed a thousand dollars toward Hayes's 1876 presidential campaign.[11]

Compounding the state party divisions after Reconstruction was the 1880 presidential campaign. With Hayes not seeking reelection, securing the Republican nomination was a possibility for several candidates; in Florida, memories of Reconstruction determined the favorite choice: Ulysses S. Grant. Most Negroes in the Florida Republican party were solidly behind a third term for the former president. Grant's opposition stemmed principally from Sen. James G. Blaine, the "plumed knight" leader of the "half-breed" Republican party faction, and Secretary of the Treasury John Sherman.[12]

Florida Republicans were as divided in their preferences for the nominee for the presidency as they had been in most other political matters. Malachi Martin, superintendent of the state prison at Chattahoochee, attended a meeting of the Florida Republican executive committee in Gainesville in January 1880. His report of the political situation showed the wide gap in sentiment. A carpetbagger Republican immigrant to Florida, Martin was hoping that Blaine would restore to national favor the old Reconstruction leadership in the southern states:

> I met most of the men who control and direct political affairs here, and I am justified in saying that by proper management a Blaine delegation can be sent from Florida to Chicago.
> The officers of the Treasury Dept. must be silent or talk John Sherman! I know of none of them who does not prefer the

former. Special agents have been here and some of them have gone to New Orleans. Conover has been trying to help the Sherman Boom, or as one of your Washington people puts it: a "Sherman Bummer"!! It will take two weeks for the Grant excitement to die out. . . .

If the friends of Mr. Blaine see fit to help us, we will be glad to have them do so. And when the Treasury Dept. is to be contended with, we need all the assistance we can get.[13]

Because the 1876 presidential election had proven to be such a close contest with Florida so critical to the outcome, the support of black Republican party members was important. None of the white party chiefs in Florida wanted Grant, though there was disagreement between the supporters of Sherman and of Blaine. Conover, ever the party maverick, was managing Sherman's campaign. Dennis, Martin, and Stearns were hopeful of Blaine's chances with Florida Republicans. But Grant apparently still commanded most of the votes in the state, and his campaign in Florida did not abate as the June nominating convention in Chicago approached. Three months after Martin had predicted an early end to Grant's bid, Leonard Dennis observed that the ex-president was the strongest candidate in the field: "It is believed he can carry this State easier than any other man. Because of this fact southern Republicans are ready to support his nomination. Blaine has many friends and admirers and it would be possible to work up the Florida delegation in his interest. I would much prefer Blaine to Grant because I regard him as the best party man."[14]

Malachi Martin disagreed with Dennis's assessment. He wrote to Chandler in early April that "political matters here are undergoing a change. The Grant boom is receiving a check. Most of our leading and thinking men are not in favor of a third term. . . . I now think we can send an unpledged delegation, instructed to vote as a unit, a majority of them Blaine men."[15]

Leonard Dennis remained adamant that Grant was the first choice in the state. He told Chandler only four days after Martin's appraisal had reached Washington, "It now looks as if the delegation might be instructed for Grant as no one cares to oppose him, and many are endeavoring to make capital by being first to suggest his name. Blaine can be second choice without opposition."[16]

During early May 1880, the state Republican nominating convention was held in Jacksonville to select delegates to the national party convention in Chicago. Sherman's candidacy never fully developed despite the efforts of Simon Conover, or perhaps because of them, and the delegate fight in Jacksonville was over Blaine and Grant. The conflict renewed once more the inherent Republican problem in the South—black interests versus white interests. As in the 1868 constitutional convention and throughout the course of Reconstruction in Florida, Negroes again failed to exert sufficient political leverage despite their numerical superiority. The delegates to Chicago were not instructed by the nominating convention to support any particular candidate, but privately they were Blaine supporters. All but three black-belt counties in the state had voted that way, and another county delegation had voted for John Sherman.[17]

The 1880 presidential race clearly illustrated the significant differences in issues between national and Florida Republicans. Nationally, the contest in Chicago centered primarily on the warring factions of stalwarts and half-breed Republicans. The former group supported by Grant under the aegis of New York's powerful Sen. Roscoe Conkling; the latter was led by James G. Blaine, though for this group John Sherman was a possible compromise choice. After numerous ballots it became clear that none of the primary contenders could marshal enough votes for the nomination; a dark-horse candidate and congressman, James Garfield from Ohio, finally received the nomination. To offset Conkling's disappointment, one of his close associates in New York, Chester Arthur, was selected by Garfield (himself a Blaine man) to run for vice-president.[18]

Machine issues and insider politics around which the national convention revolved bore little resemblance to politics in Florida, aside from the fact that corruption and unseemly favoritism in government were common to both. National Republican party chiefs wrestled for control of an emerging unity, while in Florida factions still fought over Reconstruction issues. Most significantly, Republicans in Florida, unlike Republicans in Washington, were still coping with biracialism.

In 1878, the congressional nomination in the first district of West Florida was won by Simon Conover, who was anxious to return to Washington. His primary campaign was strangely reminiscent of Republicanism in the 1867–68 period in Florida. Two radicals opposed Conover, Edmund Weeks and Robert Meacham, members of the early radical faction known as the mule team. In November, Conover fared poorly, gaining little or no support from Meacham or Weeks in his bid against Robert Davidson, a Bourbon Democrat.[19]

In the second congressional district, however, the racial divisions of Reconstruction were better able to influence elections, even though fewer blacks were voting than previously. Horatio Bisbee, federal district attorney from Jacksonville, ran a close but successful race against Democrat Noble Hull, the lieutenant governor under George Drew. Hull protested the election outcome before the House of Representatives, but Bisbee was permanently seated in January 1881. Two years later, Bisbee won another close race, this time against Jesse Finley, former congressman from the second district, who had won elections in 1874 and 1876. Finley also contested the election, but on 2 June 1883, the House of Representatives again ruled in favor of the Republican incumbent.[20]

In each of these elections, new and old political forces were operating, especially in East Florida's black-belt counties. Leonard Dennis and Josiah T. Walls, the white and black Republican chiefs in Alachua County, the largest black-belt county in East Florida, had begun to work against Horatio Bisbee. Representing their Reconstruction constituency of freedmen and carpetbaggers, Dennis and Walls widened their criticism to include Republicans who had been rewarded with federal appointments under Hayes and then Garfield and Arthur.[21] They labeled Bisbee a ring politician by virtue of his federal appointment. Senator Chandler was kept informed of the opposition campaign of Dennis and Walls throughout 1880 and 1882. During Bisbee's 1880 congressional race, James Bell, a Republican, wrote to Chandler that he doubted that Dennis could much affect the outcome even though he was "on the warpath" against Bisbee. Bell pleaded with Chandler, who had been one of the Republicans' visiting statesmen in 1876, to return to Florida and help quiet the rampaging factionalism. With such aid, Bell advised, "we can carry the State even for Conover [who ran for governor against Bloxham in 1880], while there is no doubt as to the National Ticket. The future of the party may hinge on Florida & how important to have you on the ground."[22] F. C. Humphreys disagreed with Bell, arguing that the Florida Republican ticket, which included Conover, Bisbee, and E. F. Skinner in West Florida, was, "taken as a whole," very poor; "a weaker one could not be found."[23]

In 1882, the splintering among Dennis, Walls, and Bisbee in East Florida grew steadily worse. While Bisbee did manage to eke out a close victory over Finley, the factional strivings of Dennis and Walls certainly cost Bisbee votes. In August, Walls had won his county's Republican endorsement to oppose Bisbee. At the district nominating convention, however, he could not gather any support from outside his Alachua County delegation, and the entire pro-Walls contingent walked out of the meeting when Bisbee won the nomination. Former Republican state comptroller Clayton Cowgill reported that throughout the rest of the Bisbee-Finley race of 1882, Dennis was "lukewarm" and Walls "secretly antagonistic" toward their party's nominee.[24]

In several respects, the tripartite Republican feud in East Florida rekindled the issues of early Reconstruction; but in West Florida, wholly new issues appeared to be influencing politics and elections. In 1880, Congressman Robert Davidson's reelection campaign encountered for the first time strains of anti-Bourbon feeling. William Bloxham, Florida's premier Bourbon Democrat, was running for governor (since Drew's conciliatory attitudes were no longer required for Democrats to win elections). Davidson shared Bloxham's Bourbon sentiments; he too had been an outspoken Confederate, ardent secessionist, and popular post–Civil War Democrat. Pensacola Republican R. W. Rute observed before Davidson's renomination that his Confederate background could hurt him with immigrant Florida voters from outside the South, meaning "it will certainly be an easy run for an Independent."[25]

Davidson won handily in 1880 but faced considerable opposition two years later from independent A. D. McKinnon, senator from Washington County. McKinnon ran in the congressional primary against Republican regular E. F. Skinner of Pensacola, who had been endorsed by the national GOP congressional campaign committee. McKinnon was a carpetbag supporter of former Governor Stearns, who was district party chairman for West Florida in 1882. In the runoff election in November, McKinnon polled more than a third of all the Republican votes cast, indicating Republican voters' dissatisfaction with federal appointments in Florida. J. Willis Menard wrote to Chandler afterward: "Skinner's candidacy was very obnoxious to a large portion of our voters in this District."[26]

By this time, independent movements had sprung up across the South, indicating widespread discontent with the Republican party as well as with Bourbon Democracy.[27] As early as 1875, some northern Negroes were questioning their participation in the GOP, and their sentiments filtered into the South. Timothy T. Fortune, editor of New York *Age,* began a formal advocacy of black independency in 1884. He attacked the Republican party for "having degenerated into an ignoble scramble for place and power. . . . I do not deem it binding upon colored men to further support the Republican Party when other more advantageous affiliations can be formed. . . . No colored man can ever claim truthfully to be a Bourbon Democrat. It is a fundamental impossibility. But he can be an Independent."[28]

A meeting of the state's Negro leadership in Gainesville on 5 February 1884 indicated how deeply ran the sentiment in agreement with Fortune. Unlike the 1877 meeting in which politics was not talked about, in 1884 political concerns were rife. J. Willis Menard, editor of the Key West *News,* was elected chairman of the meeting. His opening address measured much of the Negroes' discontent about current developments in the GOP. Menard recalled how Negroes had stood with the Republican party throughout Reconstruction, a relationship that had promised mutual benefits for southern blacks and whites. Conditions in 1884 warranted a shift, however; there was "an emergency which the colored had to contend with."[29] The emergency that Menard defined for his eager listeners was the decline of black influence in Florida politics, a change similar in direction and degree to changes elsewhere in the post-Reconstruction South. Fewer and fewer Negroes were allowed to vote in elections. They were being disfranchised not only by new state constitutions but also by developments in statute law.[30] In Florida, Negroes arrested for vagrancy and other petty offenses were excluded from voting at the whim of local justices of the peace (at that time normally white Democrats in black-belt counties). To change this pattern, Menard argued, Negroes in Florida were prepared to "affiliate with any liberal party who would give them recognition."[31] The resentment among blacks at the Gainesville meeting was observed by white Republicans. One white Republican in attendance noted that Negroes had begun formulating a response to the national political strategy that had cut them adrift: "To a man [they] are in favor of cutting loose from the federal officeholders as a class, and will refuse to be led by them any longer. . . . Our intelligent colored men have no confidence in these would-be white leaders. . . . The resolutions of the convention were almost unanimous in favor of joining the Independents, entirely unanimous."[32]

By 1884, Republicans—black and white—were splintering throughout the South, and an anti-Bourbon sentiment had arisen among Democrats. In Florida, increasing numbers of young Democrats were becoming concerned with the hegemony in party affairs of the ex-Confederate, wealthy Bourbons led by William Bloxham. Because Florida's 1868 constitution permitted the governor so many political appointments, there were few chances for these younger men to break into state politics.[33]

A number of factors discomfited the Democrats, primarily the fear that Bloxham and his Bourbon administration would turn over the resources of Florida, especially land, to outside speculators at unreasonably low prices. The sale by Governor Bloxham in 1881 of four million acres to Hamilton Disston at twenty-five cents per acre was the main example. Bloxham defended his sale to the wealthy Philadelphia developer and financier on the grounds that it would rescue Florida from bankruptcy. During the Civil War, the Florida Railroad Company, which was owned principally by Sen. David Levy Yulee, went into receivership, primarily as a result of the heavy demands for its iron and steel by the Confederate government at Richmond, inadequate working capital, and an insufficient number of customers throughout its network. Florida Railroad bonds were guaranteed by the Internal Improvement Fund of the state. Francis Vose, a bondholder, successfully prevented the fund from selling any more Florida land for speculative purposes until it paid him what had been owed by the railroad. From 1870 (when Vose originally secured the court decision in his favor) to 1880, the interest on the state debt from this and other failing railroad claims climbed to $1 million. The debt was paid when Disston negotiated his purchase.

Disston's and similar purchases touched off protest among Democrats already angry with Governor Bloxham's Bourbon politics. The governor's appointive power, written into the constitution by Republicans in 1868, was the subject of a Democratic party caucus in 1884. The caucus recommended a constitutional convention to curtail this power. Bloxham, however, refused to call such a convention.[34]

Many farmers around the state were becoming increasingly unhappy with the railroads, particularly with the rates charged to haul fruits and vegetables to market. Agrarian discontent had been growing in Florida, in the South, and in the West for decades before the rise in the 1890s of the reformist People's party. The Grangers had appeared in the South and West during Reconstruction, and they had made their way into Florida by 1873. Although the Grange disavowed any political activity to seek redress for farmers' grievances, its members were widely accepted. By 1875, there were 5,000 Grangers in the state organized into almost 150 units. *Florida Agriculturist,* the Grange newspaper, was widely read by Florida's farmers. But lacking political leverage, the Grange failed in Florida and throughout the nation. The abuses against which it fought, however, continued to plague small farmers into the 1880s.

An "indignation meeting" of Columbia County vegetable and fruit growers was held on 22 March 1881. The convention protested rising costs for produce shipments on the Southern Express Company's railroad. Delegates to the meeting passed a series of resolutions condemning Southern Express for raising its rates on vegetable shipments more than 60 percent and for attempting to "throttle the enterprise of raising early vegetables for market." They promised "to remedy the evil by negotiating with the Florida Dispatch Company, or some other company that will ensure us a speedy transportation of our garden products at less rate than the present unjust one suddenly forced on us by a company that has heretofore enjoyed our undivided patronage."[35] In June 1884, an action by Putnam County's Democratic farmers served as another example of their discontent: they withdrew from their party's political caucus and formed their own independent group.[36]

On 18 June 1884, all of the various dissenters—Republicans split from the federal officeholding ring; Democrats deprived of political power by Governor Bloxham's Bourbon tactics; Negroes fearing for their political, economic, and social future; small farmers upset by the railroads' dominance over their lives—gathered in Live Oak and established a new Independent party. Candidates for state offices were nominated and a party platform listing political grievances was put together. (It demonstrated well how disparate were the elements that had come together.) Bourbons and radicals alike were castigated. The two major political parties, the platform declared, no longer were "guided by the principles that gave them existence and are utterly lacking in all the elements which invite intelligent, patriotic support." The Bourbon Democrats were attacked for their failure to reform "the present autocratic constitution," for the sale of land to Disston and for "lavish" land grants to railroads, for their use of "party hate and racial antagonisms" for political ends, and for their opposition to a free press. The platform advocated reforms to correct these and other real and perceived abuses—free ballots, full votes, fair counts, constitutional reform, a free press, a railroad commission to regulate rates, a local option law dealing with temperance, reforms of suffrage laws by removing property and educational restrictions, reforms of the election code of Florida, an end to land sales to speculators, and increased immigration into the state.[37]

The Independents tried to soothe tensions among themselves.

Frank Pope, Democratic senator from Madison County, was chosen as the Independent gubernatorial nominee; and Jonathan C. Greeley, Republican businessman from Jacksonville and one of the founders of the Union-Republican Club, was selected as his running mate. In his acceptance speech, Pope argued that the alignments of the other two political parties were artificial extensions from the Civil War and Reconstruction years and were not responsive to the challenges of the 1880s. Therefore, he stated, he would conduct his campaign by talking not about Bourbonism and radicalism or racial supremacy but rather about the needs for more schools, fairer election laws, and full voting rights for all Floridians.[38]

Florida Republicans were left in a quandary by developments at Live Oak. Factional disagreement over Pope's candidacy hindered their search for political order. During the national GOP presidential convention held in Chicago in 1884, Florida's delegation split over the issues of the Independents and the cronyism of ring Republicans. Senator Blaine triumphed over Arthur for the presidential nomination, but the chief issue for Floridians was the question of who would fill the opening on the national executive committee. The federal ring faction in Chicago was headed by Dennis Eagan. The anti-ring faction was led by Joseph Lee, a Negro attorney from Jacksonville and head of the entire Florida delegation. Eagan wanted to seat Edward Cheney, longtime chairman of the Florida GOP state executive committee; Lee wanted a leading member of the anti-ring faction, ex-Congressman Josiah Walls. Neither the ring nor the Independent factions could prevail. In the end, a compromise choice, J. D. Cole of St. Augustine, was selected.[39]

The question of formally joining the new Independent party plagued most Republicans, but the schism was especially critical in the black-belt counties of East Florida. At a Jacksonville meeting of the second congressional district nominating convention on 9 July 1884, a majority of the Republican delegates supported incumbent Congressman Horatio Bisbee. Representing Alachua County's freedmen and, he thought, most Negroes in East Florida, Josiah Walls once again refused to accept Bisbee as his party's nominee. Bolting the regular Republican convention, Walls and Leonard Dennis announced the formation of Walls's Independent campaign for Congress, dividing East Florida Republicans even further. Opposing Bisbee and Walls was a Volusia County Democrat and eventual winner of the seat, Charles Doughtery.[40]

Two weeks later, the Republican state nominating convention met in Tallahassee. Instead of choosing a candidate to oppose Pope and Democrat Edward Perry, Pope was simply endorsed, though not without considerable protest from Republicans who resented the Independent movement. F. G. Hines of Putnam County offered the original resolution that Pope and Greeley be supported with "undivided attention" by Florida Republicans, but the opposite action followed the ensuing debate. Leonard Dennis, who was managing Josiah Walls's Independent campaign in East Florida, vehemently opposed Pope and Greeley for dividing the party. Bisbee, on the other hand, denounced Walls for destroying party unity in East Florida but supported the Independent ticket. Ironically, it was Walls who found the solution that saved the Tallahassee meeting from degenerating into serious conflict: "The Republicans of my county sent a delegation to Live Oak to nominate Pope and Greeley, and we are here today instructed to endorse that nomination. They are now candidates of the Independent party, as such we can elect them; but the moment we nominate them by call of the counties, they become our candidates, and you give the Democrats a club to break their heads."[41]

With sound advice from Walls, the Republicans decided to endorse but not officially nominate Pope and Greeley. The *Florida Journal,* a pro-Independent newspaper, summarized the GOP conundrum: "Bisbee supports the Independent State ticket [Pope and Greeley] and is the regular nominee for Congress. Dennis opposes the Independent State ticket and supports the Independent nominee for Congress [Josiah Walls]. Edward Cheney opposes all 'Independents' and goes for straightout Republican nominations or nothing. Eagan favors an 'Independent' ticket, but opposes Pope." The writer sarcastically concluded, "So you see, things are a little mixed."[42]

Edward A. Perry, who had been one of Confederate Florida's most popular officers, was chosen on 25 June 1884 at Pensacola to be the Democratic standard-bearer. A compromise candidate, he was nominated to reconcile differences between William Bloxham and George Drew. His candidacy served to unify Bourbon political rule. Perry's campaign was simple and familiar—attack Reconstruction, Republicanism, and Negro rule. Perry and many newspapers around the state insisted that the new Independent movement was essentially Republicanism with a fresh face, despite Pope's Democratic background. The Tampa *Tribune* characterized the new party's style as "Republicanism with a thin veil."[43] Charles Jones, partisan editor of the pro-Democratic *Florida Times-Union,* connected Pope with James G. Blaine, who symbolized the epitome of machine Republicanism for Jones; Jones imagined Blaine's opponent, Grover Cleveland, to be the quintessential reformer. Blaine, said Jones, had surrounded himself with the most "nefarious gang of political freebooters ever brought together in any age or country."[44] Turning that strategy around, one pro-Independent newspaper, the Tallahassee *Economist* drummed for support for Frank Pope by writing that Hamilton Disston was a political supporter of both James Blaine and William Bloxham.[45]

Independents found themselves in a political situation that became harder to escape as the 1884 campaigns wore on. In West Florida, Independents required the support of fence-sitting Democrats to win, yet the fact that Republicans composed an important part of the movement alienated many Independent-Democrats and eroded strength for Pope and Greeley. At the same time, the West Florida Independent candidate for Congress in 1882, D. L. McKinnon, was attacking William Chipley, railroad magnate and owner of the Pensacola and Atlantic Railroad. According to McKinnon, state comptroller W. D. Barnes underassessed the value of Chipley's railroad by as much as 20 percent. Though many Independent-Democrats across West Florida agreed with McKinnon's anti-railroad stand, the fact that he and Pope were allied with Republicans overwhelmed other, more positive factors. J. N. Stripling, the new party's executive committee chairman, traveled the first district appealing for funds and unity, but the issue of Republicans on the ticket compounded the Independent party's problems. Nor were feelings soothed when E. O. Locke of Monroe County won the Independent nomination for the first congressional district. Locke, a Reconstruction-era Republican judge, wrested the nomination from Malachi Martin of Gadsden County and S. C. Cobb, an Independent-Democrat from Escambia County.[46]

Inevitably, in both the congressional and the gubernatorial races, the "Negro question" was raised. Bloxham warned Democrats to hew to the party line or else suffer once again through Reconstruction: "Another night of gloom and despair . . . shall cast its dark mantle over our fair state, and we stand silent witnesses of her degradation and dishonor, amid the hellish orgies of an ignorant and ruthless fanaticism."[47] Edward Perry also drew the color line. Speaking to audiences around Florida, Perry pointed out that Negroes could earn higher wages under Democratic governments because industry and railroads provided more jobs and income for Negroes as well as for whites. Frank

Pope tried to respond by ignoring the question of Negroes altogether. As he canvassed the state, he concentrated upon Bourbonism, Bloxham, and the Disston purchase. Finally, however, Pope was forced by Republicans and Democrats to speak out on the subject in Bartow. He declared to a South Florida campaign rally composed of whites and blacks that he intended to appoint qualified Negroes to office.[48]

Besides the fact that Democrats accused Pope of murder,[49] many Republicans around the state who had been prominent during Reconstruction refused to support him. Edward Cheney, Republican war-horse and longtime state executive committee chairman, preferred that Republicans go down in defeat in 1884 rather than ally themselves with Independents. But by 1888, Cheney felt that Republicanism in the South would recover without having to resort to alliances with Democrats. Dennis Egan was not supporting Pope; he and Pope had been rivals in Madison County politics throughout Reconstruction. From New Smyrna in Volusia County, George Alden, ex-secretary of state under Harrison Reed, announced that he too could not follow Pope.[50]

Pope actually was hurt most by Republican brawling in the black belt, especially between Josiah Walls and Horatio Bisbee. Both Republicans ignored their Democratic opponent, Charles Doughtery, throughout the campaign, attacking each other instead with special vengeance. Bisbee accused Walls of being in the race only to ensure Doughtery's victory by splitting votes, and he challenged Walls to a series of debates. Walls accepted in mid-August, denying the charge of leading a bolt against Bisbee. From his political headquarters in Gainesville, Walls began publishing his own campaign newspaper, the *Farmers' Journal*. His initial editorial lambasted Bisbee and failed to mention Doughtery at all. Walls encouraged Negroes in East Florida to show Congressman Bisbee that "we can act upon political matters without fear; that we will not vote for or endorse the nominees of corrupt and lying ringsters and politicians simply because they have secured the declaration that they are the regular nominee."[51]

Bisbee opened his reelection effort in Jacksonville on 1 September. Walls had agreed to debate him there; but because of his wife's severe illness, he sent Leonard Dennis instead. When Dennis attempted to speak before the partisan hometown crowd, he was shouted down. Prior to leaving, he predicted things would be very different when the congressman toured Alachua County: "Bisbee is on his own ground here, and is boss; but he'll be up in Alachua at the end of the week, and if we don't give him a picnic then you may set Dennis up for a flunk."[52]

Bisbee did arrive in Gainesville the following weekend, and the crowd before him was largely pro-Walls. They refused to let Bisbee speak until he allowed Walls to share the platform. By this time, Bisbee had charged Walls with accepting bribes to stay in the race and split votes. In Bisbee's presence and from his platform, Walls answered the charges:

> Colonel Bisbee says the *Farmers' Journal* published by me and paid for by me, is paid for by Democratic money. When he says this he lies. I say he lies! I say he lies!! I say he lies!!! . . . Intelligent people—you people before me—we know what he wants; he wants only to elect himself. He can go to hell. He cannot know whether a Democrat ever paid me a cent. I am able to fight him, and I mean to fight him to the death. We will kill him. We will fight him till the election night. . . . He has lied to me, and he has lied to you, as if we are fools. I know about these things. What are your interests? Are they not identical with the interests of the people among whom you live? Let Bisbee go to Hell.[53]

The bitterness between the two Republicans distressed other members of the party. S. H. Adams wrote Henry Sanford, editor of the *Florida Journal,* that "Gen. Walls and Bisbee are fighting hard and had we funds, could defeat Bisbee. No money from the National Committee and Bisbee has managed to kill off most of our Republican friends . . . who were disposed to help us."[54] During a Jacksonville rally on 18 September, Walls declared his preference for Doughtery over Bisbee.[55] On 14 October in Fernandina, while going to address another crowd, Walls was approached by one of Bisbee's advisors and was tendered a bribe to withdraw. When he refused, the band that Walls thought had been hired to play at his rally marched off down the street to a pro-Bisbee meeting.[56] Meanwhile, one newspaper candidly recorded, "Doughtery scoops in the votes."[57]

Democrats across Florida won easily and convincingly in November. Pope's campaign against railroads and Bloxham's attitudes toward Bourbonism and land speculation did not catch hold in Florida. As one black news editor suggested of Frank Pope, the Independent candidate was only "a pitiful negro Cleveland Democrat."[58] That label was indicative of the Independents' weakness. The party was more a catchall for widespread dissent than an emerging political force for reform.

Shaping Dissent and the Search for Order   93

Pope proved unable to spread himself across the Independent spectrum. While he supported Democrat Grover Cleveland for the presidency, he lost ground over his support for appointing Negroes to office. His past Democratic affiliations also placed him apart from broad Republican support. The net result was Perry's convincing victory by more than five thousand votes.[59]

The 1884 campaign was the last effective third-party movement in Florida until George Wallace's American Party in the 1970s. Florida Independents failed to hold together because they "had little in common other than being out in the political cold."[60] Republicanism in the state would move even farther into the cold in succeeding decades.

7

Republicanism in the Solid South

THE YEAR 1884 marked a turning point in GOP fortunes. A new political age brought with it changes in party leaders, political philosophy, and election strategy. For the first time since the Civil War, a Republican candidate for president failed to win. Republicans managed to acquire a few more seats in the Senate, but Democrats claimed a majority in the House.[1]

The presidential contest between Grover Cleveland and James G. Blaine had been one of the bitterest in American electoral history, each candidate repeatedly attacking the personal integrity of the other. A popular slogan had suggested that the election would go to the party that could "cast the most stinkpots." Cleveland, accused of fathering a bastard child, refused to acknowledge that he was its father but continued to provide financial support for mother and child nonetheless. GOP hard-liners took up a new chant: "Ma, Ma, where's my Pa? Going to the White House!! Ha, Ha, Ha!"[2]

Blaine received equally rough treatment from pro-Democratic newspapers. Rumors circulated that his first child was born six months after his marriage, and exposés were published about his personal finances. The New York *World* added novelty to the election by making Blaine the first presidential candidate to find himself caricatured on the front page of a leading newspaper.[3]

Important changes followed the election. Within a year, Ulysses Grant, Chester Arthur, and Senate kingpin John Logan had died, and two other powerful Senate Republicans had been swept aside. Added to that, the transformation of William Chandler into a political reformer who advocated lower campaign expenditures and opposed the influence of big business in his party caused a new Republican polity to emerge. Best exemplified by Mark Hanna and Mathew Quay, these new Republicans organized their politics around their business conservatism. Republican leaders accepted the corporate ethic of the late nineteenth century: "Prosperity for business means prosperity for the nation." Social programs for America's less fortunate were eschewed in favor of social Darwinism. It became increasingly clear that the GOP in Washington would undertake to do little to sustain the remnants of Reconstruction in the South.

Across the South, Democrats moved to bury the last vestiges of radical Reconstruction. In state after state, new conventions were called to undo constitutions that had sanctioned Negro participation in the political process. Each state enacted various laws amounting to disfranchisement: poll taxes, exclusionary voter registration practices, and the so-called eight-ballot-box laws. Together, these laws eliminated Republicans from state election campaigns altogether, producing a solidly Democratic South.

Yet in Florida, the Republican party managed to retain a measurable degree of political vitality, in part because it had never been as radical as its counterparts in other southern states. Despite the constitutional convention of 1885, President Cleveland's use of patronage to remove Republicans from federal appointments, and Frank Pope's failure to capture the governor's office, the Florida GOP polled 40 percent of the votes cast in the state and national elections of 1888.[4] The same year, Duval County Republicans elected their entire local ticket, which included Negroes, to the Jacksonville city council.[5] Much of this was due to solid party leadership and the role Republicans had played in the Florida constitutional convention of 1885.

It was not the Independent party's 1884 coalition of Negroes, white Republicans, and anti-Bourbon Democrats alone that prompted revision of the 1868 state constitution. Ever since 1876, there had been pressure on Democrats, especially those who resided outside the black-belt counties, to rewrite the document. In these white-dominated counties, Democrats complained most about the governor's appointive power, outmoded since the overthrow of Reconstruction. Black-belt Democrats, on the other hand, feared quick restoration of home rule to Florida counties. Without protection, the Negro majorities in these counties would return Republicans to office. The issue of a new constitution had not been settled during the Pope-Perry campaign: Both parties and their candidates adopted the proposal for a new state constitution early in the race.[6]

The constitutional convention met in Tallahassee on 9 June 1885, long before similar conventions in other southern states. One reason was that Pope had been somewhat more successful than Independent candidates in other states. Independents were elected to the Florida legislature, and there was even some Democratic opposition to restricting votes among Negroes and Republicans. When Jefferson County's Samuel Pasco gaveled the convention to order on 9 June in the capitol, a number of experienced black and white Republicans were among the delegates. Former Senator Simon B. Conover, Union-Republican Club cofounder Jonathan C. Greeley, and Thomas Vann Gibbs, son of the former secretary of state, represented their districts. So did former Chief Justice Edwin Randall; Representatives Henry Baker, Samuel Petty, and H. W. Chandler; Milton's Mayor Hannibal Rowe; Nassau County Commissioner Charles Lewis; and James Challen of Duval County, who had recently moved his prosperous law practice from Cincinnati to Jacksonville. Among the twenty Republicans were seven Negroes.[7]

The entire constitution was rewritten between June and August. A number of the issues before the delegates did not reflect party affiliations or racial differences. The issues that mattered most to Republicans and Negroes were suffrage, poll taxes, and the governor's appointive power. The black-belt counties were the major points of contention. To the Democrats living in Alachua, Duval, Gadsden, Jackson, Jefferson, Leon, Madison, Marion, and Nassau counties, the argument rested on concise logic. More than 50 percent of Florida's population resided in these counties, and 75 percent of these residents were black. Yet these were also wealthy agricultural counties that generated half of the state's taxable income. Ninety percent of the white population (22.5 percent of the total) earned 45 percent of the total personal income, but only 38 percent of the voters in these counties were Democrats.[8] Without restrictions to prevent Negroes from controlling elections, constitutional revision would fail.[9] The key to the problem was "the safety of the black belt."[10]

The poll tax controversy illustrated the nature of the division among white-county Democrats, black-belt Democrats, and Republicans. The committee appointed to examine the poll tax was composed of six Democrats (only two of them residents of the black belt), three Independents, and two Republicans. Thomas V. Gibbs was the sole Negro. The committee eventually submitted three reports to the convention; two of them reflected the white-county–black-belt-county Democratic split. The majority report, written by Austin S. Mann, a Democrat from predominantly white Hernando County, argued forcefully that a poll tax referendum should be separate from a vote on the new constitution. Mann, chairman of the committee on suffrage, felt that a separate vote would be the only way to guarantee ratification of the new constitution. His Democratic opponent on the committee was Samuel Turnbull, a planter and political novice from Jefferson County. Turnbull not only insisted that the poll tax be incorporated into the constitution but wanted it to be even more restrictive than the existing one. He advocated a two-dollar tax per voter to be paid three years in advance.[11]

Republicans joined Mann and other white-county Democrats on the convention floor to defeat Turnbull's harsh proposal. Edwin Randall introduced a memorial "of the working people of Jacksonville," a white group opposed to the tax. They argued that it would prove to be a hardship on low- and moderate-income groups, tending to promote "aristocracy and despotism." Only Thomas V. Gibbs held to the earlier Republican principles of Reconstruction. Alone, he offered a report stressing the negative effects of a poll tax upon Negroes, urging that any form of poll tax be rejected.[12] The outcome of the debate was to authorize future sessions of the Florida legislature to adopt a poll tax law. There were 21 Republicans and 16 white-county Democrats who voted against the resolution. However, as a relative compromise, they managed to have the tax proposal changed from two dollars to one, due and payable in the year preceding an election year.[13]

Republicans were even less successful in dealing with other issues that divided the convention delegates. In an effort to prevent total ruination of Republicanism in the black belt, Jonathan Greeley introduced a measure that would have both curtailed the governor's appointive power and bridged the differences between white-county and black-belt-county Democrats. Greeley's idea was disarmingly simple: he advocated restricting future governors to appointing at most three commissioners in each county from a single political party. The purpose was to ensure Democratic representation in black-belt counties and Democratic sweeps in predominately white counties. But the restriction also would have gained black-belt Republicans at least minority representation on each of their five-member county commissions. After much deliberation, Greeley's proposal failed by 48 to 42 votes.[14]

Marion County's state representative, H. E. Miller, was unsuccessful in his attempt to revise Florida's elections laws concerning governors and lieutenant governors. Miller suggested that governors should continue to be elected by the largest electoral vote but that lieutenant governors should be elected according to the combined electoral vote of both parties. His measure failed without discussion. Nor were Gibbs and William Thompson, Leon County's tax assessor and state representative, able to persuade the convention to guarantee permanent public institutions of higher learning for blacks. Also unsuccessful in the end was Edwin Randall's proposal, which would have put Florida in support of "impartial instruction of white and colored children."[15]

In the first legislative session that convened after the constitution was ratified, Republicans were unable to prevent Democrats from gerrymandering legislative districts to prevent future Republican resurgence at the polls.[16] Moreover, on the last day of the 1887 session, an annual registration statute similar to the exclusionary tactic adopted in South Carolina was inserted into the election code: the Florida statute required voters to carry registration certificates to the polls in order to cast their ballots. Moreover, the certificates had to be renewed each year.[17] One white-county Republican legislator offered a humorous note as he attempted to secure an amendment to this registration bill: "Provided that when any person shall apply to the supervisor of election to be registered, it shall be the duty of the said supervisor to register him and also to brand him on the north part of his person with the initial letter of the party to which he belongs; if a Democrat, with the letter 'D'; if Republican, letter 'R'; if Mugwump, letter 'M'; and if Knight of Labor, 'Let Her Up.'"[18]

By 1889, Republican chances for success in Florida elections were virtually nil. Prior to the 1888 state campaign, Democrats had increased their fraud tactics at the polls in conjunction with the anti-Negro–anti-Republican laws. Registrars either refused to register blacks during regular office hours or required them to produce white witnesses who could testify about residency. Republican ballots were rejected in precinct after precinct, sometimes on the most ludicrous pretexts. For example, if names were written in red rather than blue ink, if ballots were dirty, or if dashes instead of asterisks were used, Republican ballots were cast aside. Philip Walter, chief federal elections officer in Florida, reported to the U.S. attorney general that at least ten Republicans in each of the state's seven hundred precincts were prevented from casting ballots and that "over 10,000 Republican votes were thrown out after they were cast."[19]

Although these tactics enabled Grover Cleveland to increase substantially his vote total in Florida over the 1884 presidential balloting, Benjamin Harrison won the election, returning the White House to the

GOP. Apart from the peculiar success of Republicans in Duval County, however, Democrats took firm control in the state, acquiring heavy majorities in the black belt. The changes that resulted were dramatic. Whereas in the 1887 legislature Republicans and Independents comprised more than 30 percent of the membership, by 1889 they were reduced to 14 percent.[20] Moreover, after a month-long campaign against Duval County Republicans, Democrats in Jacksonville assisted by Governor Fleming replaced the duly elected Republican city government with a Democratic one.[21]

With Democrats from the black-belt counties elected in sufficient numbers to the 1889 state legislature, even more stringent anti-Republican measures were passed, including a more severe registration act. An eight-ballot-box law was also rammed through, courtesy of Democratic representative William Marvin of Jackson County, son of the provisional governor who had been appointed by Andrew Johnson early in Reconstruction.[22] In the election year of 1890, Republicans attempted to counteract the laws arrayed against them by paying poll taxes for Negroes, by organizing registration drives in the black-belt counties, and by holding seminars on the new voting requirements in each district. Despite their efforts, the Florida GOP was buried by a Democratic avalanche.

As some political observers had predicted, the overall voter turnout was much less than before the exclusionary legislation. For the first time since early Reconstruction, fewer than 50 percent of the eligible voters came to the polls. The *Florida Times-Union* candidly attributed the huge Democratic majorities in 1890 to the new election laws. Editor Charles Jones commented that the "poll tax prerequisite was undoubtedly the greatest factor in the Republican defeat in Florida." Jones was also pleased by the results of the new eight-ballot-box law in the black-belt counties: "A large number of Negroes could not read and placed their ballots in the first box they came to. The new election law is a God-send to the state, as it prevents ignorance from ruling and controlling the destinies of the Land of Flowers."[23]

The anti-Republican program devised during this period worked well enough to ensure continuous Democratic victories into the twentieth century. Republicans were forced to deal with the immediate problem of surviving as a political organization. They responded by withdrawing almost completely from state elections and concentrating instead on carrying Florida for Republican presidential aspirants and rewarding themselves with federal patronage positions. No Republican figured as a gubernatorial candidate until William J. Howey in 1928. Moreover, in 1920 the Florida Supreme Court refused even to recognize the existence of the Republican party in the state. Under these conditions, the Democratic party co-opted politics in Florida. Uniting only when necessary in order to defeat minor Republican opponents during a general election (if any Republicans ran), Democrats smoothed out their internecine differences prior to nominations or during primary campaigns.

Two main factions operated within the Democratic party as the nineteenth century closed. Sen. Wilkinson Call and future governor Napoleon B. Broward headed the progressive wing, gearing their attention to the problems of Florida's small farmers (the crackers) and the growing urban population. They argued for reforms in many areas. On the other hand, there were still the traditionally conservative Democrats who had supported William Bloxham during Reconstruction and who now allied themselves with Governors Fleming, Perry, and Mitchell and Sen. Samuel Pasco.

Because Democrats were able to incorporate most of the prevailing political sentiment into their party organization, Republicans and other political groups went unrepresented in Florida. Following Reconstruction, Democratic administrations found it unnecessary to institute major changes because previous Republican administrations had been moderate. Railroad developers and land speculators, though they had been encouraged to build under the Republicans, found the Democrats even more receptive. Nor was there an agrarian demagogue in Florida to compare with Tom Watson in Georgia or Theodore Bilbo in Mississippi who might stir up the crackers. None of the dissenting farm groups, including the Grange, the Farmers' Alliance, or the Populists, was overly successful either. With the Populists' failure in the 1890 campaigns, Democratic bridges across Florida's political waters were secure. Agrarian reformers, Bourbon conservatives, urban progressives, and conservative businessmen all found their places within the Democratic party. Of course, blacks were excluded. The few blacks who continued to play a role in politics found themselves in a Republican party that no longer desired their support and no longer wielded political influence.[24]

The effects on Florida Republicans were obvious and direct. As the party's influence waned in state campaigns, concerted political activism broke down into factionalism reminiscent of Reconstruction days. There were two major factions, though their labels belied their composition: the Lily Whites supported Negro exclusion despite having Negroes as supporters; the Black and Tans were a mixed political bag of Negro and white Republicans, almost all of whom had been prominent during the halcyon years of Reconstruction. Not all of the Black and Tans were freedmen or carpetbaggers, as one might have expected.

The 1888 gubernatorial campaign also illustrated the effectiveness of the new anti-Republican constitution and exclusionary voting laws. Lacking anyone more qualified or interested in waging a campaign that could not be won by any Republican, the state GOP nominated V. J. Shipman in Ocala during the first week of August. Shipman, a strawberry grower from Lawtey, opposed Francis Fleming in the November general election. Shipman was a carpetbagger and ex-Union officer from upstate New York who had been one of the early Republican organizers of Bradford County's freedmen. Never more than a minor figure in state Republican circles and an unsuccessful applicant for a federal appointment as collector of customs in Fernandina in 1882, his most genial qualities seem to have been his great love of stump speechmaking and his great weight—more than 300 pounds. Many who saw him that fall agreed with his self-description as one of "Barnum's white elephants."[25] Understanding that he had no chance for victory, Jacksonville's *Florida Times-Union* recognized his nomination approvingly, characterizing the candidate as "gallant, clean, and honorable."[26]

The Shipman-Fleming race initiated a number of new aspects into Florida politics. It was the first post–Civil War campaign in which Florida Democrats could afford to be overtly racist in their appeals to white voters, now that Negroes could no longer influence elections. A typical cartoon appearing in the Tallahassee *Weekly Floridian* showed the impact of this fact upon the Solid South. Pictured were a black man and a white man dancing arm in arm over the caption "The Head and Tail of the Mongrel Ticket." Charles Jones, crusty editor of the anti-Republican *Florida Times-Union* of Jacksonville, also seized the opportunity to flail Republicans. In fact, he was worried that Republicans might quit politics in Florida altogether. Prior to the GOP's Ocala meeting, Jones had urged Republicans to "acquit themselves like men, and not plead the baby act."[27]

He further suggested that they should campaign for fun if not for victory: "Things may look a little discouraging, but you mustn't forget that there's going to be lots of fun in the campaign if you'll just go into it with a vim and good humor, even if you should come out a bad second best in the matter of votes." Jones's diatribes against Negroes and his personal insults against white Republicans grew worse as the campaign wore on, in part because of his concern over Grover Cleveland's presidential race against Republican Benjamin Harrison. Even Horatio Bisbee, long accustomed to political attacks, felt obliged to answer Jones. He charged the editor with "flagrant and outrageous falsehoods, touching the character of Republican conventions, for the purpose of disgusting white men and preventing their joining the Republican Party." [28]

Shipman lost heavily, of course, but Grover Cleveland carried the black belt, the first Democratic presidential candidate to do so since the Civil War. Despite Josiah Walls's advice that Negroes should vote for Shipman and the other white Republican candidates and ignore blacks who were running for local offices and state legislative seats, Negroes still received the blame for the GOP debacle. "As long as the Negro clings to his party traditions, regardless of the question of right or wrong, he can never reach the plane of good citizenship and his liberty becomes license," wrote Jones in an editorial.[29]

There were other GOP weaknesses of strategy in 1888 besides what to do about Negroes or anti-Republican legislation. The party had transformed itself in the South from liberal to conservative following Reconstruction. Out of this transition would emerge eventually the twentieth-century southern Republican—white, conservative, and business-oriented. Despite the fact that on the national level Republicanism completed this transition well before 1890, Florida Republicans clung to Reconstruction issues with enough tenacity to fracture party unity. Divisions were created over more than simply the question of Negro participation in party affairs. Shipman himself is an interesting case in point. At the Ocala convention in 1888, Republicans adopted a platform supporting the railroad companies and their right to charge freight rates unencumbered by federal or state regulations, a position which most Florida farmers opposed. Yet Shipman, himself a farmer, received the endorsement of J. J. Holland, Florida's field representative of the Knights of Labor. Moreover, there also was some support for Shipman's campaign among members of the Farmers' Alliance.[30]

Conditions worsened for Florida Republicans during the 1890s. As South Florida developed into a major fruit-producing region, it grew away from North Florida's cotton belt economically, socially, and politically. But the GOP either could not, or would not respond, even though many South Florida newspapers warned Democrats about their political futures. Unlike the cotton-producing regions of North Florida with their steady supply of Negro labor, the rapid increase in citrus production in South Florida produced a severe labor shortage. Public officials who did not support immigration to remedy this problem, one South Florida paper warned, were not "likely to be returned" to office.[31]

Washington politics still served as the focal point of Florida Republican interest. Once Harrison had returned the White House to the GOP, a brief flurry of activity designed to reinvigorate southern Republicanism was instituted. President Harrison was committed to reversing former President Hayes's southern strategy by reinstituting federal intervention in southern elections. Widespread electoral fraud and corruption had not diminished with Democratic redemption of the Reconstruction South. Even with the passage of anti-Republican–anti-black exclusionary legislation, Democrats in Florida continued to hassle Republican voters. Votes were altered, thrown out, or miscounted by Democratic election supervisors. Voters were either denied the right to register or found their names purged from registration lists if they were Republican. Negroes continued to be targets of violence. In 1890, a black federal marshal was killed by "an unknown person or persons" in Quincy. Later, Marshal Edmund Weeks, who was assigned to investigate the murder, was refused hotel accommodations in the city.[32] As the fall elections approached, the Orange City *Times* warned Republicans to register carefully: "The fact that your name was there [on the registration books in each county courthouse] is no proof that it is still on the books. The names of hundreds of Republican voters have been stricken from the books and yours may be one."[33]

President Harrison had three sound reasons for advocating a new federal elections bill in 1890: the southern strategy had failed to increase measurably the numbers of ex-Whigs who might have joined the GOP; Congress, dominated by the Republican party, wanted to guarantee support for higher protective tariffs, a position opposed on economic grounds by most Democrats; and the president wished to block the fraudulent tactics of southern Democrats and keep them from infiltrating elections in the North. Sen. Henry Cabot Lodge of Massachusetts introduced a "force bill" in June 1890. It provided for a federal elections supervisor and federal review courts to hear petitions sponsored by a minimum of one hundred citizens in each congressional district. Even though the responsibility for state and local elections would have remained in the hands of state officials, the bill's effect could have provided the impetus for a Republican resurgence in the South. Democratic opponents of the measure argued that its passage would be the initial step toward reinstituting Reconstruction, and a successful Senate filibuster by southern Democrats was undertaken. After weeks of fruitless debate, a Republican Senate caucus voted to postpone the measure's consideration, even though a similar bill had been passed by the House on a straight party-line vote. It proved to be Harrison's last attempt to overturn the bulwarks of the Solid South.[34]

Failure to get the measure approved discouraged Florida Republicans. The party ran candidates in the November 1890 elections, but only one, O. B. Smith of St. Johns County, was elected to the Florida legislature.[35] In 1892, the state GOP decided to protest the voting laws and the federal government's failure to protect voters in the South by refusing to draft any candidates. At their state convention in Tallahassee in early April, a simple resolution was adopted: "We consider it utterly useless to put tickets in the field for officers, state, congressional, or national and hereby decline to do so until our rights are protected and our liberty secured to us by enactment of an efficient national law."[36]

Jacksonville was the one exception in Florida to this decline in Republican fortunes. Negroes and white Republicans managed to maintain a voice in Duval County politics and Jacksonville city politics to a degree unmatched elsewhere in the state or in the entire South. Even as laws dealing with poll taxes, ballot boxes, and voter registration were being written, Jacksonville's GOP joined in March 1887 with other reform groups in the city, including the Knights of Labor and the so-called Straightout Democrats, and established a political coalition known as the Citizens' Ticket.[37] The issues in the mayoralty race between John Burbridge, president of the Jacksonville & Atlantic Railroad Company, and William Dancy, the Democratic nominee, were remarkably free of Bourbon politics and were concerned instead with urban needs such as law and order, a full-time mayor, expansion of the city limits, and a professional fire department. Burbridge's acceptance speech before the nominating convention indicated the broad concerns that had united his coalition: "Fellow-citizens, a movement like this is going on in all the principal cities throughout the whole country. Wherever men have taken possession of the city government and the duties of the officers are not discharged in accordance with the wishes of the people, the citizens have assembled and nominated tickets that have swept the old officeholders from power." Burbridge also promised his audience that the reform group, composed of Negroes and whites, would attempt to limit further discrimination against blacks: "I shall know no one on account of his color and I shall make no distinctions. . . . The colored man can get justice from me as well as the white. Whenever he deserves it, I shall do him justice. Why? Because they have rallied around us in this fight and saved us from a government not of the people but of a clique. . . . Had it not been thus, the opposition would have overridden us and driven us from the field."[38] Burbridge beat Dancy in the spring elections by a slim margin of 210 votes.[39]

Jacksonville's new city charter, under which the Burbridge government came into office incorporated three new predominantly black residential areas inside the city limits, but whites still dominated the city government and city council. Under the charter, new elections were approved on 31 May 1887. By December, it was apparent that Republicans in Jacksonville were thriving. Of eighteen new councilmen, seven were Republicans, including five Negroes.[40]

Heavy Democratic pressure developed to discredit the coalition. C. B. Smith, Burbridge's successor as reform mayor, was often accused in the local press of running a carpetbag regime.[41] Charles Jones, editor of the *Times-Union,* who had been a member of the reform group despite his anti-GOP prejudices, resigned and was replaced by J. J. Daniel, a member of the regular Democratic faction. Daniel's appointment as editor resulted in sharper attacks against the city government. A splintering of the coalition came in 1888, when a yellow fever epidemic struck the city. White residents were able to escape to temporary refuge centers outside the city limits, but blacks were denied entry. By September, blacks outnumbered whites in Jacksonville by three to one. In November, they dominated the elections, electing Negroes to the positions of clerk of the criminal court, clerk of the circuit court, justice of the peace (three), and constable (six). Moreover, Benjamin Harrison carried every city precinct by a substantial margin over Grover Cleveland in the presidential balloting.[42]

Shortly thereafter, Democrats in the 1889 session of the Florida legislature introduced a bill that would empower incoming Gov. Francis Fleming to remove the Republican-dominated city government in Jacksonville and to appoint a new council by executive fiat. The *Times-Union* made no effort to hide the bill's anti-Republican purpose: "We might go so far as to concede for the sake of argument . . . that the bill is intended to overthrow the Republican Party in the city. . . . For eight long years of the reconstruction period the solid black mass of newly-enfranchised ignorance and impudence defeated every measure for the welfare of the State. Here in Jacksonville, where ninety-nine hundredths of our visitors and immigrants are white men, two-thirds of the 'guardians of the city's welfare' are negroes! On the dark continent—in India—everywhere save in Jacksonville alone, the white man is supposed to be (at least!) quite as good as the negro."[43]

Several state legislators traveled to Jacksonville in the spring of 1889 to ascertain whether in fact such a bill would ensure a Democratic majority and thus white supremacy. After their return to Tallahassee in May, the measure was passed by the legislature. Aided in 1890 by Florida's election laws, Democrats in Duval County won both the county and state elections with little trouble. Following their sweep, a petition campaign was initiated to repeal the disfranchisement law. The municipal franchise was restored, finally, in 1893.[44] Although at least one Negro Republican occupied a seat on the Jacksonville city council until 1907, in the end the result was the same that had befallen Republicans everywhere else in Florida.

Florida Republicans responded weakly when, on 23 July 1893, Congress passed a judicial redistricting act aimed at Charles Swayne, a Republican judge in Florida who had insisted on prosecuting Democrats for flagrant violations of the state's election code. Introduced by Congressman C. M. Cooper from Orlando, the bill called for a drastic reduction in the size of Judge Swayne's jurisdiction. Florida had been divided into two federal judicial circuits of roughly equal size. In the northern district, Swayne, appointed by President Harrison in 1890, presided over court cases from Jacksonville to Pensacola. Judge E. O. Locke, a conservative Republican appointee of Grant, was in charge of the southern circuit, which included the Keys and the southern portion of the peninsula. Swayne variously convened his court in Jacksonville, Pensacola, and Tallahassee. Locke, a lifelong resident of Key West, convened his court both there and in Tampa.[45]

Many Democratic and Republican attorneys felt inconvenienced by the shift in districts and resented the blatant political intent of Cooper's bill. One Democratic attorney, Arthur Odlin, wrote to William Eaton Chandler on 9 December 1893: "The real object of this bill is simply to prevent Judge Swayne . . . from sitting at Jacksonville. In fact, the passage of this bill will so limit his jurisdiction as to leave him almost nothing to do. He resides in St. Augustine and it will compel him to make a change to Pensacola. One reason . . . is the fact that he was born in the North, another reason is that the Florida legislature [in 1891] . . . sought to bring about the impeachment of Judge Swayne on political grounds. . . . They are determined to punish him."[46]

Specifically, the bill provided for removing twenty counties from Swayne's circuit, including Duval County, where his major opposition resided, and St. Johns County, where he lived with his family. Under the new law, Swayne was forced to move across the state, since by law federal judges had to reside within their judicial districts. Swayne moved to Pensacola and in 1900 resettled his entire family there. His temporary quarters, however, served as one of the major arguments for his opponents when they attempted to impeach him in Congress in 1904. He was acquitted of all charges in a brief trial before the Senate in December 1904.[47] A number of Democratic lawyers opposed the impeachment effort as they had previously opposed the reduction of Swayne's judicial circuit; for them, it meant greater distances to travel, unnecessary delays, and an unwelcome backlog of cases in Judge Locke's court. One Democratic attorney argued in a letter to Senator Chandler that "The Democratic members of the bar of Florida are far from unanimous in supporting the bill which has been introduced in the lower house. . . . In my opinion the republican members of the bar are practically united in opposition to the bill. It seems . . . that this is a matter upon which the judgement of the bar is more trustworthy than the opinions of editors and politicians."[48]

One federal appointment in Washington during this period allowed Florida Republicans an opportunity to exploit Democrats for a change. Sen. Wilkinson Call headed the liberal, or populist, wing of the Florida Democratic party, and Sen. Samuel Pasco and Gov. Henry Mitchell led the conservatives. When Swayne's impeachment troubles arose, Republican executive committee chairman Dennis Eagan's term as collector of revenue in Jacksonville was nearing its end. Senator Pasco and Governor Mitchell wanted to appoint George Wilson, Democratic chairman of the second congressional district, but Senator Call was opposed. A number of Republicans hoped to take advantage of the Pasco-Call standoff to repeal the redistricting law and possibly also to ameliorate the more noxious elements in Florida's election code. Both Pasco and Call promised to support these moves in exchange for Republican support for the Wilson appointment. Senator Chandler was besieged with conflicting advice from Florida Republicans wanting to capitalize on the Democrats' divisiveness. Eagan supported Call's efforts to overturn Wilson as his replacement, writing to Chandler: "Up to this time I have taken no interest in this democratic fight, but the time has come when we can turn it to our advantage. Call and his friends have joined with republicans for the repeal of our infamous eight ballot box law, which repeal was passed through the state senate but defeated in the state assembly on the advice of Governor Mitchell and Senator Pasco." [49]

Jonathan Stripling, who was of the same opinion as Eagan, wrote Chandler that opposing Wilson for tax collector would "tend to widen the breach and intensify the feeling now existing in the ranks of our democratic brethren, and render the possibility of reconciliation even more remote. I trust that you and our other republican friends in the Senate will stand by Senator Call in his fight against this confirmation." Stripling perceived that the issue would lead to "an open declaration of war between the democratic factions": "The machine element of the organized democracy will be with Governor Mitchell, while Senator Call's strength will be with the rural classes. There are a lot of reasons for believing that there will be two democratic candidates for Governor at the next election, each of which will be disposed to be very courteous to republicans. This is our only hope in this State." [50]

Stripling changed his mind when Congressman Cooper introduced his judicial redistricting bill, throwing his support to the Wilson nomination and Senator Pasco. Pasco had launched a propaganda campaign around his intention to reform Florida's anti-Republican election laws and oppose Cooper's bill. By mid-April, Stripling was urging support in the Senate for Wilson's confirmation, vowing that he would "make almost any concession that will honorably secure its [the Cooper bill's] defeat." [51] Even Henry Flagler, who by this time had begun to establish his hotel and railroad empire on Florida's east coast, saw fit to inform Senator Chandler that Wilson's appointment was a critical issue in Florida politics. Through an intermediary, Flagler let it be known that he supported Pasco's position and that a defeat of the Wilson appointment would be "a very bad thing for the Republican Party." [52]

Even though Wilson eventually was confirmed and the Democratic breach continued to widen, Republicanism failed to take root in Florida. One reason was that Republicans themselves were as badly fractionated as Democrats in the 1890s. As in other southern states, Florida Republicans generally were separated into two camps, each of which supported part of the national party philosophy. Lily Whites, as the words imply, were Republicans committed to building upon former

President Hayes's southern strategy by attracting moderate whites of Whig origins and excluding blacks, and by attaching themselves to the symbols of Reconstruction. In the other camp were the Black and Tans, who had shaped Florida's return to the Union and who refused to accept a diminished role for that reason. It was to the second group that Harrison's effort to have Congress pass a stiff federal elections law in 1890 was most appealing. But, as the 1896 elections in Florida showed, neither camp held fast to its principles.

For example, Negroes played an important role in the Lily Whites' nominating convention. Mathew Lewey, black editor of the *Pensacola Age,* was elected permanent chairman of the faction's convention held in May in Ocala. At that meeting, Edward Gunby was nominated for governor and a Negro, former Reconstruction state representative John Wallace, won the nomination for Florida attorney general. The Black and Tans met the next month, also in Ocala. A Negro lawyer from Palatka, J. W. Purcell, was elected to chair the meeting, and George Allen, a Jacksonville-born Floridian from Key West, was nominated for governor.[53]

The differences between the Lily Whites and the Black and Tans should have resulted in gubernatorial candidates clearly unlike in philosophy or politics; Gunby and Allen were different but not as reflections of their respective factions. Allen had had little political experience and was in fact a prototype of the businessman Republican. He was born in 1854 in Jacksonville and migrated to Key West, where he founded the First National Bank of Key West after the Civil War. His sole encounter with Florida electoral politics was a four-year term in the state senate from 1878 to 1882. Edward Gunby, on the other hand, displayed more of the traits common to the other faction. He was a carpetbag Republican who had settled in Orlando in 1883, where he had a law practice. His political background suggested a previous connection with the old-style ring Republicans who curried federal appointments and engaged energetically in party affairs. He had been a member of the Republicans' 1890 national delegation and had served as collector of customs in Tampa from 1889 to 1894.[54]

That Gunby and Allen were running for governor in 1896 indicates that the Florida GOP retained some viability. Still, it was hardly a match for the Democrats, even though the destructive eight-ballot-box law had been repealed a year earlier. Moreover, it soon became clear that no matter which Republican was nominated, his party would not benefit much from dissension among the Democrats. Unable to wrest a compromise candidate from the ranks of Call's or Pasco's alliances, Democrats turned once again to their Bourbon war-horse, William D. Bloxham. With the ageless master's nomination for a second term, Democrats ensured themselves another victory.

National events more than political opportunities resulting from dissension among Democrats persuaded Florida Republicans to throw off their lethargy. The repeal of the eight-ballot-box law restored some optimism, but William McKinley's confident campaign and predicted sweep of Nebraskan Populist William Jennings Bryan produced even more. At the meeting of the Republican state executive committee on 16 January 1896, chairman Dennis Eagan explained GOP thinking: "The situation warrants it. The members present are also in favor of it, and I think that what they say will have its weight with the party throughout the state." Eagan's reference to the rank-and-file's influence included Negroes, as reflected by the fact that the state executive leadership reelected Joseph Lee as state secretary and John R. Scott as secretary of the second congressional district.[55]

The 1896 Lily White platform of Edward Gunby illuminates southern Republican positions on a number of state, sectional, and national turn-of-the-century issues. Florida Republicans reaffirmed the party principles of Reconstruction, if not the actual practice of equality. Following national GOP guidelines, Florida Republicans advocated higher protective tariffs to stimulate domestic industry and business, including two cents per pound on Egyptian cotton. Because of growing concern with Cuba's revolution, Florida Republicans in 1896 called for increases in military spending. Other vital planks provided insight into the Republican response to Populism and the growing issues of reform.

Hoping to stifle Populism in Florida, Gunby's platform advocated direct election of U.S. senators, federal aid to public schools, opposition to the brutal convict-lease system (which southern Democrats had erected as a substitute for slavery), a new state-run penitentiary, a youth reformatory, community home rule, and direct election of local officials. The GOP also advocated a law requiring public officials to publish semiannual reports of their official expenses. Altogether, the platform was an amalgam of current Republican, southern, and Floridian thinking.[56]

On 29 July, George Allen and his Black and Tans capitulated to Gunby and the Lily Whites in a belated but unsuccessful effort to achieve party unity. In a letter addressed to Gunby's campaign chairman, John Stillman, Allen wrote that he wished to avail himself "of the opportunity now of helping to discourage in every way possible dissension in the ranks of the party." The remainder of Allen's slate—E. C. Weeks and Josiah T. Walls, candidates for presidential electors, and Joseph Harden of Polk County, who was running for state commissioner of agriculture—also resigned voluntarily.[57]

Not that it mattered one way or the other. Edward Gunby fared poorly in the general election in November, even though McKinley carried Florida handily for the national GOP. Yet the 1896 effort is instructive and significant in the history of Florida Republicanism. The Florida GOP failed during the campaign to attract or merge with Florida Populists in the manner that had produced political success, including the election of a coalition governor, in North Carolina.[58] There were isolated coalition tickets, especially in central Florida (Lake, Volusia, and Orange counties), but no statewide alliance was created.[59] Most important, however, was that Republicans in 1896 demonstrated once again their inability to work together. The Gunby-Allen split was but another reminder that Reconstruction factionalism could not be erased by time or circumstance. The truth of Florida's "political atomization," the lack of party unity and permanency, the shifts in alliances due to whim or expediency seemed to indict Florida Republicans. Nevertheless, it could be argued that if Republicans had been allowed to play a more critical role in state politics in the 1880s and 1890s, they would have adopted the lessons on party unity learned from Reconstruction. What the Lily Whites and the Black and Tans proved, however, was that once again Republicans were first and foremost their own worst enemies.

8

Presidential Republicanism in Florida

PRIOR TO the presidential election in November 1896, Mark Hanna, Republican kingmaker and William McKinley's campaign manager, undertook to allay fears among certain Republican businessmen who felt uneasy about the new political movements that were sweeping the nation—Populism, agrarian radicalism, William Jennings Bryan's attack on the eastern establishment, and anticorporatism. Frightened that these combined currents could induce a tidal wave of antibusiness, anti-Republican protest, GOP businessmen heard Hanna remark contemptuously, "There won't be any revolution. You're just a lot of damn fools."[1]

Hanna was right; McKinley swamped Bryan that November. Republicans nationally had become the standard choice of the electorate. The Grand Old Party was seemingly grander than ever. Warm relations and an unusually cooperative atmosphere flowed between the president and Congress. McKinley's much desired tariff legislation to protect domestic industry was enacted with a minimum of debate and rancor; and when the president asked for a declaration of war against Spain over the issue of Cuba, Congress and the nation agreed.

There were other, less-welcome trends that arose from the 1896 campaign. Some Americans experienced what has been called a "psychic crisis" in the last decade of the nineteenth century.[2] A kind of antiparty, antipolitical malaise afflicted voters of both parties, manifesting itself at all political levels. While other social institutions in America were becoming more bureaucratic and centralized, politics was not. Party bosses, their political machines, and their attempts to corrupt the democratic process were increasingly resented. Many reforms—direct election of U.S. senators, woman suffrage, nonpartisan municipal elections—were intended to weaken the traditional political structure.

To a large degree, the reformers, including Populists and progressives, succeeded in their goals. Yet in the years following the 1896 campaign, there occurred a massive dropping out of American voters, and the two-party system that had existed in many states outside the South degenerated as a result. The wide-ranging functions of the political parties in the social fabric—including patronage, welfare programs and charity, and sheer entertainment—were either surrendered to or usurped by other social institutions. Straight party voting and party identification waned, and voter turnout noticeably declined. Voter participation seemed to correlate to income levels; it was lowest among the poor. What emerged remains a phenomenon even today; it has been called a crisis of participation.[3] Of course, in the South, voter shrinkage had taken place before 1896. All the exclusionary and restrictive voter laws prevented more and more poor whites and blacks from voting. Politics and government became once again the provinces of the powerful. Yet that politically elite class was unable to contain the discontents engendered by the social stress of industrialization in the late nineteenth century.

When Theodore Roosevelt came to the presidency in 1901 after the assassination of McKinley, he tried to toss a lifeline to floundering southern Republicans, setting out to revitalize the southern GOP with a patronage policy calculated to exclude Negroes. He was encouraged by a large number of southern whites who were nominal Democrats but who were vehemently opposed to the Democratic party's tariff policy and to Bryan's radical agrarian reform policies. Roosevelt believed that eliminating black Republicanism and boosting Lily White organizations would lead to a southern Republican renaissance.

His attempt failed, largely because he refused to remove all southern Negro officeholders. Roosevelt persistently supported qualified blacks, such as Minnie Cox, postmistress at Indianola, Mississippi. This policy, and episodes like inviting Booker T. Washington to dine at the White House, left Roosevelt with few powerful friends in the South, many of whom agreed with the Indianola sheriff, who described the president as "a fourteen carat jackass."[4] Roosevelt on many occasions defended his appointments of blacks, calling them honorable. To Robert C. Crist, South Carolina banker and Democratic mayor of Charleston, Roosevelt attempted to justify his retention of William Crum as collector of customs in that city. Crum was a prominent physician and Negro leader. He was county Republican chairman and had been a delegate to every national Republican convention since 1884. "I cannot consent by my action," wrote the president, "to take the position that the door of hope—the door of opportunity—is to be shut upon all men, no matter how worthy, purely upon the grounds of color. . . . The question of 'negro domination' does not enter into the matter at all."[5] Roosevelt changed his mind during the campaign of 1912 when he saw that blacks would have to be removed from southern Republican organizations before whites would consider joining in appreciable numbers.

In 1912, when Theodore Roosevelt bolted the Republican party to run for reelection as the nominee of the Progressive Bull Moose party, the GOP split between William Howard Taft and Roosevelt, resulting in the election of Woodrow Wilson, a southerner and a Democrat. This campaign illustrated once again the frustrations and ineptness of southern Republicans.

The Florida GOP met in early February 1912 to select delegates to the national Republican nominating convention set for June in Chicago. Roosevelt had not yet bolted, but his intention of seeking a second term was widely known. Florida Republicans, like Republicans across the nation, were aligning themselves with either the New Yorker cowboy hero of San Juan Hill or the incumbent, genial, overweight William Howard Taft. Each man could claim support from Florida Republicans. As the incumbent, Taft had the advantage in wooing the delegates' support for his nomination. Roosevelt, on the other hand, enjoyed immense popularity in Florida stemming from his combat role in the Spanish-American War.

The Florida Republican party had broken apart completely by 1912. The factions were too numerous to count, and none rested on solid political ground except for the so-called post office group led by Joseph Lee, the black customs agent from Jacksonville who was secretary of the GOP state central committee.[6]

The first of several state conventions claiming to be official met in Palatka on 6 February 1912, and Lee was chosen its chairman. Taft and Roosevelt supporters were equally visible, though Lee himself was supporting Taft. Lee quashed the Roosevelt supporters' hopes of gaining control of the meeting and sending their delegates to the Chicago convention. There were several contested delegations at Palatka, including those from Columbia, Escambia, and Hillsborough counties. Lee ruled in favor of seating the Taft delegations but refused to seat the pro-Roosevelt Republicans,[7] led by Herbert L. Anderson, a Jacksonville attorney. Anderson's followers then bolted, accompanied by a band, and marched down Palatka's main street, tossing hats in the air and shouting for a "square deal" in Florida. The mood was more indicative of a holiday than of a political rebellion. That afternoon, Roosevelt's supporters reconvened in another hall.[8]

On 18 May, Anderson's faction held its second convention at the Odd Fellows Hall in Jacksonville. Roosevelt by this time had formally announced his candidacy on the Progressive party ticket, and Anderson was quickly elected Progressive party chairman for Florida. He faced open dissent at the convention from a Negro lawyer and progressive Republican, Charles Alston of Tampa. Alston, like Anderson, had refused to submit to Joseph Lee's tactics on Taft's behalf at the Palatka meeting. Representing many Negroes who still were able to participate politically, Alston insisted that Anderson's Progressive party permit whites and blacks to meet in unsegregated support of Roosevelt. But Anderson refused, organizing two racially separate conventions instead; blacks would meet in St. Augustine on 26 July, whites one day later in Ocala. At their meeting, Alston's black progressive Republicans endorsed Roosevelt's candidacy and reportedly agreed to accept Anderson's segregated policies.[9]

At Ocala the following day, however, Alston and a few of his followers attempted to crash the convention. Repulsed, Alston organized another convention, this time without reference to Anderson's group.[10] Anderson in turn repudiated Alston and declared that there should only be two political parties in the South, Progressives and Democrats, both white.[11]

Ormsby McHarg, a New York attorney who served as Roosevelt's chief organizer in Florida, reported that "there is no Republican Party in Florida for all the great number of delegations."[12] Roosevelt himself offered no public comment on the actual events[13] but committed himself and his party to a Lily White alliance. Negro Progressives in Alabama, Georgia, and Mississippi adopted similar positions.[14] As a result, when the Progressive convention was held in Chicago on 4–6 August, Charles Alston's black delegation was denied seating. Alston had previously failed to gain admission to the national GOP meeting in June, unsuccessfully challenging Joseph Lee's pro-Taft delegation.[15] Ironically, Herbert Anderson's delegation was also denied admission on the grounds that his calling two separate meetings in Florida may have been illegal. As a result, no Florida Progressive delegation was part of the national convention that nominated Roosevelt. Alston had refused the credentials committee's compromise that would have allowed his Negro delegates to sit as "supplemental delegates." He replied, "If we attend the convention merely as spectators, we prefer to buy our own tickets."[16] After leading an "indignation" meeting of spurned Negro Progressive groups from Florida, Mississippi, and Alabama, Alston left Chicago to work to elect Woodrow Wilson, probably taking some Florida Negroes with him to the Democratic party.[17]

Much of the factionalism was a reflection of the split between Roosevelt and Taft, but not all of it. A political impasse developed between those few remaining Negro Republicans and Alston. Even among white Florida Republicans, there was more to the 1912 campaign issues than Taft or Roosevelt. A power vacuum of sorts had been in evidence in the state party organization since the death of James Coombs, Florida's national Republican committeeman. With Coombs's death, the position of national committeeman was conferred upon Henry S. Chubb, the state Republican party chairman since 1900. The merger did not defuse Republican dissent because these had been the two most important party positions for Republicans in the state. Throughout the next several years, each of the Republican factions as represented by the Taft-Roosevelt split of 1912 fought over these posts and the federal patronage power each carried.[18]

The years following the 1912 fireworks were uneventful for Florida Republicans. In 1916, another statewide slate was chosen at the convention at Palatka, but the GOP nominee for governor, George W. Allen, stood little chance despite bitter Democratic dissension. Five Democrats were in pursuit of the gubernatorial nomination that year, but only one, Sidney J. Catts, aroused party members. Catts was a newcomer to Florida. Having had no success in prior efforts to attain political office in Alabama, he had moved to DeFuniak Springs in 1911 to become pastor of the First Baptist Church.[19] Catts's chief campaign issue in 1916 was his anti-Catholicism, and he made political capital by promising to defend Florida against "Romanizing" influences. Of course, Catts did not invent religion as a hot political issue; he merely took advantage of deep-seated prejudices already in place. Georgia's Tom Watson actually had been the one to politicize religious bias.[20] During the primary campaign against William Knott, state comptroller and former state treasurer, Catts propelled Florida's politics in new directions. Along with his demagoguery, he was the first campaigner to discover the potential power of Florida's "forgotten man," the ignored and usually silent voter of the hamlets. Shrewdly aware that the bulk of Florida's electorate did not, or perhaps could not, read the Miami *Her-*

ald or Jacksonville *Times-Union,* Catts forcefully argued his case against Catholicism and conservation and for prohibition, economy in government, higher taxes on corporations, and larger pensions for Confederate veterans. Although the Florida Supreme Court ruled that Knott was the winner of the first Democratic primary, Catts beat Knott handily in November. Candidate George Allen was never a determining factor, receiving slightly more than 10,000 votes out of more than 100,000 votes cast.[21]

As usual in the post-Reconstruction era, the Florida GOP was shaken briefly from its somnambulism by a presidential election. The 1920 campaign, which resulted in the election of the affable but incompetent Republican Warren G. Harding, was no exception. It was also usual that Florida Republicans could not agree on their candidate. Once again the party splintered before the June national convention. This time, however, the issue was less a question of Harding's or of General Leonard Wood's candidacy than of the federal government's future attitude toward the League of Nations. Harding and the national Republican party firmly opposed the nation's entry into the league, while James Cox, the progressive Democratic governor from Ohio and his party's presidential nominee, stood solidly in favor of Wilson's dream of international unity. Herbert Anderson, back in the Florida Republican fold since 1912, again spearheaded division. He controlled the Florida delegation at the Chicago convention, but in the process he lost his influence among state Republicans interested in Florida politics. Anderson refused to back Harding on the league question and eventually left the GOP altogether, coming out in support of Cox.[22]

Replacing Anderson and other old-guard Republicans after 1920 was George W. Bean of Connecticut, who became a postmaster in Tampa and an unsuccessful congressional candidate in 1912. He replaced Henry Chubb as national committeeman in 1918 following Chubb's death, and with the passing of Joseph Lee in 1920 he was able to establish firm control over much of the Florida Republican organization despite unceasing opposition from other factions. With Bean's help, Daniel T. Gerow was elected state party chairman, the second position vacated by Chubb's death. Because of these circumstances, Bean gained more strength than any other Florida Republican party official since Edward M. Cheney during Reconstruction.[23] Herbert Anderson remained Bean's main opposition, however.

Under Anderson's prompting, if not his actual directive, J. Eugene

Merrill, a disgruntled member of the state central committee, filed suit against Daniel Gerow in 1920, claiming that Gerow's election as state party chairman during a January meeting of the committee in Palatka was illegal. Merrill's suit also contested the legality of the entire GOP slate and central committee. He based his case on Florida's election law of 1913, which stated that a political party lost its status if it did not poll more than 5 percent of the total vote in the previous general election. Since no Republican had polled the requisite percentage in 1918, Merrill argued, the party organization itself was null and void in 1920. The suit before the Florida Supreme Court claimed the chairmanship for Merrill in an attempt to overthrow Bean and Gerow.[24]

The case illustrates the desperation of all of southern Republicans in the era of the Solid South. Presiding Justice Jefferson B. Browne refused to rule, maintaining that the court had no jurisdiction in the controversy. Instead, the justices unanimously stated that the conflict was between two individuals because there was no Republican party to fight about: "Having gone out of existence as a political party in the eyes of the law, its officers, as such in the eyes of the law, went out of existence with the party. The law does not know such a political party as the Republican Party; it does not know its officers; it has no control over it or its internal affairs."[25]

Browne's ruling strengthened Bean and weakened efforts to rebuild a viable state party. The court's decision in *Merrill v. Gerow* made the Republican party a private affair under Bean's control inasmuch as he held the crucial patronage position vis-à-vis the national organization and administration. In a legal sense, the Florida Republican party died as a result of the 1921 case but remained as a patronage organization; post office Republicanism in Florida had arrived.

As Republicans looked forward to 1924 and another presidential election, it became clear that Warren Harding's administrative transgressions would be difficult to overcome. The Teapot Dome scandal had sent some of the president's cabinet officers and close advisors to prison and others scurrying for cover. Harding himself announced his intention not to seek reelection and died shortly before his term expired. That proved fortunate for the Republican party because Vice-President Calvin Coolidge entered the White House possessing a respectability and integrity his predecessor could never have matched.

In the midst of these events, George Bean rested comfortably in control of his state's political patronage power. He continued to ignore the restiveness among some Florida Republicans who resented him. On 15 March 1924, he issued a circular to the members of the state central committee, as the GOP executive committee was now formally called, and to all county chairmen:

> Regardless of all that may be happening in Washington and the many rumors afloat at the present time, the effect has not in any way lessened the popularity of President Coolidge for our next President. I think it is generally conceded that this will be a great Republican year. We in Florida are in better shape than with any other Administration. The Organization has worked hard during the last four years; we have kept up Republican clubs and have been recognized 100% by the Administration.
>
> Not one of our recommendations for appointments has been turned down by the President or by the Senate. This is a record of which we can well be proud.
>
> I am particularly anxious that the coming State Convention shall be the biggest we have ever held, both in point of representation and in the enthusiasm manifested for Republicanism. There is very little opposition to the Organization anywhere in the State and the little existing opposition is from a very few individuals confined to about three counties. There is no occasion even for this small amount of opposition; the Organization is always ready and willing to welcome every one into the Party. Reports are coming to me from every part of the State of the activity of these few men, but in every instance the report states their efforts have had no effect in breaking up the splendid feeling to the Organization that now exists.[26]

Privately, Bean was concerned and worked to suppress internal dissent in his organization. When James Gavin, secretary of the Wakulla County Republican executive committee, reported to him that an effort was being made to unify the different factions there via a series of meetings in Crawfordville, Bean replied that such unofficial gatherings outside the state GOP were a waste of time and money and would not help in the fall: "The thing to do is make a concentrated effort to build up the party, not pull down same." He stressed the GOP's record in past presidential elections: "The Republican organization in this State has worked hard to build up the Republican Party, the results of its efforts showing in the difference between the vote of 9,000 cast for Roosevelt and Taft combined in 1912 and that of the vote between 44,000 and 45,000 cast for Harding in 1920."[27]

Bean's refusal to approach seriously the visible if small minority of Florida Republicans who desired a more effective state party cost him his position as national committeeman. During the 1928 state convention held in Daytona Beach, a small group of dissidents led by Glenn B. Skipper of Lakeland engineered a coup against Bean. Skipper's success, coupled with the likely success of Republican presidential nominee Herbert Hoover (the widely admired engineer and relief specialist of World War I) against Democrat Alfred E. Smith (a Catholic, anti-prohibition, New York governor and Tammany Hall politician), led many Florida Republicans to believe that they might capture some state offices. Instead, the election of 1928 is remembered as one of the most bigoted and embittered in American history.

Skipper, a successful cattle rancher and businessman, had been Bean's vice-chairman on the GOP state central committee for several years. He possessed few aspirations for developing a state party organization but attracted many Florida Republicans who did; he wanted to succeed Bean as national committeeman. Well before the state convention in June, Skipper had begun secretly recruiting and organizing anti-Bean Republicans into a reform coalition. He had already chosen a likely gubernatorial candidate: William J. Howey, a citrus entrepreneur, real estate developer, and political neophyte from Lake County. In mid-March, Skipper called together a number of leading Florida Republicans, including Howey, in the DeSoto Hotel in Tampa.[28] Armed with a list of convention delegates who would be in Daytona Beach in June, which had been procured from state party secretary James Gavin, Skipper outlined his plans for capturing control of the Florida GOP.[29]

Several issues were discussed by the anti-Bean conspirators. It was agreed that Bill Howey would become the gubernatorial nominee regardless of whom the Democrats appointed. At the time, it was still unclear which of the Democratic aspirants—Doyle Carleton, Fons Hathaway, or Sidney J. Catts—would receive the nomination. Howey's chances were thought to be good because of Hoover's immense popularity and Florida's religious bigotry as well as the fact that Howey himself personified the new Floridian—a northern businessman without previous political connection to post office Republicanism. Skipper was sure he would do well to ride on Hoover's coattails. The other Republicans present at the DeSoto meeting, including Peter Miller of Tampa, Clarence Pitts of Sebring, Sidney Brown of Orlando, A. F. Knotts of Yankeetown, R. E. Burchard of LaBelle, and Elvey E. Callaway of Lakeland, agreed.[30]

Party structure, patronage, and finances were discussed as equally important topics. Skipper insisted on becoming Bean's replacement on the national committee and the primary organizer of the reform ticket, and there was apparently no opposition to his demand. Party structure, although of little interest to Skipper personally, was critical to most of the others who attended. For the first time in several elections, it was decided to run a full slate of candidates for all elective offices in Florida, not just for governor and senator as had been the practice. That decision led to a discussion of finances. Howey and Skipper were relatively wealthy men, and Callaway's law practice was prosperous, but the strain of supporting an entire GOP slate was beyond the desire, if not the capacity, of the small group. Eight years earlier, Governor Catts had been successful in raising money among rural Floridians, and Skipper was convinced that the issues of Smith's Roman Catholicism and his opposition to Prohibition would induce many small-town Floridians to break their Democratic tradition and to support the Republican slate financially. Moreover, Skipper guaranteed financial support from the state's Ku Klux Klan.[31]

In 1928, George Wentworth of Pensacola, whose family had been active in Florida Republican politics since Reconstruction, became chairman of the state GOP. Following *Merrill v. Gerow,* Gerow had resigned and Bean had placed Wentworth in the position. Aware of Skipper's plans to overthrow Bean, Wentworth declined to attend the state convention in Daytona, feigning illness. Although Bean was aware of Skipper's intentions, events showed that he did not know fully what the reform faction planned to do at the state convention. On 18 April, Bean issued another circular addressed to Florida Republicans around the state, hoping to cut off Skipper. His letter explained the actions taken at the state central committee meeting in Jacksonville, which had been held in March and had unanimously endorsed his position as national committeeman. Bean attacked Skipper vehemently: "The meeting had hardly adjourned when it was learned that G. B. Skipper (who was present when the vote of confidence was taken) was an active candidate for National Committeeman, using the same malicious tactics that he used four years ago at which time he was a candidate for National Committeeman; he stating in his campaign then, that it would do no good to re-elect me as he had the goods on me and I would be in the Federal Penitentiary within thirty days. . . . He is again a candidate and using even more contemptible tactics."[32]

Also attending the Daytona Beach convention was another faction of Florida Republicans who were equally disenchanted with Bean and Skipper. This group, from Palm Beach County, had begun efforts to organize support for a third or compromise candidate for national committeeman, J. Leonard Replogle, a Pennsylvania steel magnate and millionaire who wintered in Florida. Replogle's chief attraction was his wealth; it was rumored that in exchange for the position of national committeeman, he would finance the entire GOP slate.[33] George Bean also attacked Replogle in his circular: "Certainly he does not know our people and as a stranger he cannot understand our problems. It is certain that our organization is not willing to sell this office for a mess of porridge, and the argument of his backers to the effect that Mr. Replogle will finance the campaign, if made National Committeeman, will not receive serious consideration from Florida Republicans."[34]

Bean then seized the offensive and replied to charges made by Skipper and others that he had sold his patronage influence for personal gain:

> The Democratic Press has charged me with selling offices. The only two cases I ever heard of money being paid for offices, I called to the attention of the Postmaster General and demanded an investigation. The result was that two Postmasters were removed and both had either paid or offered money to Skipper, supposedly for me. As God is my judge, no man or woman in Florida has ever been asked to give or has given me a cent for a Federal office. If officeholders have been imposed on by others who told them the money was for me, I can only say, I am sorry.[35]

Nonetheless, when the Daytona Beach convention opened on 9 May 1928, Bean's hold on his position was tenuous. Wentworth was either ill or, having been warned by Skipper of the approaching events, was feigning illness; in any case, he was absent, giving Skipper, as vice-chairman of the state central committee, control of the parliamentary proceedings. Except for the party chairman, all of the prominent Republicans in Florida were on hand, including old post office types like Bean and Fred Cubberly as well as Replogle. By this time, of course, the Negro's presence had disappeared entirely.[36]

Skipper opened the convention at the Clarendon Hotel. There were five major issues to resolve: the election of a national committeeman, the nomination of a Republican candidate for governor, seating contested delegations from Dade and Pinellas counties (which represented another fight between Bean and Skipper), election of delegates and alternates to the national Republican convention scheduled for June in Chicago, and election of chairmen for each day's convention proceedings. In addition, of course, a full slate of candidates and a platform remained to be drawn up.[37]

Both Bean and Skipper wanted the national committeeman post. Bean announced confidently to news reporters upon his arrival that "only personal political enemies and the Democratic Press are fighting me. There is no sentiment in the state to disturb our present splendid organization except in a few counties." The Daytona Beach *Weekly Journal* editorialized that delegates would not depose Bean only to install Skipper, no matter how great the dissension between the national committeeman and his party: "Both men have drawn their strength from practically the same source and the opposition to Bean is not friendly to Skipper."[38] Watching the proceedings carefully in the interest of forthcoming nominee Herbert Hoover was Rush Holland of the national Republican campaign committee.

The issue over who would be the first day's chairman was resolved with little controversy. Although a few delegates supported retired Sen. Lawrence Sherman, formerly of Illinois, Daytona Beach Republican Judge Noah Bainum was awarded the honor. Fireworks commenced on the second day of the meeting. Precisely at 11 A.M., after nervously checking his watch several times, Skipper called the convention to order. Timing was essential; at the same moment, down the block at the Williams Hotel, Bean was convening a meeting of the credentials committee concerning the contested delegations from Dade and Pinellas counties. Without Bean's presence on the main floor at the Clarendon Hotel, Skipper was free to carry forth his plan. Without debates or delay, A. F. ("Dad") Knotts of Yankeetown was elected as chairman for the day and another Skipper supporter, Fred Britten, was chosen as secretary. Few members of Bean's faction were present when the balloting took place. Only Fred Cubberly protested that he, not Knotts, was entitled to chair the session.[39] A motion to adjourn until

1 P.M. so that Bean and his forces could assemble was quickly quashed by a voice vote from the largely pro-Skipper crowd.

Shortly before noon, George Bean appeared at the Clarendon Hotel, having finished the credentials committee meeting. Taken by surprise by Skipper's action, he nonetheless declined to protest the proceedings. Instead he stood in the doorway and called loudly "for all red-blooded Republicans" to get up and follow him back to the Williams Hotel. Only a handful among the 200 delegates did so, while the others remained in a state of turmoil. Knotts was unable to restore order until the band began to play.

Meanwhile, Bean convened his supporters at the Williams Hotel, taking over the dining room as a rump convention site. Reporters hovered around him as he sat in a corner, contemplating his strategy and seeming a bit flustered but not overwhelmed by the events. When asked why he had demanded that his supporters return with him, Bean offered only a lame excuse: "Some of the delegates didn't want to stay over there in the hall and listen to all that noise, so they came here." Bean's faction had dwindled to no more than thirty, so carefully had Skipper laid his plans. When Bean was asked if he had lost control of his party, he replied loftily, "The real delegates are right here with us. We are not worried. We don't recognize what those other fellows have done. Ours is the only legal convention." It was his estimation that the credentials committee at the Republican National Convention would uphold his faction; it did not. Bean's rump meeting nominated delegates and alternates for the national convention, and Bean refused to surrender his rump convention's records to Glenn Skipper and the state central committee.[40]

Skipper, however, was thwarted ultimately in his drive for Bean's position. A significant number of Florida Republicans refused to support either Bean or Skipper and the coup ground to a halt, leaving the national committeeman's position open. Barclay Warbritton, millionaire mayor of Palm Beach, who had promised to accept the nomination for the U.S. Senate, refused to do so unless the convention approved Replogle for national committeeman. Their combined wealth could not be ignored. Beleaguered and frustrated, Glenn Skipper agreed to accept Replogle without further challenge.[41]

The remainder of Skipper's plans were successful. Howey won the nomination for governor without controversy, receiving only token opposition from W. C. Lawson of Orlando, a Bean supporter. Including

Howey and Warbritton, a full slate of candidates was chosen to run in November: J. J. Lawless (Pinellas County) for attorney general; Glenn Hanley (Brevard County) for secretary of state; Clarence Bradford (Dade County) for superintendent of public instruction; F. A. Stout (Osceola County) for state treasurer; Gage Denny (Manatee County) for state comptroller. Also nominated were candidates in each of the congressional districts, six presidential electors, and four delegates-at-large to the Republican National Convention at Chicago.[42]

The platform adopted by Florida's Republicans in 1928 contained twenty-one planks and indicated conservative thinking as well as a united GOP. President Coolidge's administration was endorsed and a statement regretting his decision not to run for a second term was included. The proposed constitutional amendment to establish prohibition was enthusiastically endorsed, adding that issue to the Smith-Hoover battle lines already drawn over religion. Other typically Republican planks were a statement encouraging development of Florida land, agriculture, and industry; an attack on Democratic waste in government spending; and expanded emphasis on education.

Of equal importance were the planks specifically relating Florida to national problems. Resolutions were adopted favoring equal rights for women; tougher banking regulations and fiduciary responsibility to prevent further bank failures; import tariffs to protect citrus and vegetable products from Florida (a position that had been opposed by the GOP representatives in Congress); abolition of the tax lien law of 1927 that made foreclosures on small businessmen and farmers too easy; homestead exemption; federal aid for swamp drainage, land reclamation, and flood control; and more equitable workmen's compensation. There were also the typical Republican economy measures calling for repeal of the federal inheritance tax, a decrease in the state's bonded indebtedness, and reductions in auto licensing fees and gasoline taxes that would have benefited successful businessmen, who usually advocated GOP principles.[43]

As the campaign took shape following the Daytona Beach convention, it soon became clear that William J. Howey was more than a token candidate for governor. Born in Odira, Illinois, to William H. Howey, a circuit-riding preacher, Howey moved to Polk County in 1908. He failed in a number of citrus ventures, finally settling successfully in Lake County in 1918. Once established as a citrus developer, having purchased some 87,000 acres of land at favorable rates,

Howey attracted Republican attention. Nominally a Democrat, though nonactive, he was recruited in 1928 by Skipper, Callaway, and Knotts to run as the Republican candidate for governor.[44]

Two political images of Howey developed in that campaign. Instead of a citrus land baron, he was often described to rural voters as just a dirt farmer who understood fertilizer. To urban voters, Howey projected himself as "the Hoover of Florida," capable of managing the state government more efficiently than the Democrats. Howey concentrated on only a few certain issues. To his credit, he never publicly attacked Alfred E. Smith's religion or approved of those who did.[45] Howey stressed the need for a higher tariff to protect Florida's agricultural products, a popular position among farmers whose income did not keep pace with costs of manufactured products that were traditionally protected by trade barriers and tariffs. Though Doyle Carleton attacked Howey for hypocrisy on the issue, pointing out that it was the Eastern Republican bloc in Congress that had quashed an agricultural import tariff, Howey continued to score heavily with rural Floridians on the subject. Moreover, he wanted to promote Florida by taking advantage of the land boom that South Florida had experienced during the mid-1920s. Howey even promised that if an elaborate $1 million advertising campaign could be financed out of donations by the state's business interests, he, as governor, would pledge his entire salary. He also promised to reduce taxation and state government expenditures, but unlike other politicians before and after, he offered a concrete if controversial program for accomplishing it. First, he wanted to abolish most of the state's commissions and boards and return Florida to laissez-faire government. His rationale was partly ideological. Many of the new commissions and boards had been created to keep pace with Florida's growth and modernization in the twentieth century, but others were merely patronage positions for the benefit of the governor. Unfortunately, Howey was unable or unwilling to discriminate between the useful and the needless commissions.

He also wanted to reduce the number of circuit judgeships in Florida, claiming that far more existed than were needed. Howey figured that these cost-cutting proposals would save Florida taxpayers $1 million during his first year in office. If not, Howey promised a Miami rally in early November, "I will resign and walk home."[46]

The 1928 presidential campaign between Hoover and Smith was vicious. Smith's Roman Catholicism was the brunt of bigoted attacks in every state, and the campaign in Florida was no different.[47] There were a few twists. Some attacked Hoover's Quakerism as well as the fact that, ironically, he had been married by a Roman Catholic priest. One newspaper in rural North Florida displayed the headline "I would rather see a Catholic elected President than a Quaker whose religion will not permit him to fight for his country."[48] Democrats around the state were forced to declare their party loyalty, and a number of incumbents refused to support Al Smith. Hoover Democrats were to be found in all precincts. As the final election results showed, Hoover carried the state over Smith, with more support in North Florida than in urban South Florida.[49]

The combination of Howey's platform proposals and political charm and Hoover's popularity worried Doyle Carleton. Carleton's campaign manager took pains to warn Democratic voters that this time a large turnout in the general election was necessary to ensure a victory over Howey: "While to be sure there is no reason to expect any difficulty in electing Mr. Carleton by a big majority over Mr. Howey, we must not forget the tendency among us Democrats to consider the primary the election and fail to vote at the general election."[50]

In his campaign's last weeks, Howey traveled through South Florida accompanied by noted American humorist and author, Opie Read, who usually introduced the Republican candidate at campaign stops, calling Howey "as capable a statesman as America holds in its borders today." Read was quick to exploit the nature of the Smith-Hoover and Carleton-Howey campaigns. At several rallies, Read described for his audience how the 1928 races in Florida were the "most explosive" in history. "The political situation reminds me of two old farmers," Read told listeners in Orlando and Miami. "One asked the other about the political situation in his section and the answer was 'status quo,' and when the other asked him what that meant, he replied, 'It's in a hell of a fix.'"[51]

Even some Republicans were repelled by the anti-Smith rhetoric of John Roach Stratton, the Baptist preacher who traveled Florida, preaching from pulpit and public stump alike that Smith's election would bring the country into hell. After hearing one such diatribe in Tampa, Frank Miller, a Republican voter in Tampa, sent a letter to the local newspaper:

> I am a Republican, a Methodist, a Mason, and a Northerner originally, but now a Southern man and live in Tampa in my own home. Yesterday, I attended the meeting in the auditorium

conducted by John Roach Stratton and heard him insult the intelligence of every man and woman who is voting or working for the Democratic cause. I heard him call every Democratic voter, man or woman, a scoundrel and a disgrace to even common decency and affiliated with the forces of hell, and I was astounded to sit there and hear a Southern audience applaud the insult.

What is the matter with us? Have we gone crazy? Where is our pride? Are we too cowardly to defend our self-respect? . . . I am going to vote for Hoover because I am a Republican, but I am an American citizen and I have not forgotten my sense of fairness to my fellow man even if he is my political enemy.[52]

In November, Howey lost despite Hoover's victory, nor did any of the Republican candidates for state office prevail. Up to the end, the nominee insisted that he was going to win and restore two-party government and politics to Florida "so that the one on the outside can watch the one on the inside." In his last public speech before the election, Howey told a Miami crowd of six thousand assembled in Bayfront Park, "I don't want your sympathy, I want your votes. There is only one way to stop me and that is to count me out. I hereby offer $2,000 for the arrest and conviction of any illegal voter in the state, whether he is for me or against me." His bravado was futile; Carleton won by more than 50,000 votes.[53]

The St. Petersburg *Times,* surveying the results, offered Florida Republicans an optimistic outlook on their future: "With a two-party system now thoroughly established, a day will probably come when Florida will have a Republican administration."[54] Not for several decades would that prediction be fulfilled, but William J. Howey's campaign had suggested to many Florida Republicans that a two-party system might overcome the one-party tradition of the Solid South.

President Hoover's success in carrying normally Democratic, conservative, rural North Florida counties mattered little to state GOP strategists, however. Political analysts were convinced that most North Florida voters had been expressing their vociferous disapprobation of Catholicism and the Eighteenth Amendment, not signaling a turnabout in voting behavior. Considering that none of the statewide Republican candidates won in North Florida, Hoover's margin clearly affected only the issue of the presidency itself. Certainly Democrats could be confident of victory in future campaigns against Republicans, exploiting the traditional anti-Republican and anti-Reconstruction prejudices of the white voters who lived there. Howey had fared poorly in North Florida, lagging well behind Hoover in practically every precinct.[55]

Republican optimism was based upon emerging new trends in South Florida. Unlike North Florida, the southern portion of the state was removed from and consequently less sensitive to emotive memories of the Civil War and Reconstruction. Immigration into South Florida had increased steadily during the first few years of the twentieth century, stimulating GOP strength. Howey kept pace with Hoover throughout much of South Florida, and in several counties the candidates polled substantial majorities. Howey carried ten South Florida counties alone against Carleton and polled over 40 percent of the total votes in nine more. His ability to match Hoover, especially in Dade and Pinellas counties, indicated sizable numbers of new Republicans in Florida who would support a state GOP administration, not merely anti-Smith Democrats crossing over to show their displeasure. Pinellas County was of special significance. In addition to Hoover and Howey, Pinellas Republicans in 1928 managed to elect a majority of their candidates, including county school board members, tax assessor, tax collector, and state senator.[56]

The relative success of the 1928 Republican campaign indicated the future possibility, under proper management and development, of reinstituting two-party politics in the state. More immediately, Howey's poll of more than 30 percent of the vote allowed Florida Republicans an opportunity under Florida election laws to hold an open primary convention in 1932.[57] The Republicans' eventual failure to perpetuate any lasting successes from the 1928 campaign was as much the fault of their inability to work together as it was President Hoover's response to the Great Depression, and the wave of anti-Republicanism that followed.

9

Two-Party Vision, One-Party Reality

NEITHER William J. Howey nor the Florida Republican party could sustain or redevelop the potential strengths they had shown in 1928. They could not build upon the promise of support from a booming South Florida, for the depression destroyed Florida's economy as it did the nation's.

South Florida had been hit hard even before the rest of the country felt the depression—the land boom of the early 1920s ended well before Wall Street collapsed. The land craze saw millions of dollars and thousands of acres change hands irresponsibly and irrationally; fortunes were ruthlessly made and unmade. By 1925, when the wild speculation and development schemes were petering out, South Florida's economy had been badly damaged. Immigration, business, and Florida's Republican party suffered as a result.[1]

The depression hurt Florida's Republican party in several ways. Lack of jobs and reluctance to spend money ruined South Florida's fledgling tourist industry and slowed the wave of retirees and northern businessmen who wanted to move into the state. Fewer northern immigrants meant fewer grass-roots Republicans coming to Florida. President Hoover's failure to prevail over the problems created by America's economic distress ended the GOP's hold on the White House, and most federal patronage positions were eliminated after 1932.

Franklin Roosevelt's New Deal politics forced southern conservatives and northern liberals into the Democratic party and brought about a new era of southern Republican impotence. Except for the 1913–21 interlude under Woodrow Wilson, Republicans had not feared a loss of federal patronage since 1896, when McKinley had clobbered Bryan. The 1932 Democratic victory would shut the door on Republican patronage for the next two decades.

Florida Republicans could not foresee their political disaster. In the years following Howey's first gubernatorial campaign, the party complacently continued its traditional, nearsighted political practices. A few sincere individuals would endeavor occasionally to promote party growth and a state Republican administration. More often, grass-roots Republicans complained that their leaders were indifferent to Florida's political affairs. Such protests engendered reform movements intent on wresting control from the old-style post office leadership on the state central committee. But mostly Florida Republicans played politics according to old rules—political patronage as their way of life and party disunity as their way of doing things.

Howey's success in winning more than 30 percent of the votes in 1928 created immediate problems. A primary campaign for Florida's Republican candidates would have to be conducted because Florida's election law required open elections rather than closed conventions once a political party had polled more than 5 percent of the total votes cast. In the wake of Howey's success and under pressure because of the approaching primary in 1930, Glenn Skipper's control weakened. Howey claimed that the renaissance of Florida Republicanism owed its strength to his gubernatorial fight against Carleton. Skipper, on the other hand, maintained that it had been the diligent effort of his campaign committee in organizing, planning, and conducting Howey's race that accounted for Republican success. Their disagreement blossomed into a full-blown feud. Howey had always remained a typical amateur politician, neither holding nor seeking political office before 1928; he had not been connected or identified with the patronage politician. Skipper was clearly a post office Republican, having served on the state executive committee even before he replaced George Bean as party chairman and J. Leonard Replogle as national committeeman. Howey had never expressed an interest in either of those strategic positions.[2]

Howey and A. F. ("Dad") Knotts of Yankeetown managed to gather together a group of disgruntled Florida Republicans who opposed Skipper's control of the state executive committee. A key issue was Howey's newly apparent desire to become a post office Republican and to control federal patronage. A meeting of the feuding leaders called for 9 March 1930 at Skipper's Lakeland residence had as its goal restoration of some semblance of political harmony before the Republican primary election scheduled for May. Each faction was present—Howey and Knotts on one side, Skipper and Elvey Callaway, a Bristol attorney who had succeeded Skipper as state party chairman following the 1925 campaign, on the other. After lengthy discussions, a compromise was reached: Skipper and Callaway agreed to resign their posts on the state central committee and risk them in the primary, and Howey and Knotts promised to remain aloof from the internal affairs of the committee unless they also chose to run for vacancies. As it turned out, Howey and Knotts refused to stick by the agreement. Howey feared that Skipper and Callaway would refuse to resign, as they had promised. The day after the two factions had reached their agreement, Howey announced the formation of another faction of Florida Republicans to contest Skipper's leadership.[3]

Howey's progressive Republican faction, as it was called, fought only briefly against Skipper's. Less than two years later, in 1932, party unity was fully restored when Howey, Skipper, and Knotts each became candidates for state offices—Howey again for governor, Skipper for congressman, and Knotts for state comptroller. In the two-year interim, however, President Hoover and the national GOP continued to consult with Skipper as the national committeeman concerning appointments of Floridians to federal positions. Party unity began reforming as early as 1930, following the primary election. John F. Harris of Palm Beach, a close friend of former national committeeman J. Leonard Replogle, won that seat in place of Skipper. George Wentworth of Pensacola returned to his old position as state party chairman.[4]

Early in January 1932, Howey, having been pressured into an early announcement by a large crowd attending a rally at his home in Citrus County, issued a statement announcing his plans to run again for governor. Shortly afterward, both Skipper and Knotts also made public their intentions to seek office.[5] In an effort to arouse even more enthusiasm and support from Florida Republicans, J. Leonard Replogle was approached to become a candidate for the U.S. Senate against Duncan Fletcher. Replogle refused, either because of poor health or because he understood that no Florida Republican candidate had much chance of winning. The Palm Beach millionaire accepted the chairmanship of the GOP finance committee instead.[6]

Florida Republicans were forced to return to their closed convention format since no Republican legislative or congressional candidates had captured 5 percent of the vote in 1930. They met on 12 April 1932 at the San Juan Hotel in Orlando. Each of the main candidates had announced already, and their nominations were uncontested during the

Orlando meeting. The major business that occupied the delegates was the platform that the party and candidates would endorse.

The 1932 platform was of special importance to the Florida GOP. By April, it had become clear that President Hoover would seek a second term and that he would be renominated at the Republican National Convention in Chicago in June. Although his election chances were considered doubtful, Florida Republicans felt, as in 1928, that Howey's chances for success would be tied to Hoover's campaign, especially in South Florida. As a result, the national administration was not only warmly endorsed by the Orlando delegates, it was vigorously defended. Hoover's attempts to cope with the depression were praised, particularly his creation of the Reconstruction Finance Corporation, his moratorium on European debt repayments (which suspended payments on loans made by the United States resulting from World War I), and the various international relief programs he had helped to sponsor. In defense of his measures and against Democratic accusations that the president and his party had created the depression, a campaign song was circulated at the convention and throughout the campaign called "Why Blame Hoover?":

> When it starts to rain at half-past four
> And spoils the picnic out of doors
> Why blame Hoover?
>
> When the stove's a buckin' and smokin'
> When the creditors want money, not jokin'
> Why blame Hoover?
>
> When time turns grey our hairy locks
> When fortune seems stuck among the rocks
> Why blame Hoover?
>
> When depression kicks us in the slats
> And yanks us about and calls us brats
> Why blame Hoover?
>
> Weren't we playing, dancing, spending
> As if to money there was no ending
> Why blame Hoover?

When bossy kicked the milk pail o'er
Formerly we kicked and damned and swore
Now we blame Hoover.

Erstwhile when things weren't on the level
We stamped and shook and blamed the devil
Now we blame Hoover.[7]

Howey himself had relied upon the platform in 1928, and Republicans felt it had been effective and could be again. Under the protective umbrella of the Solid South, Florida's Democratic party had not bothered to have political campaign platforms since 1900. Howey's use of the platform as a campaign tool reversed that tradition among Florida Democrats, and James B. Hodges, Democratic party state chairman, created a platform committee to answer GOP criticism over the issue.[8]

Like the 1928 Republican platform, the 1932 Democratic platform was considerably more modern and forward-looking, and more liberal, than Republican conservatives today might appreciate. Although women's suffrage had been ratified by an overwhelming number of states, the Florida legislature continued its formal opposition to what would become the Nineteenth Amendment. At Orlando, GOP delegates went on record in support of this extension of the franchise. The convention also endorsed the concept of a constitutional amendment permitting a state income tax on individuals and corporations "in line with the policy of the national government and other progressive state governments." Furthermore, three years before the Florida legislature finally repealed its noxious poll tax, Florida Republicans adopted a party plank demanding its abolition.[9] A position also was formally adopted concerning two-party government in the state, revealing in another fashion how deeply sure Republicans were that Howey's 1928 foray had not been a fluke:

> For more than a half century, the white voters of Florida, the best strain of purest American blood, have been in the throes of a system of political officeholders . . . wrapped in a package of a portion of the Solid South, tied neatly with thongs of tradition, sealed reverently with the sacred seal of precedent, and stamped with the marks of prejudice. . . . In the 1928 election, goaded beyond endurance, the voters of this State tore off the

shackles, smashed the seal of precedent, obliterated the stamp of prejudice, and proclaimed their political freedom by voting the Republican ticket. . . . They are in revolt and are determined to bring to Florida permanently a Two-Party system of government. The best interests of this State demand two vigorous independent parties, each pledged to definite policies and platforms and each stimulating the other to elect to all offices, only clean, capable, honest and unselfish men and women. To this end we pledge our constant and best endeavors.[10]

Other events encouraged Florida Republicans in 1932. A district judge in Jacksonville ruled that all election boards in Duval County had to include Republican representatives, basing his decision on his affirmation that Florida Republicanism had become a viable political organization.[11] Coming only ten years after *Merrill v. Gerow,* in which the supreme court refused to recognize the existence of Florida's Republican party, the Duval County decision was of momentous importance. Strength increased among North Florida Republicans. Local GOP county organizations were formed in several areas for the first time since Reconstruction. County executive committees were established, local and district candidates were nominated, financial support was generated in unprecedented fashion, and actual campaigns were undertaken. The normally Democratic *Gainesville Sun* remarked, "It is the opinion of thousands of Floridians that a warmly contested two-party fight would be a good thing for Florida Democrats. One thing is certain; it should develop unity of action in addition to educating Democrats in matters of Democratic ideals and principles. Bill Howey will prove a worthy foe."[12]

As previously, Howey aimed mostly at familiar themes and topics, including the reduction of spending by state government. He set forth again his notion that reduction in expenditures could be accomplished without sacrificing efficiency. He pressed his familiar key points—cutting the numbers of circuit court judges from forty-two to twenty-one, abolishing most of the purely regulatory agencies whose costs had multiplied as Florida grew, and merging the remaining agencies into fewer but larger departments. Howey contended that state agencies were used by Democrats for patronage positions much as Republicans used federal posts and that these agencies were not responsive to the overall needs of Florida's citizens. Furthermore, as in 1928, he demanded that Florida's citrus industry be given maximum tariff protection and that Florida's gasoline tax be reduced by 50 percent.[13]

Although he had planned to open his formal campaign after Labor Day, Howey actually spent his summer actively seeking support. He traveled extensively around the state and campaigned in many small communities in North Florida.[14] During the summer, he separated his own campaign headquarters and its finances from the party's. Perhaps Howey knew that his personal popularity would be enhanced if he could cut free from his political affiliation with President Hoover. He publicly announced his intent to allow John Harris and the state campaign committee more time to concentrate their efforts and resources on other Republicans who were running for office. Privately, he may have decided that Herbert Hoover had become an albatross, but publicly he pledged his "fullest cooperation" to the state committee and all other GOP candidates, including the president.[15]

In July, Democrats selected David Sholtz to run against Howey in the November general election. Sholtz was a relative unknown who had finished second in the first primary, behind ex-Gov. John Martin and ahead of ex-Gov. Cary Hardee. Their primary runoff grew especially bitter when Martin attempted an anti-Semitic smear against Sholtz. He produced documents allegedly proving that Sholtz's parents had immigrated from Germany and that he was hiding his Jewishness.[16] Martin's tactics failed; Sholtz won the runoff election and turned to the general campaign against Howey.

Howey wasted little time in attacking Sholtz's business experience. He accused the Daytona Beach attorney and businessman of gross mismanagement practices that had put him $200,000 in arrears. He further claimed, but never substantiated, that Sholtz had borrowed heavily from several Volusia County banks during the early 1920s to underwrite several business ventures. When they failed, according to Howey, Sholtz avoided formal bankruptcy by signing over all his personal possessions to his wife's family.[17]

More telling was the GOP charge that the Democratic nominee was a tool for corporate interests in Florida, despite Sholtz's assertions that his administration would care for the common people and those who were economically distressed. Outgoing Governor Carleton had been clearly favorable toward big business interests, and Sholtz had campaigned through the primaries on the issue of doing more for the "little guy." However, Sholtz stood impassively by while Governor

Carleton promised Floridians that his successor would not break with tradition and "would follow my policies."[18] According to Howey, "Florida can expect no relief in its present crisis from the lawyer-politician nominee. The voters face exactly the same situation they did four years ago. . . . It is my impression that Florida has awakened, that there is a distinct determination for a complete housecleaning at Tallahassee and that the people do not propose at this moment to continue their allegiance to exactly this thing that has caused our State governmental breakdown."[19]

Nor was Howey exaggerating the extent of the crisis in Florida precipitated by the depression. Carleton's administration had been forced into deficit spending, in direct violation of the constitution of 1885, because Florida's revenue had shrunk. Towns and cities across the state were in no better fiscal condition; more than 150 municipalities had defaulted on their bond obligations. St. Petersburg's Board of Education had begun charging tuition to parents able to pay for public education, pleading with childless adults to help pay tuition costs for the others. Wages declined and working hours increased. An ad in a Miami newspaper asked for dry-cleaning attendants willing to work nine hours a day, six days a week at $1.50 a day.[20]

Howey felt that his own business experience in Florida equipped him to handle the crisis. In contrast with Sholtz's alleged failures, Howey argued that he had been more successful and more efficient: "I propose to apply the same principle should I be elected governor that I have applied in business. In other words, I will put into effect the same elimination and reduction in the costs of operation which may, in governmental affairs, involve some refinancing. Whereas my business operation costs five years ago were at the rate of $1 million a year, today they have been cut to $101,000 a year. I have distributed in payrolls, salaries, and supplies in 10 years in Florida, more than $6,000,000 and have paid in taxes $389,000."[21]

Howey's financial condition may not have been as sound as his campaign suggested. A report on his business activity filed with the Florida Securities and Exchange Commission was made available to the state Democratic chairman, James B. Hodges. According to Ernest Amos, state comptroller, Howey had lost more than $200,000 in the fiscal year that ended 31 May 1932. Hodges believed the data could prove useful during the campaign: "Mr. Howey is not as good a businessman as he would lead the public to believe," he wrote to the chairman of the Duval County Democratic campaign committee.[22] The Republican candidate also began complaining about the lack of financial support from the national GOP committee and from the Florida executive committee. He argued that he had spent $50,000 of his own money in 1928 and had agreed to his renomination on the condition that further aid would be forthcoming. Howey reportedly was "highly dissatisfied" with the $800 spent by the national Republican campaign committee for his campaign in Duval County. Contributions were down in all other counties as well. He threatened to quit campaigning altogether if his office payroll fell behind by more than two weeks and to mail out copies of the *Florida Beacon,* the Republican newspaper in Jacksonville financed largely by Edward Ball and the Du Pont interests, to Democrats instead.[23]

Looking back, it is difficult to believe that William J. Howey and the Florida Republican party thought they could be successful at the polls in 1932. Hoover's antidepression program amounted to little more than corporate volunteerism and neglected deeper social miseries. Appalling unemployment and poverty spelled certain defeat for the president and his party. "Hooverize" in 1928 meant to economize, a reflection on Hoover's successes after World War I and his policies as secretary of commerce. "Hoovervilles" in 1932 were the rural shanty towns put up across the nation by millions of unemployed Americans, the epithet indicating how commonly Americans had come to blame Hoover for the depression.

Despite this, Howey remained optimistic that Florida's voters would reject Sholtz. In the first Democratic primary, Sholtz finished second in his three-man race with Martin and Hardee, and most Democrats did not bother even to vote. Unwilling to see that this situation was unlike 1928 when Democrats were divided bitterly in their chaotic primaries by Sidney Catts, Howey conceived Democratic apathy as a restiveness that could be turned into Republican votes: "I cite the fact that . . . there remain more than 200,000 registered Democrats who either voted against the nominee or refused to vote at all, thus establishing the striking fact that the Democratic nominee was so named by a significantly small minority vote."[24]

An interesting sidelight developed in the Howey-Sholtz contest. Since Reconstruction, Democratic candidates had attacked Republicans constantly for their support and solicitation of black voters. Naturally, Republicans had become defensive about the role of Negroes in their party. But in 1932, the situation was reversed. Republicans, including Howey, began accusing Democrats of "Negroizing" Florida politics. Democrats, on the other hand, played on the race issue by charging that if Florida Republicans succeeded in establishing a two-party system, blacks again would hold the balance of power between divided whites. Republicans were invited to join Democrats to preserve white supremacy. The GOP counterattacked with its own racist charges:

> In Florida, the "Negroizing" of the [Democratic] party is well under way. The negro paper of the largest circulation is owned and its policies controlled by a white Democrat. Negroes are being lined up and organized by the Democratic leaders to support their candidates. . . . Organizations are being formed in other parts of the State which are endorsing Roosevelt, Garner, and Sholtz. It is stated that negroes joining these clubs are promised that funds will be provided with which to pay their poll tax.[25]

Sholtz swamped Howey by a two-to-one margin in November; Democrats won every office. Roosevelt carried Florida over Hoover by a substantial margin. Despite the Democratic victory, Howey's original optimism had not been unfounded. His personal popularity apparently had not diminished since 1928. His gubernatorial vote percentage was down only slightly, less than 6 percent from his previous total. He did even better in North Florida than in 1928, though he fared worse in depression-plagued South Florida. In contrast, Hoover fell from almost 57 percent in 1928 to just over 25 percent in 1932.[26] These results show that William J. Howey had indeed maximized the Republican potential in 1932. His appeal and popularity were genuine and sustained. Had he chosen to run as a Democrat, he might have been elected.

Soon thereafter, Bill Howey removed himself from active politics. Although he ran for the post of national committeeman in 1936, he was defeated by John Harris at the state Republican convention. He showed no further interest in becoming a candidate for any state or national elective office. He resumed his varied business ventures; he died in Umatilla on 7 June 1938, the victim of a sudden heart attack while at work.[27] In nearly a century between Marcellus Stearns and Claude Kirk, Bill Howey was the only viable Republican candidate in Florida.

The 1932 defeat ended the Florida GOP's brief encounter with two-party politics. The *Florida Beacon*'s editor bravely wrote: "The

Republican Party neither dies nor surrenders. It has just taken a swell licking, but neither goes away nor changes its address."[28] A. F. Knotts confided more truthfully to his diary: "Election day. Democrats win everything." For the next two decades, even post office Republicanism lay dormant as Roosevelt and then Truman helped to reshape politics in the South. The two-party vision had come; a one-party reality remained.

10

Primaries and Patronage, 1932–1952

IN A SENSE it was unfortunate that William J. Howey could not continue as an amateur politician. Following his second and final campaign for governor, he too was subjected to scorn, villification, and, eventually, blame for GOP misfortunes. His own political ambition thrust him into the mainstream of Florida's Republican factionalism, and his former supporters attacked him viciously. He was accused of having been too liberal and a secret supporter of Franklin Roosevelt. Other Republican leaders publicized Howey's campaign for national committeeman as an abortive attempt to "sabotage" their party, and these attacks grew increasingly shrill as he tried to unseat John Harris in 1936.

The former candidate felt that his two unsuccessful yet serious gubernatorial campaigns entitled him to the position of Republican national committeeman. He began to try to unseat John Harris at the 1934 state convention held in Jacksonville. Most of the GOP leaders quickly opposed him; former party chief George Bean led the anti-Howey movement. Bean persuaded other Republican delegates and reporters covering the meeting to reject Howey's candidacy. During one press conference, Bean even suggested that Howey had never been a stalwart Republican: "I have always had serious doubts as to the sincerity of Mr. Howey's Republicanism."[1]

The post-1932 reaction to Howey and the political factionalism within Florida's Republican party that persisted for two decades had several roots. One, the election of Franklin Roosevelt and the creation of the New Deal marked the birth of a new alignment of conservatives with Republicans across the South. Although no organized southern resistance to Roosevelt appeared during his first term (except from the left in the person of Louisiana's Huey Long), many southerners quickly were disenchanted with the New Deal; by 1936 a formal grass-roots movement was formed in Georgia to encourage protest. (As William Havard has pointed out, this term "grass roots" cropped up over and over again in other states, culminating in the 1948 Dixiecrat campaign of Strom Thurmond.)[2] In Florida, Republicans supporting an open primary and presidential aspirant Douglas MacArthur used the identical term in 1952.

Part of the antipathy Howey experienced was also nothing less than a reaction to his sincere interest in developing Florida into a two-party state. Between 1932 and 1952 only a handful of Republicans in Florida considered such a goal to be feasible. With total Republican registration in those years never exceeding 10 percent of the number of registered Democrats, those few two-party advocates found it difficult to institute party reform.[3] There was to be in this period a sustained fight between Republicans who wanted two-party viability in the form of open primary elections, generally characterizing themselves as reformers, and those who wanted to ensure GOP patronage by working only in presidential campaigns and endorsing closed conventions.

The latter group of old guard Republicans were committed to the principles espoused in the written declaration of John Harris endorsing patronage politics and presidential campaigns. Harris's "Declaration of Principles" intended to serve as a broad encompassment of Republicanism in Florida and the South by setting forth basic approaches to education, individualism, and economic nationalism. It condemned social experimentation, fiscal stinginess, and, of course, the New Deal:

> We cannot call up the spirits of the great departed who if living would hurl themselves into this fray to preserve the Nation, but we can and do implore all who hold in solemn reverence the advice, the conduct of Grover Cleveland, Theodore Roosevelt, and those who supported them in their lives, to follow eternally just admonitions, and the only effective way they can do so is to vote for those pledged to act in case of their election in accordance with the views so clearly and frequently expressed during their lives by them.[4]

Two special points about Harris's lengthy document are obvious by their omission. One is that there was no reference to Abraham Lincoln as an integral part of the southern Republican tradition. By the 1930s, not even Florida Republicans were making pretenses of wanting to solicit black votes. Howey himself had declared his interest in keeping Negroes out of Republican elections by inquiring if Florida's secretary of state was empowered to prohibit Negroes from voting by simple resolution.[5] Democrats already had excluded blacks from their primary elections. New Deal advocate James B. Hodges commented upon hearing of Howey's request, "I am very glad that the Republican Party is trying to rid itself of the negroes, so that they are only welcome in the New Deal, having been repudiated by both the Democratic Party and the Republican Party." In 1934, Hodges himself had managed to have Negro voters' names purged from Democratic registration lists in Duval and Escambia counties.[6] The other missing item was the mention of two-party aspirations. Harris ignored this issue altogether, a testimony to Republican rigor mortis in Florida elections. None of the Florida Republicans who attended the convention insisted upon a statement concerning two-party politics, a marked contrast with Republican rhetoric in the two previous campaigns for governor, 1928 and 1932.

Howey, symbolizing the floundered hopes for two-party equality, was neither welcome nor especially popular among Florida Republicans. Past friends and supporters refused to support him against Harris. William G. Underwood, editor of the Jacksonville *Florida Beacon* and an ardent Howey supporter in the previous two elections, turned bitterly against him when he announced for Harris's seat. Instead of encouragement, the *Beacon's* editorial pages were filled with anti-Howey statements claiming that he had always been a Roosevelt progressive.[7] Howey himself published a series of letters in the *Beacon* addressed to all Florida Republicans explaining how and why he opposed Harris.

Howey wanted the national committeeman to continue pursuing party parity with Florida Democrats. After a fruitless search for a suitable candidate other than himself, he decided to enter the race. No doubt, he did not search very earnestly. The *Florida Beacon* attacked his motives mercilessly: "If he expects to conduct his campaign upon a basis of misrepresentation, abuse, and cheap jokes . . . it is well that the *Beacon* is on the side lines to shed its light on the record."[8] Elvey Callaway, GOP gubernatorial nominee in 1936 and a close friend of Howey since 1928, delivered a speech before a large group of Pinellas County Republicans picnicking at Madeira Beach in early August. Callaway called upon Howey to renounce his bid to unseat Harris and defuse the factionalism his campaign had engendered.[9] Peter Miller, former collector of revenue in Jacksonville, member of the Republican state executive committee, and another Howey associate, claimed that Howey's candidacy was damaging party unity and that he should withdraw.[10]

The 1936 state Republican meeting in Orlando was convened in late April. By the time the delegates had gathered, Howey knew that his political opportunities had vanished. He removed his name from consideration, a move that none expected, but in turn he nominated J. Leonard Replogle to oppose Harris. Replogle had been endorsed by other southern Republican state conventions as a potential vice-presidential candidate in 1936. He refused to contest with John Harris. Addressing the assembled delegates, he praised Harris's contribution to Florida Republicanism and announced his support for him, "first, last, and all the time."[11] Harris won reelection unanimously; Howey's political career was finished.

John Harris's role in Florida politics is obscured by the fact that no southern Republican during this era of political isolation rose to prominence, but there is little doubt that his personal attitudes concerning party patronage shaped the Florida GOP. Every national committeeman who followed Harris until the post-Goldwater era insisted upon the same set of priorities he had put forth. In response to demands from disgruntled state Republicans (probably led by Howey), Harris in November 1935 identified three main goals for Florida Republicans: presidential politics, first; then senatorial and congressional elections; and state and local races, of least importance. These priorities were not just in terms of common interests but, more critically in terms of how monies were to be allocated, how campaign staffs would be utilized, and above all how the Florida Republican party viewed its role in government and politics.

Patronage was the key issue, and John Harris defended its pursuit openly and without remorse. He disagreed, for example, when Bayard Pitts, a member of the state executive committee from Tampa, called for an end to the closed "machine-like" exercise of patronage politics and a beginning of a "Great Forward Movement and a New Moses who would lead the Florida voters out of the wilderness, across the Red Sea of dirty politics, into the Promised Land of Victory."[12] In a letter published in October 1935, he wrote: "You write that it looks to you as if the desire is for a machine to control Federal Patronage only. This is meant to be, I take it, somewhat of an offensive statement. The purpose of those with whom I am associated is . . . perfectly proper for the individuals who bear the heart and burden of the day to be rewarded with such Federal, State, and other appointments as they desire and as are available."[13] The activity of Reconstruction's ring of federal officeholders was carried on by its post office successors.

For the next thirty years, the stream of Florida's Republican politics meandered aimlessly. Only the issues of patronage and presidential elections raised its level now and then, but never much. In 1936, Elvey Callaway of Bristol was nominated to oppose Fred Cone in the governor's race. Though he campaigned on a platform of modernization, including a minimum foundation for public school spending, civil service examinations for all state employees, and lessened political influence in state government, it was really Cone's Democratic primary win that ensured his victory against his Republican opponent. Cone was aided by the Du Pont interests in Florida since two of Callaway's planks threatened Edward Ball and the Du Pont empire. Callaway's campaign promise was to remove the Florida Highway Commission from the list of political patronage positions and to emphasize the construction of primary roads between Florida's urban centers more than construction of secondary roads. Du Pont timberlands in rural Florida might have lacked paved roads for a long time if Callaway had been elected in 1936.[14]

Lacking more important and more substantive political issues, Florida Republicans during the 1930s and 1940s occupied themselves with one long factional struggle. Emory Akerman, founder of the Young Republican organization in Florida, and William Gober, party vice-chairman in 1938, adopted a position favoring open primaries to select delegates and candidates for offices currently held by nominees of the state executive committee and state convention. They felt that the patronage control exercised by John Harris and J. Leonard Replogle, who finally succeeded Harris in 1939, was far too restrictive. Their efforts to loosen the party machinery were aided by Democrats in the Florida legislature who further reduced the percentage of votes required in a previous election for a party primary campaign to occur, from 30 to 15 percent of the registered voters in any congressional district. "We've got republicans in Florida and we can't shoot 'em," editorialized the *Tallahassee Daily Democratic*. "We want to keep them out of the democratic party where they might have the balance of power."[15]

The major disagreement in this pro- versus anti-primary struggle was over the selection of delegates from each congressional district to

GOP national conventions. As long as national committeemen, party chairmen, and the state executive committee controlled the process, patronage during any Republican presidential administration would remain in their control. Florida's election law in 1940 required that delegates from districts having fewer than 100 Republicans registered to vote had to be chosen by closed conventions run by the state committee; in districts with more than 100 registered Republicans, delegates had to be elected in a primary election. The nomination process was a prime patronage function.

The issue exploded during the meeting of the Florida Republican executive committee in Orlando on 18 March 1940, when the committee appointed Florida's delegation to the national convention, scheduled to meet the following June. Leading the opposition to the closed convention selection process was Elvey Callaway, who attacked the state patronage managers before the executive committee had taken action. He claimed that the state committee had violated the law by appointing Florida's national Republican slate in the third congressional district. The committee responded that fewer than 100 Republicans were registered in that district, thereby necessitating nominations by the committee in a closed session. Callaway argued that more than 1,800 Republicans lived in the sixteen rural counties that comprised the North Florida congressional district.[16] Although he was wrong (most North Floridians who voted Republican in presidential elections had registered as Democrats in order to be able to vote in the state's Democratic primary), Callaway used the issue to attack his party's leaders. Had Florida Republicans adopted the concept of an open primary rather than closed conventions, he argued, the Republican party's "moral integrity might have been saved, and you wouldn't have had the political head of fascism that we have right here in our party in Florida."[17] Although the executive committee eventually named Callaway as a member of Florida's national delegation, he refused the honor.[18]

For the next several years, the primary versus convention procedure was the battle prize of Florida's Republican party politics. Forces favoring primaries won a quasi-victory in 1947. J. Thomas Watson, Florida's attorney general, offered an advisory opinion that the state executive committee did not have the right to block primary elections to select delegates to national conventions. He added that it did have the right to select delegates-at-large but that selection could occur following an enabling resolution passed at the annual state convention.[19]

Watson's opinions did not have the force of judicial decrees, however, and the practice of closed conventions continued with the election of G. Harrold Alexander of Fort Myers as state party chairman in 1948.

Alexander was hardly a neutral figure in Florida Republican history. Molded in the tradition of strong GOP chiefs like Edward Cheney during Reconstruction and George Bean during the 1920s, Alexander attracted strong support and sometimes stronger opposition during his tenure. His record over the sixteen years during which he served as party chairman and as the most powerful member of the state executive committee was spotty. GOP registration increased significantly across the state, and several local and county organizations, especially in central and southern Florida, developed into virtual Republican bastions. In 1954 William Cramer was elected the first Florida Republican congressman since Reconstruction, and he was soon followed by others—Burke, Frey, Gurney, and Young. Alexander also wielded political clout in Washington, particularly during the Eisenhower administration, supplanting the national committeeman as the most influential Florida Republican. He chaired the Florida Republican delegations at the 1952, 1956, and 1960 national nominating conventions. More significantly he directed three winning campaigns in Florida for Eisenhower and Nixon in those years. Alexander also encouraged cooperation among southern Republicans, founding and serving as the initial chairman of the Southern Association of Republican Chairmen. He became the most powerful Florida Republican of the twentieth century, perhaps in the entire history of the party.

Throughout his career, however, Alexander refused to accept the notion that Florida's Republican party could ever become more than a patronage organization structured to work in presidential elections. From his initial successes to his final overthrow by the Young Republicans, Alexander's opinions never wavered. A postelection interview following Eisenhower's victory in 1952 offered the GOP chairman, like John Harris before him, an opportunity to defend his style of patronage politics. Alexander attacked those who wanted an open primary system for not recognizing that Florida Republicans had a long way to go before they could become competitive with the Democratic party. He cited several reasons: (1) fewer than one in ten of Florida's registered voters was a Republican, and as long as Floridians continued to perceive the Democratic primary as the state's major election, this ratio would not change; (2) the costs of running a campaign for state office prohibited many candidates from joining with Republicans in a risky venture; (3) there were more poorly qualified candidates dragging down the entire party than qualified candidates building it up; (4) party discord, long an issue in Florida Republican politics, would increase with Eisenhower's inauguration and result in a patronage scramble that would interfere with healthy party development in Florida. For these reasons, better control over Republicans affairs in Florida could be achieved through the present convention system, not through an open primary.[20]

Some Florida Republicans disagreed with their party chairman vociferously. In 1952, a small number of Republicans from Dade County challenged Alexander's right to appoint the national delegation. Headed by Florence Garrison, president of the Florida Federation of Women Republicans, the Grass Roots Republican Committee was created in response to the faction-torn state executive committee's decision in February to send its handpicked delegation to Chicago. Garrison's group was uncommitted to any of the GOP presidential aspirants—Sen. Robert Taft of Ohio, Gen. Dwight Eisenhower, or Gen. Douglas MacArthur. The state executive committee, meeting in Gainesville, overwhelmingly supported Taft. With Alexander as chairman in full control of the proceedings, three delegates-at-large were appointed: Alexander himself became the party chairman; C. C. Spades of St. Augustine and Helen Lieb of Tampa were elected to the national committee. The other delegates were to be selected by the various district conventions but they had to be ratified by the state committee. Garrison's group wanted to open delegate selection only in the presidential preference primary, considering the three candidates' wide appeal in Florida, but was overruled by Alexander.[21]

On 15 April 1952, in Orlando, an organizational meeting of the Grass Roots Committee was convened in the San Juan Hotel. Its main goal was to decide whether Alexander's delegation's right to be seated at the national convention should be challenged. A motion to contest its legitimacy carried unanimously. Garrison headed the dissident faction's steering committee, while her husband, Wesley, was elected district chairman from Miami. By this time, the Grass Roots Committee had expanded beyond Dade County. Others at the meeting who also opposed Alexander's control of the party machinery included James Bent, St. Petersburg; Thelma Kolby, Jacksonville; Ray Stephens, Pensacola; A. B. Sias, Orlando; L. Garland Biggers, Palm Beach; Pearl Yeager, Sebring; and A. W. Shulte, Williston.[22]

Alexander wasted little time in responding to this challenge. Harry

Swan, the GOP gubernatorial nominee, had accepted an invitation to address the insurgent group. The party chairman issued a public reply noting that John Booth, Spessard Holland's GOP senatorial opponent, had come out in support of Alexander and the actions of the state executive committee. Booth's statement read in part: "I feel that if the Republicans do not win the 1952 election that it will be the end of the Republican Party and that there will be an entirely new political alignment. I do not think this is the time to have internal dissension in the Republican Party, regardless of personal opinions. I do not think personalities or personal likes and dislikes should be permitted to interfere with the Republican Party presenting a united front." [23]

Booth acknowledged that he had originally supported Mrs. Garrison's legal suit, filed in January before the Florida Supreme Court, to overturn Alexander's delegate selection.[24] He pointed out, however, that the court had ruled that the state party chairman was not in violation of Florida law. Booth subsequently withdrew his support of the Grass Roots movement: "The Supreme Court of the State of Florida settled the law applying to the rights of the state committee to select delegates. I wish to see unity in the Republican Party and I am opposed to a contesting delegation for many reasons. I will not take part in any movement to select such a delegation." [25]

None of the three main Republican presidential committees in Florida was involved in the Grass Roots protest. Alexander's delegation had been uninstructed but generally pro-Taft. This position was popular with Florida's more conservative Republicans, if not popular with all Floridians. As the June national convention approached, however, Eisenhower's broader appeal and more ebullient personality began to overtake Taft's intellect and experience. There seemed little doubt that Alexander's delegation would switch to Eisenhower without difficulty. The only outsiders interested in the Grass Roots Committee's protest were the MacArthur presidential committee. Led by C. Lewis Fowler of St. Petersburg, the committee supported the Garrisons' efforts, calling itself "Fighters for MacArthur: The Dixie Rainbow Southern Division."

Alexander attempted to stifle contact between the two committees, more to defeat the Garrisons than to damage MacArthur sentiment in the state. One member of the Grass Roots Committee complained about the GOP chairman's tactics: "One of Alexander's approaches [to stopping the contesting delegation] is to get the MacArthur people called off. He is getting to be a regular message boy." [26] The MacArthur strategy in Florida resembled the general's national campaign— in the event that neither Taft nor Eisenhower could muster enough support to win, he wanted to be the likely third choice. The Grass Roots Committee, needing support from all of Florida's Republicans, accepted the support by MacArthur's people, but they remained uncommitted nonetheless.

The Florida Republican primary was held on 6 May 1952. Harry Swan won the gubernatorial nomination with ease but stood no chance in the November general election. The runoff primary was on 27 May, but few Florida Republicans turned out to vote. Even in Pinellas County, the largest center of Florida Republican strength, fewer than 36 percent of those registered bothered to cast ballots. In Dade County, where the Grass Roots Committee had originated, the results of the turnout were even more disappointing: only one-fourth of the GOP voters cast their ballots. The Grass Roots group blamed the low turnout on Alexander's refusal to allow a presidential preference primary to determine candidates and delegates to the national convention. H. G. Rupert, president of the Republican Club of Dade County, pointed out that the results proved that most Florida Republicans had registered as Democrats so that they could vote in Democratic primaries. In response to Alexander's claim that the small May turnout indicated a renunciation of the Grass Roots Committee and their concept of a primary, Rupert stated that it "smacks of the most unmitigated gall possible. He is castigating Republicans for not exercising a privilege which he denied them." [27]

The significance of the issue of open primaries or closed conventions was obvious. Republicans who wanted a viable two-party state could not conceive of it without open primaries. When in 1952 the Florida legislature had refused to modify its anti-Republican stance, it was argued that more than 80,000 Florida Republicans were effectively disfranchised and unable to participate in their party's national political affairs, thanks to Alexander. Without the power to elect their national convention committee and delegation, a strong party chairman like G. Harrold Alexander could maintain an iron grip. His personal clout had increased immeasurably during the elections, especially when all three candidates were courting southern delegates in order to gain the GOP nomination. All that Republicans in Florida could do without a primary was to nominate meaningless candidates for local and state offices who stood no serious chance of winning.

The Grass Roots Committee failed in its bid to overturn the Alexander delegation at the national convention in June 1952. None of their basic goals had been accomplished: instead, Alexander's delegation went to the floor in Chicago and the state legislature failed to repeal the noxious 1949 antiprimary law that enabled the party chairman to continue dictating Florida Republican policy. While no new tide of Republican candidates committed to party growth had appeared, there were changes in the wind. Within the next decade, Florida's Republican party would experience a fresh breeze and a new breed of party members.

Part Three. Reformation

11

The New Breed and the Old Problem

FEW REPUBLICANS in Florida understood how Barry Goldwater, their party's presidential nominee in 1964, failed to carry their state. By the mid-1960s Florida had become a paragon of presidential Republicanism, having delivered its electoral votes twice to Dwight Eisenhower and then to Richard Nixon in 1960. Senator Goldwater's defeat, which was a narrow one, appeared to many Florida Republicans as important proof of their party's political impotence and bankruptcy under the leadership of G. Harrold Alexander and his handpicked successor, Tom Fairfield Brown. In the wake of Goldwater's defeat, a new breed of Florida Republicans swept into power and managed to elect an unprecedented number of Republicans to local, state, and congressional offices; those successes paved the way for the first Republican gubernatorial administration since Marcellus Stearns ended the era of Reconstruction.

Goldwater's campaign pointed up the fact that, in Florida and the South generally, Republicanism had begun taking on new significance. Slowly but steadily, new and traditional pockets of GOP strength had begun emerging to influence elections. Traditional Republican strength in the South centered in the Blue Ridge and the Smokey Mountains—the result of leftover unionism during the Civil War. Following Reconstruction, these mountaineers continued their patterned opposition to major Democratic movements, such as had the Bourbons in the late nineteenth century and the Solid South in the twentieth. The mountaineers had been the spine of Republicanism in the South. And, despite the various state-by-state drives to eliminate blacks from the party, a large number of older Negroes still clung out of sentiment and tradition to the party of the Great Emancipator, though the New Deal had managed to siphon off most younger southern blacks.

New political groups had been enfolded by the GOP in the South by the middle of the century: old-style Populists who had not been able to make a comfortable transition to the Democratic party following the agrarian protests; northern immigrants who had settled in the South unencumbered by any memory of Reconstruction and its bitterness; conservative businessmen opposed to the New Deal; and, most significantly, bigoted white southerners enraged by the civil rights commitments of the Democratic party under John Kennedy and Lyndon Johnson.

Several factors set the field for Senator Goldwater's appeal to the South and to southern conservatives. In the Dixiecrat campaign of 1948, South Carolina's Sen. J. Strom Thurmond's apostasy in opposing the incumbent President Truman as well as New York Republican Governor Thomas E. Dewey had dislodged a number of formerly confirmed southern Democrats. The Dixiecrats reminded many political observers of the Hoovercrats of 1928: they too had forsworn their traditional political affiliations and they too had been moved by prejudice (though religious, not racial). Thurmond disguised his anti-Negro campaign as one that championed states' rights, but the message was clear: southerners would accept neither a Truman-supported Fair Employment Practices Commission or civil rights law nor a too-liberal New York Republican. Throughout the Deep South, Thurmond prevailed.

Though the South was made to seem still "solid" by Thurmond's apparent success, a fracture lay hidden beneath the surface. In states that had led the region in secession and civil war, Thurmond's campaign was especially well received; but in the fringe states bordering the Deep South, among them Florida, Thurmond's appeal in 1948 was greatly reduced. A voting pattern that was to continue through the next several presidential elections already had changed the electoral habits of a significant number of southerners. The traditional Democratic hold on the South was broken at last, and the Solid South was cracked into two parts. In the next five presidential elections, Republicans ran well, achieving important breakthroughs in local, state, and congressional campaigns.[1]

Another factor that explains Goldwater's impact on southern Republican strategy was that the rise of the urban voter in the South became a critical factor of GOP support. The cities of the South were diametrically opposite politically from northern cities, usually voting Republican, while northern cities usually voted Democratic. The same opposition occurred in reverse in the rural regions: Republicans tended to do poorly in the rural South, and Democrats lagged behind in the nonurban North.

A partial reason for this difference lay in the fact that the traditional composite elements of northern cities—immigrants, working poor, organized union groups, and minority labor forces—were not found in most cities in the South, including Florida's urban centers specifically. Generally lacking these elements that had made the New Deal coalition so successful, southern cities usually contained smaller industries and plants that required more skilled and white-collar labor and depended less upon mass production. Instead of factory workers, cities like Tampa, St. Petersburg, and Ft. Lauderdale lured Yankee retirees—elderly business managers and professionals—whose political preferences in the North had been Republican. The seedbed of modern Florida's Republican support lay here, among people who had had little in common with New Deal Democrats in the North and even less with southern Democrats. These Republicans tended to be economically and socially conservative, but unsympathetic to the passions of Reconstruction.

These conditions existed throughout much of the South but were magnified in Florida. By the mid-1960s Florida was rapidly becoming two separate regions politically, socially, and economically. The northern portion of the peninsula continued to be part of the Deep South, manifesting little political difference from southern Georgia and Alabama. Southern and Central Florida developed steadily and rapidly under the combined influence of warm climate, homestead tax exemption, and no state income tax. By 1953, William Cramer of Pinellas County had won the first GOP congressional seat since the turn of the century. He was followed by others, including Edward J. Gurney of Winter Park, who later became Florida's first Republican senator since Reconstruction's Simon Conover. Cramer, Gurney, and the other few successful GOP politicians who had won seats in Florida's legislature and in Congress did not owe their elections to the Florida Republican party, however. They won because of individual initiative, appeal, and effort. The party itself continued to falter under G. Harrold Alexander and Tom Fairfield Brown despite the growth in the numbers of Republican voters. Barry Goldwater's defeat finally galvanized political reform among the state's GOP sufficient to produce, at last, a viable two-party system.

Goldwater had bungled his campaign in Florida. By speaking out against Social Security in St. Petersburg, for example, the senator alienated many local residents living on Social Security or fixed incomes. By campaigning against federal welfare, he alienated many black voters. By voting and speaking against the 1964 Civil Rights Act, Goldwater appealed to racists and conservatives but repelled many moderates. But, in the end, it was his opposition to welfare programs for the elderly that cost him Florida's electoral votes.

Goldwater came close to carrying not only Florida but the entire South. By lashing out against urban riots that had wracked the nation the previous summer and attacking the civil rights legislation championed by Presidents Kennedy and Johnson, and aided by George Wallace's withdrawal from the presidential campaign, Goldwater managed to carry Louisiana, Mississippi, Alabama, Georgia, and South Carolina. As in Florida, he barely lost in Tennessee, Arkansas, and Virginia. Goldwater drew 49 percent of the total popular vote in the eleven states of the ex-Confederacy.[2]

The key to Goldwater's victory was to have been his southern strategy. At the San Francisco nominating convention Goldwater's southern supporters literally drove Nelson Rockefeller, then New York's governor, from the convention floor. Rockefeller's defeat was more than a personal victory for Goldwater; it symbolized for southern Republicans their own triumphant return to power. But in appealing only to reactionary elements, Goldwater alienated the new urban Republican in the South, especially in Florida, which cost him the election in that state. His speeches in Tampa and St. Petersburg attacking Medicare programs for the elderly cost him more even than his anti-Negro position.

Overlooking Goldwater's mistakes, Florida Republicans blamed his defeat on the party's state executive leadership, G. Harrold Alexander and Tom Fairfield Brown. Most of the direct criticism was reserved for Brown, the party chairman. Elected in 1962 to succeed Alexander, Brown was often considered aloof, accused of running the state party in dictatorial fashion and of being uninterested in developing the Florida GOP into a truly competitive organization. As Alexander's protégé, Brown, a wealthy Tampa attorney, had continued the tradition of post office Republicanism, concentrating only on presidential elections. Until Goldwater's debacle, Republicans in Florida had been doing well; but his campaign's failure in 1964 menaced Brown's reelection as chairman two years later.

During the four years he was the head of the Florida GOP, Brown never once called the entire executive committee into session, a failure that reflected the minority control of party machinery. The rules under which the Florida GOP operated in the mid-1960s allowed for gross inequity in representation. There were just over 45,000 registered Republicans in the state in 1962, and the state executive committee was composed of 132 state committeemen, all of whom had equal votes in determining policy. The vast majority of Republicans lived in four counties—Hillsborough, Pinellas, Orange, and Broward—but since each county was represented by the same number of committeemen, some 250,000 Republicans were represented by only eight votes while 103 registered Republicans in ten North Florida counties controlled twenty votes. Brown and Alexander could safely ignore the majority will under these conditions. When confronted by the fact that he had never bothered to call a meeting of the state executive committee, Brown's reply revealed his attitude toward the rank-and-file members: "Only the froth would come out."[3]

Unequal representation was only one of the reasons that Tom Brown fell into disfavor with the majority of Florida's Republicans. In 1964, the state party headquarters had distributed less than $20,000 in campaign aid to the various candidates for local, state, and congressional offices, including Charles Holley, the GOP gubernatorial nominee. At the same time, Brown spent more than $78,000 in operating expenses for the GOP's headquarters in Tampa. Charles Holley, who had polled over 40 percent of the vote against Farris Bryant without party help, announced his intention to run against Brown for the chairmanship at the June 1966 state convention.[4]

A number of other prominent Florida Republicans were angry at Brown. Holley and George Petersen, the 1958 gubernatorial nominee who had also polled more than 40 percent of the vote, claimed that even a small amount of extra help from party headquarters would have meant the difference between losing and winning. Congressmen Edward Gurney and William Cramer also acknowledged that the chairman had not assisted their campaigns, and Cramer's supporters even claimed that Brown had campaigned actively against him in Pinellas County. The organizers of a fundraising dinner for Gurney in Orange County in 1965 had voted not to invite the state chairman. None of the Republican candidates received back even the amount of their filing fees from Brown's office: they had paid $77,235 in qualifying fees to state party headquarters in 1964, but their total reimbursement was only $5,565. Across the state a growing number of Florida Republicans were becoming restive under the abuses of Brown and his committee and were in agreement with Pinellas County committeewoman Thelma Fischer's statement that "We can't jump from election to election every four years and accomplish anything.... We must eat, sleep and talk Republicanism from day-to-day, week-to-week, month-to-month."[5]

Not all of Brown's adversaries could settle upon Charles Holley as their candidate, however. Fearful that Holley would cater to the faction led by William Cramer and discriminate against other groups, a small number of younger party members began holding a series of meetings in Bartow shortly after Goldwater's defeat. At first less than a dozen attended, including Willard Dover of Dade County, Lou Frey of Winter Park, Bob Corselius of Dade County, Fred Hagen of Orlando, Bill James of Delray Beach, Bill Shields of Fort Myers, Hal Stayman of Dade County, and Bill Taylor of Jacksonville. Three issues motivated them: Goldwater's defeat, the ineptitude and unresponsiveness of the senior leadership in the state party and on the executive committee, and the lack of an effective, statewide Young Republican Federation. The last was a special concern because the national Federation of Young Republicans was going to hold its convention in June 1965 in Miami.[6]

As they continued to meet in John's Restaurant in Bartow, there emerged a consensus view of how to change Florida's GOP. Their first goal was to elect a candidate who could take control of the Florida Federation of Young Republicans and reactivate younger party members around the state. Consistent with that was their interest in hosting the national convention and the money that needed to be raised for it. Second, they wanted to defeat Tom Brown for state party chairman in 1966, though they did not support Charles Holley. Third, it was hoped that by 1970 at the earliest a Republican candidate for governor, backed by an effective party organization, could win and make Florida once again a two-party state.[7]

The Young Republican Trust Fund, as this insurgent faction wished to be known, set out to accomplish the goals its members had adopted. The Florida Federation of Young Republican Clubs was scheduled to meet in May 1965, only a month prior to the national gathering. A non–Trust Fund member, David Wells of Jacksonville, was nominated to head the reform slate. Duval County had a large and potentially powerful Young Republican Club organization, and Wells's nomination as federation president was designed to build unity among North and South Florida Young Republicans. Wells won against Lou Frey, a Trust Fund member and a member of Edward Gurney's Winter Park law firm. Although disappointed over his defeat, Frey continued to work with the Trust Fund and with David Wells.

The Trust Fund furthered its aims vis-à-vis the state party at the national meeting of Young Republicans when the Florida Federation, led by David Wells, managed to elect several candidates to positions of importance within the national organization. Moreover, Bob Corselius and Hal Stayman, both active fundraisers for Young Republican candidates, met with Marquita Maytag, wife of the president of National Airlines, about plans to elect a Trust Fund candidate as state party chairman.

Wealthy, conservative, politically active, and shrewd, Maytag also was very angry over the GOP's failure to carry Florida for Barry Goldwater and blamed Alexander, Brown, and the state executive committee. She listened sympathetically over lunch while Corselius and Stayman outlined their plans to assume control of the Florida Republican party. Thereupon she wrote a check for $25,000 to the Young Republican Trust Fund.[8]

With this money, two field-workers were employed to reinvigorate Young Republican Clubs in all of Florida's sixty-seven counties. Because he could communicate with Florida's crackers, Charles Nerguard was to organize the northern counties; Hal Stayman managed the efforts in South Florida. Nerguard, working out of Wells's office, was executive secretary of the Florida Federation of Young Republicans, and Stayman became the executive director of the Young Republican Trust Fund. Their purpose—to overthrow Tom Brown and prevent Charles Holley from succeeding him—was kept secret. Both Nerguard and Stayman traveled extensively to persuade county committee members uncommitted to Alexander's faction to oppose Brown. Neither man fully outlined the conspiracy underway for the Tampa meeting in June 1966.[9]

By late 1965, the state party chairmanship issue had split Florida Republicans into several factions. The old guard led by G. Harrold Alexander no longer supported Tom Brown for a second term. Siding with GOP state treasurer Helene Morris, Alexander dropped Brown over charges that he had mismanaged party funds.[10] To replace Brown, the old leader put up another candidate, Tallahassee attorney Wilfred Varn. Alexander, unaware of the strength of Holley's faction and of the

Trust Fund's, fully expected his candidate to win. Indeed, Varn refused to campaign actively for the post at all, assuming that Alexander's hold on the state committee would ensure his victory.

Meanwhile, Charles Holley gathered support in his bid for the party chairmanship. His campaign in 1966 was backed by many older Florida Republicans who had long protested the exclusive power of Alexander and Brown. Helene Morris had become a stalwart supporter of Holley long before Alexander agreed that Brown should be replaced. Following the Goldwater defeat, Morris had attempted to remove Tom Brown as chairman. In the spring of 1966, she filed suit in circuit court in Tampa to restrain Brown's spending at party headquarters, arguing that it was unnecessary and unlawful. She wanted an investigation of Brown's failure to return candidates' filing fees.

At first Brown ignored the accusations; then, when court action seemed near, he replied to the charges in an open letter:

> Up until this time, I have felt the best action to proceed in the light of blasts by Mrs. Morris was not to respond, as such controversy in the press is not conducive to Party unity and in the best interest of the Party. For your information, the State Headquarters has been maintained at my insistence and over the objections and opposition of Mrs. Morris. It is obvious to anyone interested in building a strong Republican Party that a State Headquarters is essential and that operation of such a facility properly staffed costs money. I have been able to keep the Headquarters open at considerable personal sacrifice through the support of a dedicated few who recognize the importance of our Headquarters' operation to the success of the Republican Party campaign throughout the State this year.[11]

Brown enclosed a copy of the auditor's report on the state executive committee filed with Florida's attorney general, which covered the year 1965, and a copy of the restraining order and court decision. The Tampa court ruled that Brown could continue to pay rent for the GOP's headquarters, employees' salaries, and utilities. In Brown's view, the court's action confirmed that "the operation of the Headquarters of the Republican State Executive Committee of Florida by myself as Chairman is in keeping with my authority as Chairman and in the best interest of the Republican Party." Not until the convention did Brown finally concede that he had misused the funds coming out of the candidates' filing fees.[12] It was because of Brown's contentiousness that G. Harrold Alexander finally dropped his support for Brown's reelection as party chairman.

Eventually, the Young Republicans settled upon William Murfin of Hobe Sound as their candidate for state party chairman. Murfin was a wealthy druggist who had three main credentials for the position: he could afford the time off to work in politics without damaging his business in Martin County; he lacked the personal ambition to be elected to political office; most importantly, he was a fresh candidate, unscarred by the party's internecine struggles. But Murfin also was something of a liability. Shy and retiring, he was uncomfortable giving public appearances. Consequently, he failed to excite much enthusiasm or support once he had become a candidate for party chairman. Nerguard and Stayman were forced to double their efforts because of Murfin's lackluster nature. Most of the state committee members who were disenchanted with Brown and Alexander had already decided to vote for Charles Holley, however.

Murfin was not the initial choice of the Trust Fund members. During the early months of planning, the most acceptable candidate was Lou Frey, who had worked amiably and cooperatively with the members and with David Wells and the Florida Young Republicans. Frey was forced out of the chairman's race in February 1966 by Congressmen Edward Gurney and William Cramer. Both men had met with the Trust Fund, and, while Gurney at first was amenable to his junior law partner becoming state GOP chairman, Cramer insisted on strict neutrality. Once Frey removed himself from the race, Cramer became an open supporter of Charles Holley at the state convention in June.[13]

In the weeks before the convention at Tampa, it seemed that the Trust Fund members had been defeated; without an effective candidate and against the opposition of Charles Holley, victory seemed impossible. A last-minute campaign took Murfin to meet individually with members of the state committee. Nerguard and Stayman, who had spent the previous year making personal contact with state committeemen district by district, hoped to convince them to support Murfin. A week before the convention, admitting that Murfin would not be able to win the election on his own, several members of the Trust Fund arranged a meeting in Fort Myers with G. Harrold Alexander. A turning point had arrived when an informal poll indicated that Murfin and Holley were about even while Varn, the old guard's choice, was a distant third. Thus, Alexander's faction found itself in the crucial swing position.

As Murfin, Hal Stayman, and Bill Shields discovered during their luncheon meeting with him, Alexander was unaware of the situation. He seemed relaxed and confident that Will Varn would carry the election despite his refusal to campaign. After all, it had worked that way for many years. Using charts and poll statistics, the three Trust Fund representatives finally managed to convince Alexander that his candidate was in serious trouble. A few phone calls to his close friends confirmed that fact, and the ex–party chief was left with a choice: he could announce his support of the Trust Fund's candidate and withdraw Varn's name from the race, or he could allow the Holley faction to win. Throughout the preceding several months, Holley's attacks on Alexander and Brown had grown increasingly strident. Alexander agreed to support Murfin instead, and the old guard Republicans on the executive committee would vote with the Trust Fund. In return, Murfin, Stayman, and Shields promised that some of the regulars would remain in active partnership with the Trust Fund after the election. Upon closing the bargain, Alexander turned to Bill Murfin and made a final request: "If I'm alive, Bill, I'd sure like to be a delegate to the national convention."[14] Murfin failed to reply. The post office era was over.

William Murfin was elected state party chairman on 18 June 1966. The actual vote at the International Hotel in Tampa was somewhat anticlimactic, with Murfin winning easily on the first ballot sixty-six to forty-seven.[15] (Varn had withdrawn his name from the ballot prior to the vote.) The remainder of the Trust Fund's slate of candidates won endorsement with equal ease: Mary Lou Hammond of Indian River as vice-chairwoman; Dorie Hostleter of Lake County as secretary; and Lou Frey, bouncing back from William Cramer's betrayal that had cost him the chairmanship of the Florida GOP, as treasurer. A few members of the old guard, in keeping with the agreement made between Alexander and the Trust Fund, were also elected to fill minor party posts in each of the congressional districts. Also up for election were the 144 seats on the state committee itself; the results indicated how willing Florida Republicans were to change their traditional practices. All but forty-six were new members committed to reform; they had supported either Charles Holley or William Murfin for chairman. Murfin seemed anxious to lay intraparty disputes aside and concentrate on the upcoming election, acknowledging a new era in the history of Florida's Republican Party: "If we fail to win this year we can blame no one but ourselves."[16]

In previous years, such statements were customary hyperbole. Two events in Florida in 1966 had made Murfin's forecast more realistic. The Democratic incumbent, Gov. Haydon Burns, had lost a runoff primary in May to Robert King High, Miami's liberal mayor. The Burns-High contest had critically divided Florida's Democrats; conservatives around the state found it difficult to endorse High's stands on civil rights, integration, and spending, which closely resembled President Lyndon Johnson's. And for the first time since William J. Howey's nomination, the Republican party of Florida had nominated a candidate for governor whose political style appealed to a large number of Florida's voters.

Claude R. Kirk's entrance into Florida politics in 1960 had been unspectacular. As state campaign manager of the Florida Democrats for Nixon, he had contributed to Florida's then unbroken chain of Republican victories in presidential elections, and he had shortly thereafter changed his party registration to Republican. Four years later, buoyed by the renaissance of Republican strength in the South despite Goldwater's failed campaign for the presidency, Kirk had challenged longtime Democratic Senator Spessard L. Holland in the fourth and final campaign of his twenty-four years in Washington. Holland had become a popular figure in Florida and had become entrenched in the U.S. Senate. Against the only man ever to serve Florida as both governor and senator, Kirk had little to offer. Although his bid for election failed, the unsuccessful GOP nominee had traveled the entire state, planting political seeds for the future.

Kirk's candidacy at first did not spark much enthusiasm among Florida's Republican voters. Few expected that Robert King High would defeat Governor Burns. Even the Trust Fund members had concluded that Florida's Republican party could not realistically expect to challenge the Democrats for any statewide office. Kirk won the nomination with little trouble or effort, defeating Paul Myers of Fort Myers and Richard Muldrew, a Brevard County commissioner, in the May primaries. In the 24 May runoff against Muldrew, Kirk won almost four to one.[17]

Kirk won early on the overwhelming support of Florida's Young Republicans. In the fall of 1965, having returned from a stay in France, Kirk charmed the delegates at an Ocala meeting of state Young Republicans with his personality and champagne. When High unexpectedly wrested the Democratic nomination from Haydon Burns, Kirk was quickly transformed into a viable candidate.

Florida Democrats were badly split because of the Burns-High primary fight. Burns had compiled a spotty record during his two years as governor. Many believed the accusations of personal corruption and mismanagement of funds leveled against him. High, the diminutive mayor from Dade County, was not well known elsewhere in the state, but his attacks on Burns succeeded in getting him the Democratic nomination. Had he not been from South Florida or a liberal or an avowed supporter of Presidents Kennedy and Johnson, he likely would have become Florida's governor; but because Robert King High was all those things, Claude R. Kirk, Jr., won the 1966 gubernatorial election.[18]

The issues in the 1966 campaign were a blend of national and state concerns. Vietnam, student rioting, and civil rights were part of the Kirk-High contest, as were purely state issues like crime, tourism, and the environment. The distinction between the candidates of which the voters were constantly reminded was that Robert King High was a liberal politician from Dade County while Kirk was a political innocent and a Jacksonville conservative.[19] Although High was tendered (and presumably utilized) the full power of the state Democratic party's machinery, not all of Florida's Democrats were with him. Outgoing Governor Burns, for example, refused to campaign for High and late in the race officially announced his support and offered his organizational workers to Kirk. Edward Ball, a dominant figure in much of Florida's twentieth-century politics, publicly denounced High and characterized the Republican nominee as one who "would be clear of control of labor union bosses, civil rights agitators, and the undesirable riff-raff of our country."[20]

Kirk opened his campaign at a Tallahassee press conference on 26 May 1966, announcing that he expected his opponent to take "down his signs and put up the issues." High began his campaign in the fashion common to Democratic candidates who had won primaries and expected little opposition in the November elections. He held a joint press conference with senior party leaders, who promised to support him, and attended a kickoff dinner in Miami Beach on 22 July. Among the few political observers who appreciated the significance of Kirk's challenge was Charles Hessee, editorial writer for the *Miami*

News: "If the people are more dissatisfied with everything from Viet Nam to the white backlash to the Johnson administratation than it appears on the surface, we could wake up . . . with a Republican governor." Even as late as August, state Democratic party chairman Pat Thomas was so confident of High's victory that he announced to the press that the candidate had been in several conferences planning his inauguration and the initial weeks of his new administration.[21]

Several factors operating in Kirk's behalf had not been available to previous GOP nominees for governor. The increases in GOP voter registration in South Florida cut severely into High's lead in that part of the state. Moreover, since Congressman Edward Gurney's opponent had withdrawn from the congressional contest in 1966, the Republican incumbent put his campaign organization in Central Florida at Kirk's disposal. In addition, the matter of financial support from GOP headquarters had been resolved with the defeat of Tom Brown as party chairman so that Kirk received the financial aid that Holley, Petersen, and other recent Republican candidates had not been offered.[22] Finally, Kirk received enormous support from "DemoKirks," those conservative Florida Democrats who would not vote for Robert King High and whose votes ultimately determined the election's outcome.[23]

Kirk's platform appealed to many. He pledged no new taxation, increased road building, better transportation planning, branch governor's offices around the state so that citizens could feel closer to their government, educational reform—including higher minimum salaries, more teacher training programs, merit pay, and better student load projections—and of course a full-scale attack on Florida's growing crime problem. Kirk promised to appoint a "blue ribbon citizens' committee" to study the issue, and he also promised "to rattle a few doors" of those public officials who had not dealt effectively with the incidence of crime.[24]

On 7 November 1966, Claude R. Kirk, Jr., was elected, defeating Robert King High 821,190 to 688,233, and carrying all but twelve counties. The final stages of the campaign revealed that the Democrats had begun taking Kirk's challenge seriously but too late. High spent more than his Republican opponent but to no avail.[25] At last, a Republican governor would oversee Florida, and hopes were high that Claude Kirk would accomplish much for the state. It did not work out that way.

12

The Kirk Years

INAUGURATION DAY in Tallahassee, 3 January 1967, was rainy, overcast, and cold, but the bad weather did little to dampen the enthusiasm of the new governor, Claude R. Kirk, Jr., his family, or the thousands of well-wishers and onlookers who attended the swearing-in ceremony. Outgoing Gov. Haydon Burns in his farewell address stressed the accomplishments of his administration.[1] He noted with pride that he was leaving office with $80 million in the state treasury, that his administration had spent $84 million on urban road development and construction, and that his economic and business policies had produced 50,000 new jobs in tourism and industry. The departing chief executive also credited himself with increasing Florida's old-age welfare assistance and public education budgets and expanding the state's water recharge system. Upon noting that his wife had been "Florida's finest first lady," Burns turned over the reins of state government to the first Republican governor in nearly a century.[2]

Governor Kirk wasted no time in bringing forth his own surprises. To the shock and amazement of his guests on the inaugural stand, as well as to many watching in person and on television, the new governor called for a proclamation ordering a special session of the Florida legislature to finish its work on Florida's proposed new constitution, and he signed one less than two hours later. This first official act as governor was his initial confrontation with the legislature; there were to be many more during the next four years.

None of the legislative leaders who attended the ceremony was prepared for Governor Kirk's announcement; the process of revising the obsolete 1885 document had been under way for several years.[3] "The cornerstone of an effective government structure," reasoned the governor, "is a modern constitution. Florida can no longer suffer the limitations of its antiquated constitution. The Florida Constitutional

Revision Commission has worked long and hard to draw new guidelines. . . . It sets the tone for returning local government to the people and serves as an example for other states to follow. It will provide a vehicle for needed governmental reorganization."

The incoming governor saw no value in delaying work on the constitution: "For the Legislature to labor sixty days next April to rewrite our laws without first rewriting our constitution is not consistent with good businesslike procedure. Constitutional revision cannot be delayed for a long hot summer of dilatory debate. It must be tackled now while minds are fresh and courage is abundant." Kirk wanted the document ready for ratification or rejection by Florida's voters in a special election to be held on 18 April. If it was ratified, government could begin under the new constitution on 1 July 1967.

Democratic legislative leaders were visibly disturbed. The governor had not consulted either Verle Pope, senate president, or Ralph Turlington, speaker of the house, prior to issuing his proclamation, knowing they would oppose the idea. Yet it was clear that they had little choice but to agree to the governor's demands—to oppose him on inauguration day would have seemed cheaply partisan. Pope and Turlington pledged their cooperation.

Some experienced political observers saw in Governor Kirk's action a gamble calculated to impress upon the legislature that a Republican chief executive could not be bullied or stampeded by the opposition party. Jacksonville's Sen. Jack Mathews, a Democrat, considered Kirk's move "aggressive" but warned his fellow legislators that the new governor's approach and style might prove popular, especially when compared with the legislature's more cautious outlook. "He certainly didn't start off well with the legislative leadership," Mathews noted when probed for his reaction, "and he may learn something. But on the other hand, this approach will go over with the people, and the Legislature may learn something."[4]

Republican supporters were delighted. House minority leader Don Reed felt that Governor Kirk had quickly established his businesslike approach to state government. "I am very excited about it," claimed the Boca Raton representative. "It seems a little silly to seek a revision after a regular session. If we adopt a constitution first and then the people adopt it by referendum, then we can enact legislation now that will be right in line with the new constitution." GOP Sen. L. A. Bafalis echoed Reed: "I am delighted. It will speed up what has been needed for many years."[5]

However correct or justified, Kirk's action was nonetheless a political ploy. The new governor wished to confront an overwhelmingly Democratic legislature with his executive power, and he also wanted to attack Florida's cabinet system. He had pushed forcefully for an overhaul of the cabinet system during a December 1966 meeting of the constitutional revision committee, arguing that since the governor was the chief executive and the cabinet his principal advisory board, cabinet officers ought to be appointed, not elected. At the same meeting, he also expressed his preference for the office of lieutenant governor (abolished in 1885) and for successive gubernatorial terms. His call for an early session on constitutional revision caught the cabinet members off guard; each had assumed that constitutional revision would not be completed until June, giving them ample time to lobby to preserve the elective cabinet system. The governor's proclamation had shortened their lobbying time drastically.

The special session preempted meetings by the legislature during which organizational details for the regular session were usually worked out. A legislative weekend conference and a meeting of the state budget commission had to be canceled. The budget commission, composed of the governor and the cabinet, had been scheduled to meet jointly with the appropriations and finance committees of each house to hear biennial budget requests from all the state agencies, but those hearings also had to be erased from the January calendar.

Governor Kirk produced a second surprise in his inaugural address when he announced his choice for director of his "war on crime." (Throughout the campaign, Kirk had publicized widely his intention to conduct Florida's first such "war.") George Wackenhut, a Miami-based investigator who headed one of the nation's largest private detective agencies, had agreed to serve as a "dollar-a-year" director.

The governor spelled out Wackenhut's duties: "It will be his responsibility to marshal the forces for this great fight—the attorneys, the accountants, and the people. Although Director Wackenhut is donating his services, I have authorized him to secure from his firm whatever manpower is needed in this campaign. The cost involved in all phases of this endeavor will be paid for from funds volunteered by interested private citizens. This means that this important and crucial fight will be led by me without additional taxes. I hereby put our underworld adversaries on notice."[6]

The "war on crime" was an ill-conceived plan which eventually generated considerable controversy and trouble for the governor. Wackenhut's personal services were volunteered, but his agency's bills to the state amounted to more than $500,000. It became obvious that private contributions would not defray the program's expenses. Because of that shortfall and because of the governor's other extravagant spending, a Governor's Club was created. Membership could be had for a $500 per annum private contribution, and originally contributions were kept secret. In the resulting storm of public disapproval, charges that no one who wanted a state contract, commission appointment, or favored treatment from the governor could avoid becoming a member eventually led to court-ordered disclosures. Among its 233 contributors were nearly 50 who had received political appointments. Several member architects and engineers had received state work contracts, and nearly 20 others had received state liquor licenses.[7]

Besides the financial embarrassment, the "war on crime" did not work. The governor had been justified in his claims that Democrats had failed to stem Florida's rising crime rate. During the campaign, Kirk had reserved his harshest criticism for Robert King High, claiming that High had tried to suppress a damaging FBI report indicating the extent to which organized crime had infiltrated Dade County's hotel and tourist business. State GOP Chairman William Murfin weakly attempted to defend Governor Kirk's plan and Wackenhut's accomplishments even after mounting evidence had shown that the program was a failure. In October 1967, when contributions to pay off Wackenhut were slumping, Kirk pointed out to reporters that "the work this guy has done would have cost the state five times as much."[8] In response to the war on crime, the Florida legislature created the Florida Bureau of Law Enforcement to replace Wackenhut, and a number of the state's corrupt county sheriffs and other local law enforcement officials were removed from office.

Kirk's war on crime and his refusal to curtail his other expenses to a level acceptable to Floridians generally—and to the Republican party specifically—forced him into deep political and financial trouble. Clarence Jones, staff writer for the *Miami Herald,* correctly observed that Governor Kirk was one chief executive who could have "beaten the system" of special-interest politics had he tried. Kirk began his term unencumbered by debts owed to special-interest groups, for his campaign expenditures had been relatively low. The primary against Richard Muldrew had been a low-budget affair, and by beating Robert King High in the general election, Jones wrote, Kirk had "paid off the mortgage [to conservative contributors], free and clear."[9]

Yet the way he spent the state's money soon eroded his political popularity. Claude Kirk liked to live in a flamboyant and theatrical style. He thoroughly enjoyed charming women and good liquor; the problem was that he enjoyed them to excess. Unable to support his life style on his governor's salary ($36,000), an allowance for maintaining the governor's mansion ($159,000), and a special contingency fund ($13,000), he soon was borrowing money from sources and in ways that created severe political repercussions. He rented a Palm Beach home, chartered a Lear jet to fly him across the United States on his vice-presidential odyssey, and spent lavishly on his friends and political associates. The governor's spending style soon moved well beyond Florida Republicans' ability to pay.

As the first Republican to enter the governor's mansion in nearly a century, Kirk and the Republican party faced many obstacles. He was opposed by a solidly Democratic cabinet, state legislature, and national administration. As governor, Kirk was responsible for making some two thousand political appointments in his four-year term, and there were too few experienced Republicans to advise him. The cutoff of funds for his extravagant spending aggravated relations between the governor and his party with the result that Kirk increasingly rejected Republican support in Florida. The final rupture came in the wake of his veto of the 1969 legislative salary bill.

Legislative salaries became an issue after reapportionment in 1967. Reapportionment had overturned the domination of the Florida legislature by small-county representatives, traditionally called the porkchop gang. Following the U.S. Supreme Court's decision in *Baker v. Carr* (which established the one-man–one-vote rule), Florida's urban population gained new and strengthened representation in the legislature. Several Republicans were elected to represent new districts in South Florida, enough to provide Kirk with a veto-proof minority in 1967. Most of these new legislators, including some who were Democrats, quickly realized that the legislature had served merely as a rubber stamp for the requests of the governor and his cabinet officers. Legislators were paid only $6,000 per year plus a county supplement in some instances, and they lacked adequate staffs and consultants for drafting effective legislation that would meet Florida's growing problems with population, crime, education, transportation, welfare, and the environment. It was hoped that higher salaries would attract better-qualified representatives. The move to increase legislative salaries generated bipartisan support; neither Republicans nor Democrats wished to make a political contest of it, and Governor Kirk had promised his support. In 1967, however, a bill to raise salaries sponsored by a bipartisan group in both houses died in committee.[10]

Salary bills were reintroduced in the 1969 session, and once again the legislature received warm encouragement from the governor. Indeed, Kirk had suggested one such plan for increases that tied legislative salary increases to raises for the chief executive. His plan was to raise their salaries to 50 percent of his own. While his measure was rejected by the committee studying salaries, there was no indication that Kirk planned to veto any bill that might reach his desk.[11]

Bills were introduced simultaneously by Republican Don Reed in the house and Democrat John Mathews in the senate on 15 April. Discussion centered upon the size of the increase, and proposals ranged from an extra $2,400 to $10,000. In a bill passed 17 April, the House of Representatives agreed to double its compensation to $12,000. The vote was 68 to 31 with nine Republicans opposed. The senate endorsed the new rate overwhelmingly by a vote of 30 to 7, with Sen. Beth Johnson of Cocoa Beach and Sen. David Lane of Ft. Lauderdale the only dissenting Republicans.[12] The bill finally reached the governor for his signature on 22 April.[13]

Kirk refused to sign, hoping for news media coverage that would make him appear to the voters of Florida as a fiscal conservative. Even though he had promised to support the salary increases, Kirk delivered his veto message before a joint session of the legislature. Speaking before a stunned and angry group of Republicans and Democrats, he rebuked the legislators unmercifully: "The Legislature passed, with almost indecent haste and no attention to public feeling, an overwhelming pay raise for its membership. . . . As Governor, I can have no alternative but to respond to the people when the people's cause is right and just. I veto this bill."[14]

In lieu of their salary increases, Kirk suggested a series of actions to regulate legislative expenses by establishing budget controls, removing conflicts of interest, curtailing purchases, and providing for a legislative audit. He warned against nepotism in legislative staff positions, a practice that he claimed added considerably to legislators' overall incomes, and closed his stinging speech with a further threat: "Just as you would be well advised against yielding to the temptation to indulge in recrimination, so I must tell you that adverse public reaction will be equally swift should you attempt to evade this veto by increasing legislative expense allowances to provide the pay increases sought in this bill." [15]

Republicans and Democrats alike were infuriated by the governor's remarks as well as by the fact that he had reneged on his promise to support legislative salary increases. Though there had been political pressure to oppose such increases, notably from U.S. Sen. Edward Gurney, the governor's turnabout was blatant confrontational politics.[16] Kirk had accused the legislators of gross political corruption, fiscal irresponsibility, and venal intent—in the same year that the governor himself had become the object of a governmental audit. That audit had disclosed that he had misspent funds on travel and services and that he had used state money for unconstitutional purposes, including his European honeymoon, flowers, Christmas cards, and food.[17]

Republican leaders were embarrassed by Kirk's veto remarks, but Democrats were outraged. They had agreed to a nonpartisan bill based upon assurances from Republican party leaders that Kirk would sign the measure. Verle Pope announced that Kirk had "Kirkumcized" the legislature, while Edward Blackburn compared the governor to one of the most infamous of betrayers: "The governor has broken his word to the leaders of his own party in his veto message yesterday; for he had promised his leaders to support this pay raise for the Legislature—and had actually suggested this compensation was not enough. . . . The governor's personal pledge to his own leaders proved to be a Judas kiss, and I believe history will reward him with no higher honor." [18]

The veto override was swift and sure. Both Republicans and Democrats viewed Kirk's assault as a public attack on their individual integrity. The vote was 35 to 10, with Beth Johnson the only Republican supporting the governor; in the house, the vote was 88 to 20, only four Republicans voting for Kirk.[19]

The salary dispute was merely the final break in what were already strained relations between the governor and Florida's Republican party. Indeed, from the moment he entered office, Kirk failed to achieve harmony with his party. Political appointments were a major irritant. Out of office for nearly a century, Florida's Republicans were naturally eager to control state governmental affairs. Patronage committees were organized throughout the state following Kirk's election to advise him on appointments, but the governor generally refused to consult them. Kirk realized that he was elected by conservative Democrats, so-called DemoKirks who would not support Robert King High. He wanted to reward them as much if not more than Florida's Republicans. Pat Dodson, head of the Kirk advisory committee in West Florida, repeatedly urged the governor to appoint more Republicans, even traveling to Tallahassee to make his appeal in person. Though Dodson himself received an appointment to the Board of Regents of the state's university system as a result, the issue continued to fester among party members.[20]

Three ideas appear to have shaped the governor's thinking about patronage and appointments. First was his belief in the significance of the Democratic vote in his election victory; it was unlikely that he could have defeated Haydon Burns if the latter had won the 1966 Democratic primary. Second, because Kirk was forced to work with a legislature and cabinet controlled by Democrats, he felt he could not ignore the opposition. Third, Kirk insisted that younger men should serve in his administration as a source of new ideas, which led to a greater number of relatively inexperienced aides. While many of his appointees performed creditably, his closest staff did more to ruin his reputation than to enhance it. Three staff appointees in particular provoked controversy: William Safire from New York City, who handled public relations; Jim Wolf, his press aide; and Tom Ferguson, his administrative assistant. These were the men most instrumental in pushing and planning the governor's vice-presidential ambitions. From the moment he became governor, Claude Kirk began running hard for the 1968 vice-presidential nomination on the GOP ticket.

Although in the end it was his vice-presidential quest that ended his political career, the nomination seemed a feasible goal when he became governor in January 1967. Richard Nixon, who attended Kirk's inauguration, was already thinking ahead to the 1968 Republican national convention. Apparently, Nixon told "Uncle Cleve," Governor Kirk's father-in-law from his first marriage, that he intended to put a young, fresh, southern Republican governor on the ticket, if he won the nomination. During the New Hampshire GOP primary in March, William Loeb, archconservative editor and publisher of the *Manchester Union-Leader*, urged a vice-presidential write-in campaign on Kirk's behalf, citing three reasons for his pro-Kirk position. It would prove to southern Democrats that the GOP "have our foot in the door in the South . . . and we intend to walk in." It would show George Wallace that "There is a difference between states rights and racism. There is a great gulf between the honest conservative and the Ku Klux Klan. We want to vote against federal encroachment, and crime, and civil disorder, and mollycoddling, but we don't have to vote for a bigot to do it."[21] And it would end Nelson Rockefeller's chances in New Hampshire, where Rockefeller was hoping for a big write-in vote for the presidential nomination.[22]

Governor Kirk tried to follow Loeb's advice. He campaigned in Alabama against George Wallace and even insinuated that Wallace's 1968 presidential bid was a plan masterminded by President Lyndon Johnson. In a series of speeches written by William Safire, Kirk charged openly that Wallace was in the presidential race as an independent only to siphon votes from southern Republicans. Wallace's campaign did exhibit a negative effect on Nixon; in Florida most polls showed Nixon ten percentage points behind Johnson in a three-man race and ten points ahead without Wallace.[23]

Governor Kirk's plan for getting the nomination by seeking national headlines failed him before 1968, when Richard Nixon made it clear that he was no longer interested in the Florida chief executive. It was Michael O'Neal, head of the state road board and political advisor to the governor, who then suggested that Kirk endorse Nelson Rockefeller. Kirk did so in a last-ditch attempt to become a vice-presidential nominee, but the endorsement was both unpopular and embarrassing. Up to the nominating convention in Miami Beach in June, the governor continued to assert his candidacy, insisting that his name was on Nixon's list of five vice-presidential possibilities. Maryland Governor Spiro T. Agnew was another.[24]

Contentiousness between the governor and the Republican party in Florida operated behind the scenes of more prominent public issues, such as his vice-presidential quest, state office appointments, and salary raises. Kirk wanted to control the Florida GOP. In 1968 when the state convention met in Orlando, the governor attempted to gain control of the party over the issue of national committee representation. Congressman William Cramer was running for reelection as national committeeman, and in an effort to assuage his feelings concerning Kirk's refusal to resign and allow him to oppose Robert King High, most Florida Republican leaders, including party chairman William Murfin, and house minority leader Don Reed, were supporting him.

The state GOP convention was meeting under the new rules of Florida's recently altered election laws. Previously, national committee elections required a statewide campaign; now the party meeting in convention could determine how national committeemen and women could be selected. Republicans decided to elect a member of the state executive committee as national committeeman and one as national committeewoman, a procedure that would save time and reduce expenses for candidates, who would no longer find it necessary to travel the state campaigning. The new law would also allow less wealthy Republicans to aspire to the positions. Along with Cramer, the regular party leaders also were supporting Paula Hawkins, president of the Republican Women's Federation, for national committeewoman.

The governor and Tom Ferguson wanted their candidates instead. Nathaniel Reed, Kirk's advisor on natural resources, and Mary Grizzle of Indian Rocks Beach, the first woman GOP state legislator, would oppose Cramer and Hawkins. Also in the contest but without much hope or support was Helene Morris, former party treasurer and national committeewoman during the Alexander era. Kirk's forces applied intense pressure on the delegates to vote for Reed and Grizzle. Tom Ferguson warned that unless they were elected, various Republicans might lose their government appointments or be removed from the governor's advisory committees and from future consideration for state jobs.[25] That Cramer and Hawkins won easily on the first ballot only indicated the distance that had developed between Kirk and the Florida GOP.

There were similar confrontations throughout Kirk's tenure. In the middle of his term, he initiated a series of late-night informal conferences at the executive mansion. The first of these meetings was between the governor and the legislative leadership of the Republican party—Bill Young, Don Reed, Bill James, and Mary Grizzle. Lieut. Gov. Ray Osborne also attended. The dinner started well with the governor obviously enjoying his role as the warm, relaxed, confident host. The conference began soon after dinner, and Kirk's initial questions raised a fuss: "What are the people saying about me in the areas you live in? What do you hear? How am I doing as your governor?"[26]

He was not overjoyed with the answers. None of his invited guests lied that everything was perfect in the minds of the majority of voters, but Don Reed's criticisms aroused the governor's ire. Reed told Kirk that his popularity among Florida voters was declining rapidly, mostly as a result of his extravagant spending, his needless controversies with the state cabinet, and his flamboyance. Bill James remembered the governor's reaction: "At this point, after the hair on the back of his neck almost began to stand up, he rushed out to the middle of the living room and put his finger down to the carpet and he ran a line across it and then stepped back and said: 'You are either with me or you can get the hell out.'"[27] The legislators walked out.

Another major confrontation came during the delegate selection process prior to the 1968 national Republican convention. A compromise had been worked out earlier in the year by which the governor would nominate one-third of the slate, William Murfin, the party chairman, would select one-third, and William Cramer, national committeeman, would choose the remainder. On Monday, 25 March, William Murfin resigned from the governor's slate, attacking Tom Ferguson and Jim Wolf for convincing the governor to quarrel over Murfin's choices. Kirk wanted to replace five members with Republicans who would support his vice-presidential bid at Miami Beach. Murfin attacked Kirk's aides as a "group of power-playing opportunists interested in their own ambitions. . . . These egotists picture themselves in Washington." Ferguson especially came under Murfin's special fire as being responsible for the damaging audit of the Florida Development Commission, which revealed gross mismanagement of funds for Kirk's out-of-state travel. Ferguson, the governor's chief aide, claimed Murfin "made 90 percent of the day-to-day decisions."[28]

Murfin's announcement sent shock waves rippling throughout the Florida GOP. Robert DeYoung, representing many Republicans' feelings, labeled the split between the chief executive and the party chairman "a disgrace":

> When personalities begin to creep in such as they have between the state chairman, Bill Murfin, and some of the Governor's aides, such as Tom Ferguson, we should take stock in what is going on.
>
> I think all of the Senators and House members along with the Governor, Bill Murfin, and the Governor's aides should sit down in a centrally located place such as Orlando and get everything on the table and come out with unity.
>
> The Republican Party has too much in stake in the State of Florida and throughout the nation this year to have this continual infighting such as is taking place. I think it behooves each of us to contact the Governor and Bill Murfin and insist we get matters settled and have proper communications from here on in.[29]

R. E. Burchard, member of the state executive committee from Hendry County, proposed a solution to the conundrum: "It is my suggestion to all party members involved in the nomination of a slate of delegates to the convention that you yield to the wishes of the Governor in this matter—without qualification. . . . Republicans of Hendry County feel that having a Republican Governor for Florida is reward enough. For such prestige we are willing to surrender to the Governor the immediate fruits of victory in exchange for long-range gains that will normally accrue to the party." [30]

Five Republicans were at the crux of this confrontation. One was Murfin himself. The chairman had appointed himself as a delegate-at-large, and Kirk knew well that Murfin opposed his vice-presidential ambitions. Sen. Tom Slade from Jacksonville, who had converted to Republicanism about the same time as Kirk, seemed to have his own political plans that troubled the governor. Freshman Congressman Herbert Burke of Ft. Lauderdale was opposed by the governor because Burke had never been a firm supporter of Kirk's administration. Burke had openly criticized some of the governor's appointments and his aides in the past. Senate minority leader Bill Young of St. Petersburg was a Kirk target because of his long-standing friendship with Bill Cramer; Murfin had nominated Young from among Pinellas Republicans to promote party unity. Young also was being mentioned as a possible primary opponent for Kirk in 1970. Don Reed was the fifth Republican opposed by the governor. As house GOP leader, Reed had tried to cooperate with both Kirk and Murfin but often got caught in the middle. Reed indicated to reporters when queried about his position in this fight that he would join a new slate constructed by Murfin in the event that Kirk refused to compromise with the party. Reed added, however, that the choice was "not a vote of no confidence for Gov. Kirk." Ideally, Reed hoped that the Republican delegation would support the governor as a favorite son for the first two ballots before switching.[31]

Murfin and other key Florida Republicans developed an unpledged slate made up of Murfin, Reed, Slade, Burke, and Young, without Governor Kirk. Nearly thirty other district representatives and ten at-large members were chosen, alternates to be selected later because of the time factor. Many observers conceded that Governor Kirk either would be forced into compromise or suffer the embarrassment of an unpledged slate. If the latter occurred, the governor might attend the

Miami Beach convention only in the role of host, not as the favorite son of the Florida delegation.

Murfin and the others wanted to avoid embarrassing Kirk. On Wednesday, 27 March, a group of GOP leaders gathered in Tallahassee hoping to end the confrontation. Their alternative slate had been completed only the previous evening. Working all night in the office of Gray Bolyston in Ft. Lauderdale, Florida GOP treasurer, Murfin and others, including Bill James, Don Reed, and Skip Bafalis, contacted prospective delegates around the state. Official filing papers were filled out and carried to Tallahassee by the chairman the following morning, and a meeting with Governor Kirk was arranged. Terms for a compromise were presented: the governor could join this slate, and the Florida delegation would support him as a favorite son through two ballots; then the delegation was going to back Richard Nixon. By this time, Kirk already had endorsed Nelson Rockefeller for the presidency, but if he wanted to attend the convention as an official member of the delegation, he would be allowed little maneuvering room.

Governor Kirk asked for time to consider the compromise. Around 1:00 or 2:00 A.M. on the morning of 28 March, several Republican leaders were roused from sleep by members of the Florida Highway Patrol and requested to come to the executive mansion. A short time later, Governor Kirk agreed to the terms of the slate compromise before leaving for a speaking engagement outside the state. A temporary truce between the governor and his party was restored. Senator Slade cooperatively resigned from the slate so that Kirk could join.[32]

Midway through Governor Kirk's administration, Florida GOP fortunes still appeared bright despite the intraparty turmoil and the governor's antics; in an April 1968 press release, William Murfin noted that there were more Republicans in Florida running for local, state, and national offices than ever before in the party's history. The chairman hailed this trend as "tangible evidence that Florida has become a two-party state." Exuding great confidence, Murfin predicted victory for the GOP in the November general elections. Besides forecasting that the Republican presidential nominee (Nixon, Rockefeller, or Reagan) would carry Florida, Murfin also predicted that the Florida GOP would gain the U.S. Senate seat being vacated by retiring Sen. George Smathers and at least three more seats in Congress, as well as achieving an even split in the state house of representatives and a majority in the state senate.[33] His optimism rested partly upon the fact that Republican registration was increasing steadily. The *Florida Republican*

Challenger, the party's official newspaper, reported that the GOP "Come Across" drive, in which Democrats were encouraged to switch parties, was meeting with marked success.[34]

Murfin was a reasonably accurate prognosticator. That November, Richard Nixon carried Florida against Humphrey and Wallace, though Wallace won in Escambia and Duval counties. Popular Winter Park Congressman Edward Gurney defeated ex-governor LeRoy Collins for the U.S. Senate seat, and Republican representation in the Florida house went from thirty-seven to forty-two. Only in the state senate were the results disappointing: Democrats gained enough seats to ensure their veto power over Governor Kirk's remaining legislative programs.

The 1968 Gurney-Collins Senate race was proof that the Florida Republican party was performing nearer its potential than ever before. Orange County and Winter Park in particular were still heavily Democratic when Ed Gurney won his first congressional election in 1964. His political conservatism, handsome features, and background as a war hero had enabled him to develop wide appeal in his district. LeRoy Collins, on the other hand, had served as governor of Florida during the tumultuous years of school desegregation. While Collins had not urged Florida's citizens to comply with the Supreme Court's decision in *Brown v. Board of Education* and had initially advocated continuing segregation, he nonetheless had been significantly more moderate than his 1954 Republican opponent, Sumter Lowry from Tampa. Lowry's intemperate remarks only aggravated the crisis while he campaigned on the single plank of maintaining segregation. He had denounced integration as "part of a Communist conspiracy to destroy the moral fiber of the nation by creating a 'mongrel' race incapable of preventing a red takeover." Lowry had supported a state interposition resolution that would have blocked federal enforcement in Florida. Collins had remained a moderate even while becoming more active in the civil rights movement. He had marched with Dr. Martin Luther King at Selma and later served as director of Lyndon Johnson's national community relations board.[35] In Florida, where many voters continued to hold anti-Negro prejudices, Collins's position on race became an easy target for Edward Gurney's 1968 senatorial campaign.

Each candidate experienced widely different kinds of primary campaigns, with Collins having by far the more difficult time. Gurney won an overwhelming May primary election against Herman Goldner, three-time Republican mayor of St. Petersburg. Despite the fact that

Goldner was the president of the National League of Municipalities, most Floridians outside the Tampa–St. Petersburg area did not know him at all. Those who did were resentful that Goldner in 1964 had refused to campaign for Barry Goldwater. In his primary race against Gurney, Goldner again stayed on the fringe of the Florida GOP: "I have no blessings from the state organization, and I want none from Kirk."[36] Gurney polled the largest majority of votes ever in a Republican race in Florida, carrying his home county (Orange) by 95 percent and Goldner's (Pinellas) by almost two to one. Overall, Gurney won 80 percent of the total vote.[37]

Collins, on the other hand, faced much stiffer Democratic opposition, especially from Earl Faircloth, Florida's attorney general. Faircloth, who once had run as a liberal, worked hard in 1968 to tag Collins with that label. Also in the primary were two unknowns, Sam Foor of Tallahassee, who once had campaigned for governor, and Richard Lafferty of Gainesville, "a 100 percent" supporter of George Wallace and author of "Lafferty's Fables," which the candidate claimed were "classics and rank with Aesop."[38] Collins beat Faircloth but became inextricably identified with Lyndon Johnson's policies and problems and branded a liberal. In the general election, Gurney managed to unite Faircloth Democrats with his own conservative Republicans to beat Collins, who had failed to disassociate himself from Johnson despite his repeated assertions that he was "running on my own merits and on my own principles and convictions."[39] As a result, Edward Gurney became the first Florida Republican to enter the U.S. Senate since Simon Conover during Reconstruction.

One Republican who might have resented rather than rejoiced in Gurney's victory was William Cramer, "dean" of the Florida GOP. He was the ranking member of the U.S. House of Representatives Public Works Committee and hoped to become its chairman. As he had in 1966, Cramer in 1968 declined an opportunity to run for another office in Florida, preferring his safe congressional seat. But Cramer was rankled by the turn of events. In 1966 he had been unable to persuade Claude Kirk to resign the Republican nomination after the Democrats had nominated Robert King High instead of Haydon Burns; in 1968 he had believed that Faircloth would beat Collins. Edward Gurney's victory, moreover, meant that he, not Cramer, might become the more powerful Washington figure and manipulator of federal ties between the national and state GOP organizations. In 1972, William Cramer, upon the urging of President Nixon, would decide to run for the U.S.

Senate seat vacated by Spessard Holland. But Lawton Chiles, an obscure state legislator from Lakeland, won in November, forcing Cramer out of Florida politics altogether.

The personality of Claude Kirk hovered over all these developments. No Florida governor before him seemed to enjoy the office more nor had any encouraged more conflict and controversy. While aides Ferguson, Wolf, and Safire contributed to the numerous tussles between 1966 and 1970, the governor himself obviously enjoyed a scrap. Bill Mansfield, Tallahassee bureau chief for the *Miami Herald,* summed up the governor's personal attitude about people and government: "Kirk is a man who likes to take a new idea and run with it—fast. Critics call him 'impulsive.' Supporters hail him as 'innovative.'" "He'll succeed or fail because of his advisors," one capital observer related to Mansfield. "If they can come up with the right ideas and have the nerve to say no at the right time, Kirk could make a really outstanding record! But they're young and mostly inexperienced in government and Kirk is so forceful they may not have the courage to tell him when he is wrong."[40]

Mansfield's comments apply not only to the man but to his administration. When he took office, Claude Kirk himself lacked experience. He had to be taught the functions, powers, and responsibilities of office, including how to veto a bill and initiate legislation and countless other details. He was in fact vitally uninterested in administration, believing that enthusiasm could substitute for experience. This attitude contributed to many political disagreements with his county patronage committees.[41] Claude Kirk immensely enjoyed the office, the limelight, the glamour of being governor, but not the everyday work.

Much that was accomplished in those years was the product of needless controversy, fueled by the governor's style and the political naïveté of his closest aides. Confrontation politics provoked deep ill will between the governor and persons who opposed him. Such confrontations sometimes produced positive results, as in the teachers' strike of 1967–68. But Governor Kirk at the same time made the crisis in Florida education better and worse.

Claude Kirk did not create the crisis in education that erupted during his administration. He reacted to it so eccentrically, however, that many Floridians believed that Kirk wanted only to play politics with the demands for more pay and improved working conditions for teachers. The teachers' crisis began in fact in the 1950s. Florida's educational system grew increasingly weaker under Democratic governors and a porkchop legislature opposed to spending money on even worthwhile causes. As more and more pupils entered school, reflecting Florida's population growth and the elevated post–World War II birthrate, financing for the state's educational program became inadequate. By 1968, teachers were humiliated by their low salaries, hindered by their lack of teaching materials, and frustrated by their overcrowded classrooms and rundown schools. The system continued to lack adequate financing, even though Gov. Farris Bryant supported an improvement program for public education, including more funds for the minimum foundation program, higher salaries, and an increased general appropriations bill. Rapid enrollment growth, an expanding junior college system, and a reluctance to increase taxes contributed to a more precipitous decline in teachers' morale in the 1960s. Gov. Haydon Burns, preceding Claude Kirk in office, endorsed further construction funds for junior colleges and the universities but ignored other needs of education.[42]

Thus were the problems in education handed to Governor Kirk. In his campaign against High, Kirk had listed among his primary goals the need to improve education, but he believed that quality education could be achieved without increasing taxes. His plan was to encourage counties to raise their school millage rates while the state cut its expenditures and passed on the savings to the local schools. In the spring of 1967, the Florida Education Association, recognizing the futility of Kirk's plan, announced that unless the state legislature appropriated more money for education, sanctions and a blacklist would be imposed. The governor and the legislature, despite their clashes in other areas, united in protesting what they deemed were unreasonable demands from the FEA.[43]

Early in June 1967, the National Education Association imposed a national sanction following the FEA's censure of the governor and the legislature. A public relations campaign against Florida was initiated to warn businesses and people with school-age children of the poor quality of the state's schools. The schools were terrible indeed; while the state ranked tenth in the nation in 1964 in per capita income and had a population growth twice as high as the national average, its expenditures for education ranked thirty-fourth. A nationwide boycott was planned by the NEA.[44]

Governor Kirk reacted with typical hostility, undaunted by the NEA and resolute in his determination to appear as a tough-minded conservative. He denounced Dr. Phil Constans, director of the FEA, as the man "who has brainwashed our teachers into attacking our state, our parents, and our children."[45] The governor successfully vetoed $132 million in educational appropriations in 1967, leaving Florida schools with less money than before.[46]

GOP Sen. Tom Slade of Jacksonville disagreed with the governor's veto, pointing out that it could have serious political repercussions if the crisis were not resolved successfully. He told a district meeting of the Young Republicans in Pensacola that taxation and education were Republican issues that must be resolved. Slade proposed five possible solutions to the crisis, which could be adopted individually or as an entire package. First, he proposed that Florida eliminate ad valorem property taxes as the funding basis for schools. Second, he wanted to establish a common school fund via a statewide tax levy of five mills to replace local financing. Third, he suggested that the state assume most of the administrative responsibility in the public schools, leaving local boards with duties only in the areas of capital outlay, transportation, and maintenance. Fourth, he proposed a tax rebate to those counties that took steps to correct their understaffed and undersupported schools. Last, he advocated a higher millage rate ceiling to permit an increase in local educational revenue.[47]

Although Slade's ideas were not receiving a full hearing, Governor Kirk's plans for resolving the crisis were. On 5 September 1967, standing before a chalkboard in a Tallahassee public school, he appeared on statewide television to make several announcements. His special report to the citizens was called "Education in Florida: Perspective for Tomorrow," which he had written on the board behind him. Kirk called for long-range planning in education and an end to politically disruptive influences in the system. He wanted the state's education goals to reflect decade-long planning rather than annual budgeting. He stressed the need for more accountability among teachers and administrators. Finally, he announced the creation of a special commission on quality education that would make Florida first in the nation by 1975.[48]

Constans and the FEA were unwilling to wait that long. Constans also appeared on statewide television from the same Tallahassee classroom to rebut Kirk's proposal with a program called "Education in Florida: Perspective for Today," which he, too, wrote on the blackboard as a symbol of the gap between the governor and the teachers.

Governor Kirk's actions during the teachers' crisis eroded much of his earlier bipartisan support. Soon after his television address he married Erika Matfield, and they began their European honeymoon at taxpayers' expense. Furthermore, his continual name-calling and personal denunciations did little to foster hope that the crisis would soon be resolved. He denounced Superintendent of Instruction Floyd Christian as a "do-nothing" and the FEA teachers as "an intellectual mafia." A brief truce was arranged on 18 October, when Kirk finally agreed to call a special session of the legislature to restore badly needed money in the educational system. In its turn, the FEA then called off its 23 October "Decision Day," when mass resignations from teachers across the state were to be turned in. The governor informed the Republican legislators that the FEA had agreed to join his quality commission "to work for a total education package program for the State." Whereas earlier he had characterized the FEA as a teachers' union, now the governor expansively commented that "the FEA has shown publicly that it is a professional association."[49]

The compromise was short lived. On 22 December, a master plan for education in Florida was presented to the governor by the commission. The report essentially called for massive reorganization of education at all levels, simplified but expanded funding structures, increased appropriations for junior colleges and universities, modern management techniques, adult and vocational education programs, comprehensive master planning for school construction, and more efficient classroom use.[50]

Governor Kirk called a January special legislative session to consider these recommendations as he had promised he would, but he turned it into his own political gambit. He threatened to veto any education bill unless the superintendent's position was changed from elective to appointive. It was a direct slap at Floyd Christian, perceived by Kirk as too cooperative with the teachers. Christian asked that the issue be left to a public referendum.[51] The spending bill itself did little to improve education, though the legislature did increase per-pupil expenditure, raise salaries, and appropriate more money from general revenue. However, there were no changes in the structure of the educational system, especially concerning taxation, which meant that the changes were merely short term. Constans and the FEA prepared to defy the governor and the legislature by going out on strike.

The governor balked at further negotiations, and a teachers' strike began on 9 February 1968. Christian urged parents and volunteers with at least a high school diploma to help keep the schools open. Governor Kirk issued a press release condemning the FEA and noting that "the people will control education in the State, not unions." A second compromise between Kirk and the FEA was worked out, and the governor agreed to tell the teachers of his latest concessions in person at a Dade County rally on 21 February. The rally was televised nationally, and millions watched as the governor arrived by helicopter—late—and touched down in the middle of the field. While the cameras whirred and attention was focused upon him, Governor Kirk taunted the crowd: "How about a good boo for your governor? How about a hiss then?" Refusing to read his prepared speech, Kirk rejected a second session of the legislature, saying "No one is going to coerce me into calling a special session." [52]

His political instincts were right, and the teachers' strike eventually ground to a halt. The teachers' demands for a special legislative session were ignored, and the governor signed into law the results of the earlier January session. While some 50,000 teachers walked out, according to the FEA, their professionalism and feelings of personal obligation to their students and their inexperience with labor-management disputes contributed to a drift-back rate of several thousand each day; but education in Florida was improved by the crisis, even if not to the satisfaction of the FEA. What was most unfortunate was that the governor had politicized the situation into what one Florida official called the "biggest crisis since the Civil War." [53]

Claude Kirk did achieve some good results in the period 1966–70. He appointed the state's first full-time advisor on education, Dr. Charles Perry, who later became president of Florida International University. Florida did move up to twelfth in the country in teachers' salaries and only slightly below that in per-pupil expenditures. Kirk also removed much of the corruption involving the state road board by appointing the first professional highway commissioner, and by creating a state Department of Transportation and setting five-year planning goals for new road construction. Bidding for road contracts became less political as well.[54] He also signed into law the nation's most stringent antipollution law and created a Department of Natural Resources and a Commission on Marine Science and Technology. Of course, Florida's new state constitution was implemented during his tenure.

In 1970, in a bitter primary battle, Kirk won renomination over Jack Eckerd, the millionaire druggist who had wanted to redeem the reputation of the governor's office and the Florida GOP. That November, however, Kirk won no more than 700,000 votes; Democrats were not willing to support him in large numbers, and Reubin Askew won the election. Claude Kirk left Tallahassee and Florida politics for his Palm Beach home. Few Republicans were sorry to see him go.

Any assessment of Claude Kirk's administration and of the period 1966–70 must begin with the character and personality of the man himself. There is an old story about a young Catholic priest, filled with the ecumenical spirit, who asked his bishop why it was improper to work cooperatively with Protestants. The bishop replied, "Because we have the Truth and they have to admit they are wrong." Claude Kirk and that bishop shared a common trait: the inability to see any value in their opponents' views. Kirk was stubborn and usually unwilling to act constructively on the advice of others. It was this singular quality that limited his ability to avoid the political pitfalls in his Governor's Club, the convention slate fight, or the war on crime. Immersed in his own brand of confrontational politics, he was often unable to place any positive value on the need for serious compromise.

Of course, there was also the problem of the man's flamboyance. Possessed of an overlarge ego and enormous energy, he refused to recognize that his becoming governor was largely an accident of fate. Without the DemoKirks, many of whom would have voted for Haydon Burns, it is doubtful that Kirk could have put himself into the office. Once there, he added to his problem by again refusing to recognize an unvarnished reality: to have been a serious and viable candidate for the vice-presidency, he only had to perform well as governor.

One thing is clear: Kirk's impact upon his political party was disastrous. As Harold Stayman, member of the Young Republican Trust Fund, pointed out, the Florida GOP was not prepared to win the governor's office in 1966. Its goal had been to prepare a deeper and larger foundation for two-party politics by first strengthening the GOP's representation in the state legislature and in local and county organizations. At the earliest, it had been planned to offer a serious gubernatorial challenge in 1970.[55] Kirk's election came too soon. As the first modern Republican governor in Florida, he lacked sufficient party strength in the legislature to enact his proposals. Moreover, the Republicans in the legislature were for the most part also new and inexperienced in the affairs of state government. Few were perceived to be strong enough to gain Kirk's great respect and attention as political advisors.

Florida in the Kirk era demanded much from its governor. Growth in transportation networks, government reorganization, educational modernization, crime, pollution, and countless other challenges would have tested any man's talents as chief executive. It would be simplistic to say that Burns, High, or anyone else would have accomplished more, but there were forces working against Kirk's success. He was a minority governor faced with an opposition cabinet and legislature. Under the Florida system, wherein the governor is one among equals in the cabinet, being the sole Republican was a serious drawback. Another factor working against him was that 1966–70 was an era of confrontational politics independent of Florida and of Claude Kirk. Militant radicalism, riots, and other types of civil violence plagued governments other than his. In that respect, Claude Kirk was perhaps more a reflection of his era than a distortion of it.

Most strikingly, the governor contributed significantly to a larger, constant theme in the history of the Republican party in Florida: he divided the party as deeply and as damagingly as anyone since the Civil War. In Reconstruction, it had been ring and anti-ring factionalism; in the late nineteenth century and the first half of the twentieth, there was the factionalism of patronage. In each period, GOP party strength and growth weakened and declined. During the Kirk era, actual party membership increased, but Kirk and anti-Kirk factionalism prevented the party from making the best use of it. William Murfin, state party chairman, accepted a Nixon appointment in Washington, and the faction led by Governor Kirk and Senator Gurney replaced him with Duke Crittenden in 1968. The new party chairman supported G. Harrold Carswell against William Cramer in the 1970 senatorial primary fight. When Cramer won, Crittenden was replaced by L. E. (Tommy) Thomas, a member of the anti-Kirk group. The net effect of this continuous intraparty feuding was that in the 1970 elections, the Florida GOP lost heavily at all levels, wiping out many of the political gains and potentials that had seemed so long-lasting in 1966.

13
Epilogue as Prologue

GEORGE BERNARD SHAW once remarked that all works have three parts—a beginning, a middle, and an end—but that they do not always fall in that order. It is fitting to end this survey of the Republican party in Florida with a brief review of the trends and developments in the Florida GOP in the decade of the 1970s, an advance look at a future companion volume. This chapter is a preview, an epilogue with an eye to the future—thus epilogue as prologue.

In the 1970s, nationally, one encounters Watergate and the misfortunes that befell President Richard Nixon and the Republican party. In 1968, Nixon won the election with 301 electoral votes: he carried New Hampshire, New Jersey, and Vermont in the Northeast; the border states of Kentucky, North Carolina, Tennessee, and Virginia; only South Carolina (and Florida) in the Deep South; Illinois, Indiana, Ohio, and Wisconsin in the east-central region; and all states west of the Mississippi except Texas, Hawaii, and Washington. George Wallace ran well in the Deep South (ten million votes, forty-six electoral votes, and five states), while Hubert Humphrey carried the traditional Democratic strongholds of the Northeast.

Wallace's success in the South was a harbinger of the seventies. The year that Nixon was inaugurated, a young campaign consultant named Kevin Phillips, attached to John Mitchell's staff, spelled out the implications of the 1968 presidential election. Phillips's book, *The Emerging Republican Majority,* forecast a new conservative tide arising in the South and West. These new conservatives, he argued, when combined with the Republicans' traditional middle-class constituency, could produce an enduring Republican majority in American politics in the twentieth century.

The Phillips thesis is hardly original in American history. Political power periodically has flowed from the East and Northeast to the South and West and back, since the election of Andrew Jackson in 1828. This intermittent flow usually has been interpreted as political protest, sometimes in the guise of third-party movements, and always more successful when assimilated by the two-party political system. The populism of the late nineteenth century is perhaps the most obvious and visible example.

The Phillips thesis, popularly called the "Southern Strategy," could have proven a reasonably accurate predictor of political trends in the seventies. Phillips argued that "wool hats" (broadly defined as Wallace voters) of the South and "hard hats" of organized labor in the urban North could be forged into the GOP with traditional Republicans from the plains, mountain, and east-central industrial states. The national GOP strategy for the seventies conceded only the Northeast, northern plains states, and perhaps the Pacific Northwest.

The validity of Phillips's idea could not be tested while George Wallace remained a viable presidential candidate, that is, until Arthur Bremer's assassination attempt cut him down in the spring of 1972. Often overlooked in the explanations of Watergate, there is little doubt that Wallace's presence in the presidential race of 1972 threatened Richard Nixon as much, if not more, than the challenge of George McGovern. If one reads history forward rather than backward, it is plausible (but not provable) that Nixon feared Wallace enough, especially prior to the nomination of George McGovern, to establish the Plumbers' Unit against leaks. As it once seemed strange that Abraham Lincoln feared reelection in 1864 during the Civil War, Nixon experienced similar fears in early 1972. Yet, without Wallace and against McGovern, Richard Nixon swept to victory, quashing the importance of Wallace in the race. But the bugging of the Democratic committee headquarters started the unraveling of the Nixon administration.

Nor could the Phillips thesis be tested in 1976 when Jimmy Carter was carried to the White House by the resurrection of the Democratic coalition of the New Deal (helped substantially by Gerald Ford's decision to pardon Nixon from all prosecution related to Watergate). In 1980, Ronald Reagan's overwhelming victory finally gave a small measure of validity to the concept of an emerging Republican majority.

The main trend in Florida's Republican party during the seventies was the passing of leadership from the old guard to the new, accompanied by the continuation of the party's internal factionalism. The best illustrations are the Florida campaigns for the U.S. Senate. In 1970, the Florida GOP primary for the seat soon to be vacated when Sen. Spessard Holland retired was contested by George Balmer, G. Harrold Carswell, and William Cramer. Balmer, a minor Republican politician from Hollywood, had no impact on the outcome. Carswell and Cramer, on the other hand, represented the opposing factions that have plagued the Florida GOP since Reconstruction.

William Cramer, St. Petersburg's congressman, was the first Republican elected to Congress from Florida since the end of the Civil War. His seat in the House of Representatives had been "safe" for many years, but political ambition motivated him to run for the U.S. Senate. Cramer had a history of poor political timing; in 1966 he had briefly contemplated running for governor before deciding not to challenge the incumbent, Haydon Burns. When Burns lost in a surprising defeat to Robert High in the Democratic primary, Cramer tried to persuade Claude Kirk to retire from the race. Kirk refused, of course, to give way to Cramer, thereby adding to the factionalism. In 1970, with the backing of Richard Nixon, Cramer felt he had an excellent chance to become a U.S. senator.

His Republican opponent was a former federal judge, G. Harrold Carswell, a national figure of sorts. Nominated by Nixon for the U.S. Supreme Court, he had run into trouble during his Senate confirmation hearings when it was revealed that he had been a member of a private social club in Tallahassee that discriminated against blacks. Despite his repeated assertions that he personally disavowed racial prejudice, Carswell became the second Nixon nominee to the Supreme Court to be denied confirmation for this reason (Clement Haynesworth of South Carolina had been the first). Carswell's supporters, led by Governor Kirk and Sen. Edward Gurney, hoped he would attract a sizable sympathy vote from Florida's conservative voters.

Cramer smashed Carswell in the primary, as the latter was caught in the backlash of anti-Kirk feeling among Florida Republicans generated by Jack Eckerd's race for the governor's office that year. Cramer's margin of victory was two to one, with George Balmer gathering fewer than 11,000 votes. When Eckerd forced Governor Kirk into a runoff, Cramer seemed to have clear sailing. But he failed to reckon with two political facts operating in the 1970 general election. First, the anti-Kirk sentiment among Florida voters led to a general disorder. V. O. Key once labeled Florida a "no-party" state, meaning that Florida voters were difficult to keep aligned in predictable fashion. Clearly, this theory was operating in November 1970. Cramer's opponent was a little known state senator from Lakeland named Lawton Chiles. Early in the Democratic primaries, Chiles had been overshadowed by former governor Farris Bryant, whom he managed to defeat in a runoff for the nomination. Chiles also began generating wide media attention; with his well-documented walk across Florida, he was soon being called "Walkin' Lawton."

Richard Nixon's presidential record in 1970 was not good enough to save Bill Cramer. Nationally, 1970 was an "off" election year (no presidential election), and across the nation the GOP lost seats in the Senate and the House. Chiles eked out a victory in November, winning over Cramer by fewer than 150,000 votes out of 1.7 million cast. With his defeat, William Cramer retired from active elective politics in Florida; he was soon established in a Washington law firm.

Edward Gurney's senatorial career ended four years later. When he was elected in 1968, the Orlando-area Republican looked forward to a long tenure. Watergate cut him down prematurely. Gurney served on the Senate Select Committee, chaired by North Carolina's senator Samuel Ervin, along with other Republicans who hoped that Watergate could not be connected to the presidency. Under the glare and constant pressure of the news media, Edward Gurney made his reputation as Nixon's staunchest defender. Although a web of testimony and evidence led inexorably to the president, Gurney remained steadfast in the belief that Watergate was only a "third-rate burglary."

Gurney's private Watergate-like scandal also hastened his defeat. Although some Republicans argued vociferously that the senator came under investigation because of his allegiance to the president, he was nonetheless indicted for campaign fiscal irregularities and mishandling of funds. Eventual clearance and exoneration came too late to salvage his political career. He declined to seek reelection while under investigation, retired from active leadership in the Florida GOP, and joined Claude Kirk and William Cramer on the sidelines in the mid-seventies.

New leadership aspirants emerged in their wake. During the 1974 senatorial primary, Jack Eckerd and Paula Hawkins squared off for the GOP nomination. Neither was new to Florida politics. The drugstore magnate had unsuccessfully opposed Kirk in 1970; the Maitland housewife had won election in 1972 to the Florida Public Service Commission over Democrat Gerald Lewis. While a member of the commission, Hawkins established herself as a strong consumer advocate, arguing for lower phone and utility rates.

Their primary contest highlighted the continuing factionalism within the Florida Republican party. Jack Eckerd picked up his support from those Republicans disenchanted with party affairs in the Kirk years. Paula Hawkins won endorsement from Gurney and his supporters. Unable to match dollars with the far wealthier Eckerd, Hawkins lost by more than two to one.

If some Republicans demonstrated gender politics in this primary, many more reacted to Watergate during Eckerd's general campaign against Richard Stone, the Democratic nominee, and John Grady from Belle Glade, running for the Wallace-inspired American Independent Party. Grady's presence in the 1974 race again confounded the Phillips thesis. Without him, Jack Eckerd would likely have won.

Eckerd would have had several advantages over Stone in a simple two-man race. First, neither was an incumbent. Second, Eckerd's personal wealth could offset any drop in funds resulting from the Watergate scandal. Third, Stone was from South Florida, traditionally a political liability in statewide races. Last, Gerald Ford's promotion to the White House after Nixon's resignation made the issue of an "off" election less significant. Without Grady's siphoning of conservative votes from the Republican nominee, Eckerd might have won. But the election went to Stone. Grady captured 15 percent; Stone won with 43.4 percent; and Eckerd took the remaining 40.9 percent. Even though Grady became the Florida GOP nominee two years later against incumbent Sen. Lawton Chiles, by the middle of the decade the promise of the Phillips thesis remained stronger than the reality.

At the gubernatorial level, the aftermath of the disastrous Kirk era continued into the seventies. Success eluded the GOP even though new Republican candidates offered themselves to Florida voters. Eckerd failed in 1970. Former state senate president Jerry Thomas tried to unseat the incumbent governor, Reubin Askew, in 1974 and failed two to one. The GOP's best chance to win the governor's office came in 1978 when the party finally patched up its factionalism long enough to nominate its two most popular candidates—Eckerd and Hawkins—for governor and lieutenant governor, respectively.

Enhancing the GOP's opportunity, the Democrats were divided between two strong candidates in the primary to select a successor to Askew: Robert Shevin, former attorney general, and Robert Graham, former senate president. Although Shevin was the early favorite for the Democratic nomination, Graham eventually won it. Eckerd and Hawkins were thus running against the lesser known of the two Democrats. Then, too, by 1978 Jimmy Carter's popularity was on the wane, a political factor difficult to measure because it was yet another "off" election. The results were revealing: although Graham and his lieutenant governor nominee, Wayne Mixon, won the election, the GOP had polled more votes in the race than any Republican ticket had since Reconstruction, excepting, of course, Claude Kirk's. Perhaps what these results indicate most was that the Florida GOP, even united, had not yet achieved parity.

While the unfulfilled promise and potential of two-party parity remained a problem for the Florida GOP, so too did the vacuum in party leadership. Paula Hawkins went on to become a successful candidate for the U.S. Senate in 1980, sweeping in with Ronald Reagan's landslide. No other Florida Republican has managed yet to achieve similar prominence in any statewide elective office. The truism that a party can be no better than its candidates still holds for Florida's Republicans. In the changing party leadership—from Kirk, Gurney, and Cramer to Eckerd, Hawkins, Thomas, Lou Frey, and others—none but Hawkins has succeeded. If the Phillips thesis—the rising conservative tide—is ever to be tested and proved in Florida, new and positive leadership in the form of solid candidates for office must appear. Only then will the promise of two-party politics become a reality in Florida.

Notes

Chapter 1. Ripon to Reconstruction

1. Richard P. McCormick, *The Second American Party System: Party Formation in the Jacksonian Era,* pp. 252–53.
2. Eric Foner, *Free Soil, Free Labor, Free Men: The Ideology of the Republican Party before the Civil War,* passim; George H. Mayer, *The Republican Party, 1854–1966,* pp. 23–47.
3. Abraham Lincoln to Ichabod Codding, 27 November 1854, in *The Collected Works of Abraham Lincoln,* ed. Roy P. Basler, 2:288.
4. John E. Johns, *Florida During the Civil War,* passim.
5. Kathryn T. Abbey, *Florida, Land of Change,* p. 293.
6. Frank L. Owsley, *King Cotton Diplomacy,* p. 47, details the use of cotton as a weapon to seek Confederate recognition from Europe. See also Gainesville *New Era,* n.d., quoted in Jacksonville *Florida Union,* 19 August 1865.
7. A. K. Allison to E. M. McCook, 13 May 1865, in Governor's Letterbook; David Levy Yulee to F. C. Johnson, 9 December 1865, Yulee to David S. Walker, 2 February 1866, MSS Box 7, Yulee Papers.
8. F. P. Fleming to M. Seton, 3 May 1865, Fleming Papers.
9. A. B. Hart to B. H. Hart, 18 December 1866, A. B. Hart Papers; Tallahassee *Semi-Weekly Floridian,* 20 March 1866.
10. *Eighth Census of the United States,* 1860, 1:54.
11. V. O. Key, Jr., *Southern Politics in State and Nation,* pp. 82–105.
12. Keith Ian Polakoff, in *The Politics of Inertia: The Election of 1876 and the End of Reconstruction,* points out that the national committee of the Republican party in Reconstruction was reluctant to interfere in the internal activity of its state committees, thereby decentralizing politics and increasing intraparty factionalism.
13. William Watson Davis, *Civil War and Reconstruction in Florida,* is the product of the Dunning school of Reconstruction historiography that viewed the Civil War in these terms.
14. William Marvin had been President Andrew Johnson's clear choice as provisional governor for Florida. He had been a judge in Key West during the antebellum period and remained loyal to the Union. Marvin was recommended to Johnson by a group of New York businessmen who knew his record. See Petitions from New York Businessmen and Marine Insurance Companies, 6 July 1865, Johnson Papers, Series I, microfilm copy, University of Florida, Gainesville.
15. Jacksonville *Florida Union,* 18 November 1865.

16. F. C. Barrett to Yulee, October 1865, MSS Box 7, Yulee Papers. Davis, *Civil War and Reconstruction in Florida,* pp. 362–65, details the specific provisions of the 1865 constitution.

17. Charles Sumner, "Clemency and Common Sense: A Curiosity of Literature; With a Moral."

18. Alfred R. Conkling, *The Life and Letters of Roscoe Conkling, Orator, Statesman, Advocate,* p. 277.

19. G. Selden Henry, "Radical Republican Race Policy Toward the Negro during Reconstruction, 1864–1872," p. 178. Henry's analysis of the Republican motives concerning the Negro in the Reconstruction South provides a clear insight into the conservative nature of all whites about race in the nineteenth century.

Chapter 2. Advent of Florida Republicanism

1. Davis, *Civil War and Reconstruction in Florida,* pp. 243–67.
2. *House Executive Document 18,* 38th Cong., 2d sess., pp. 3–5.
3. Chicago *Tribune,* 17 November 1863.
4. New England Loyal Publication Society Broadside No. 126 (10 October 1863), quoted in George Winston Smith, "Carpetbag Imperialism in Florida, 1862–1868," p. 274.
5. President Lincoln issued the plan as part of his proclamation of amnesty and pardon on 8 December 1863. See Basler, ed., *The Collected Works of Abraham Lincoln,* 7:53–56.
6. John Hay to Abraham Lincoln, 8 February 1864, vol. 142, Lincoln Papers.
7. *Senate Report 47,* 38th Cong., 1st sess.; see also accounts of the Olustee engagement in Davis, *Civil War and Reconstruction in Florida,* pp. 268–95, and Johns, *Florida during the Civil War,* pp. 190–220.
8. Polakoff, *The Politics of Inertia,* passim.
9. Peter D. Klingman, *Josiah T. Walls: Florida's Black Congressman of Reconstruction,* passim.
10. John F. Reiger, "Deprivation, Disaffection, and Desertion in Confederate Florida."
11. Ella Lonn, *Desertion During the Civil War,* p. 231.
12. Richard L. Hume, "Membership of the Florida Constitutional Convention of 1868: A Case Study of Republican Factionalism in the Reconstruction South," p. 12.
13. Union-Republican Club of Jacksonville, Proceedings.
14. J. Richardson, *The Negro in the Reconstruction of Florida, 1865–1877,* pp. 97–111.
15. Charles Wesley, *Negro Labor in the United States,* p. 48.
16. Elsie M. Lewis, "The Political Mind of the Negro, 1865–1900."
17. Union-Republican Club of Jacksonville, Proceedings.
18. Philip D. Ackerman, "Florida Reconstruction from Walker through Reed, 1865–1873," pp. 76–79.
19. Jerrell H. Shofner, "The Constitution of 1868," p. 358.
20. Tallahassee *Sentinel,* 15 July 1867.

21. J. Cory to Schuyler Colfax, 25 December 1867, J. Cory, Jr., folder, MSS Box 19.
22. *Congressional Globe,* 38th Cong., 1st sess., pp. 2102–5.
23. Samuel S. Cox, *Three Decades of Federal Legislation,* pp. 517–18.
24. John Wallace, *Carpetbag Rule in Florida,* pp. 53–57; Davis, *Civil War and Reconstruction in Florida,* p. 497; New York *Tribune,* 5 February 1868.
25. Shofner, "The Constitution of 1868," p. 373.
26. Ibid.
27. Wallace, *Carpetbag Rule in Florida,* p. 58.
28. Shofner, in "The Constitution of 1868" and *Nor Is It Over Yet: Florida in the Era of Reconstruction,* describes the splitting and reunification of the factions.
29. Declaration of Rights, Constitution of 1868, *Compiled General Laws of Florida* (Atlanta, 1928), quoted in Shofner, "The Constitution of 1868," pp. 370–74. References to specific provisions are from this source.
30. *United States Statutes at Large,* 15: 73–74.
31. Tallahassee *Weekly Floridian,* 20 August 1872.
32. Each of the state studies of Reconstruction done in the Dunning school of historiography early in the twentieth century are still available for comparisons in detail: Davis, *Civil War and Reconstruction in Florida;* James W. Garner, *Reconstruction in Mississippi;* C. Mildred Thompson, *Reconstruction in Georgia;* Charles W. Ramsdell, *Reconstruction in Texas;* and Hamilton J. Eckenrode, *The Political History of Virginia during Reconstruction.* Modern studies by Maddex, Shofner, and Nathans are revisions and do not add substantial new materials to details of the 1868 constitution-making period in the South.

Chapter 3. Republican Factions and Reconstruction Politics

1. Key, *Southern Politics in State and Nation,* pp. 82–105.
2. Andrew Wallace Crandall, *The Early History of the Republican Party, 1854–1856,* pp. 51–53, 59–61.
3. Klingman, *Josiah T. Walls,* passim.
4. Eric L. McKitrick, "Andrew Johnson, Outsider," in *Reconstruction: An Anthology of Revisionist Writings,* ed. Kenneth M. Stampp and Leon F. Litwack, pp. 48–58.
5. Harrison Reed to David Levy Yulee, 18, 22 April 1867, Yulee Papers.
6. Davis, *Civil War and Reconstruction in Florida,* pp. 534–36.
7. Tallahassee *Sentinel,* 14 August 1875; S. A. Willcox to O. B. Hart, 23 January 1873, W. Rogers to H. Reed, 12 July 1870, J. T. Magbee to Reed, 13 July 1871, A. C. Lightboan to J. C. Gibbs, 7 October 1872, all in Records of the Department of State, Office of the Secretary of State, Tallahassee; E. J. Vann to D. H. Hamilton, 19 January 1869, Ruffin-Roulhac-Hamilton Papers.
8. "Florida," *The American Annual Cyclopedia and Register of Important Events 1861–1874,* pp. 270–71.
9. J. S. Adams to Horace Porter, 6 October 1872, Attorney General's Appointments Papers.

10. David Montgomery to Ulysses Grant, 5 October 1872, Ossian B. Hart to Grant, 9 October 1872, Marcellus Stearns to Grant, 9 October 1872, Josiah Walls to Grant, 5 October 1872, ibid.
11. Tallahassee *Floridian,* 10 January 1871.
12. Ibid., 15 September, 15 December 1868.
13. Cortez A. M. Ewing, "Florida Reconstruction Impeachments," p. 302.
14. Davis, *Civil War and Reconstruction,* pp. 547–56.
15. Garth James to his parents, 31 December 1868, Garth James Papers; *State of Florida v. William Gleason,* 12 Fla. 190 (1868).
16. Ewing, "Florida Reconstruction Impeachments," pp. 304–5.
17. Davis, *Civil War and Reconstruction,* pp. 614–15.
18. Tallahassee *Floridian,* 11 May 1868.
19. Wallace, *Carpetbag Rule in Florida,* pp. 99–100.
20. John F. Stover, *The Railroads of the South,* p. 55.
21. Florida *House Journal,* Extra Session, 1869, pp. 9–10.
22. Florida *Acts and Resolutions,* Extra Session, 1869, pp. 31, 32, 36.
23. Paul E. Fenlon, "The Notorious Swepson-Littlefield Fraud: Railroad Financing in Florida, 1868–1871," pp. 231–61; see pp. 236–42 for Swepson's other venture.
24. Tallahassee *Sentinel,* 22, 29, January 1870; Davis, *Civil War and Reconstruction,* pp. 614–16.
25. Florida *Assembly Journal* (1872), pp. 19–35.
26. Wallace, *Carpetbag Rule in Florida,* pp. 142–43.
27. George Raney to Edward L'Engle, 8 February 1872, L'Engle Papers; Yulee to George Glavis, 10 April 1872, Yulee Papers.
28. Florida *Assembly Journal* (1872), pp. 252, 263.
29. Tallahassee *Sentinel,* 10 February 1872; Tallahassee *Weekly Floridian,* 13 February 1872.
30. Tallahassee *Weekly Floridian,* 20 February 1872.
31. Florida *Senate Journal* (1872), p. 47.
32. See John A. Meador, "Florida Political Parties, 1865–1877," p. 206, citing an unnamed contemporary Democrat for this thesis.
33. Tallahassee *Weekly Floridian,* 22 August 1871, 23 July 1872.
34. Wallace, *Carpetbag Rule in Florida,* p. 165.
35. Tallahassee *Weekly Floridian,* 25 January 1870.
36. Wallace, *Carpetbag Rule in Florida,* pp. 276–77.
37. Tallahassee *Sentinel,* 1 August 1874; Tallahassee *Weekly Floridian,* 11 November 1873.
38. Klingman, *Josiah Walls.*
39. The Tallahassee *Sentinel* of 20 August 1870, carried a complete account of the Republican convention in Gainesville.
40. Ibid.
41. Mayer, *The Republican Party,* pp. 179–82.
42. William E. Parrish, *Missouri under Radical Rule, 1865–1870,* p. 310.

43. William Bloxham to Robert M. Davidson, 30 July 1872, misc. MSS Box 15, P.K. Yonge Library.
44. Thomas Osborn to William Eaton Chandler, 11 July 1872, Chandler Papers.
45. Biographical Sketch of Honorable Ossian B. Hart, late governor of Florida.
46. Alva A. Knight to Chandler, 15 September 1872, Chandler Papers.
47. Tallahassee *Sentinel,* 21 September 1872.
48. As a result of the 1872 campaign, there were thirteen Republicans and eleven Democrats in the state senate and twenty-eight Republicans in the lower house. Democrats retained control of the lower house.
49. Wallace, *Carpetbag Rule in Florida,* p. 216.
50. Ibid., pp. 291–95.
51. Meador, "Florida Political Parties," p. 256.
52. Tallahassee *Weekly Floridian,* 18 August 1874.
53. Wallace, *Carpetbag Rule in Florida,* pp. 329–32.
54. Tallahassee *Sentinel,* 17, 24 June, 29 July, 26 August 1876.
55. Davis, *Civil War and Reconstruction,* pp. 713–15.
56. *House Miscellaneous Documents,* 45th Cong., 3d sess., part 4, p. 343.
57. Jerrell H. Shofner, "Florida in the Balance: The Electoral Count of 1876."
58. Ibid., pp. 146–47.
59. Key, *Southern Politics in State and Nation,* pp. 82–105.
60. Klingman, *Josiah Walls,* p. 87.
61. Klingman, "Ring versus Anti-Ring: Jacksonville Republican Politics, 1870–1875."

Chapter 4. Politics of Reconstruction

1. Jacksonville *Tri-Weekly Florida Union,* 22 June 1871. I am indebted to the excellent summary and evaluation of Reconstruction in Florida contained in Richardson, *The Negro in the Reconstruction of Florida, 1865–1877,* pp. 199–224.
2. Davis, *Civil War and Reconstruction,* pp. 534–36.
3. Ibid., pp. 587–609.
4. *House Reports,* 42d Cong., 2d sess., no. 22, pt. 13, pp. 70, 103–4, 123, 132–34, hereafter referred to as *House Report 22.*
5. Ibid., p. 156, testimony of Frank Myers.
6. *House Miscellaneous Documents,* 42d Cong., 2d sess., no. 34, pp. 52–53.
7. *House Report 22,* pt. 13, p. 222.
8. Allen W. Trelease, *White Terror: The Ku Klux Klan Conspiracy and Southern Reconstruction,* offers the most recent and detailed analysis of the political motives of the Ku Klux Klan in Reconstruction.
9. Richardson, *Negro in the Reconstruction of Florida,* p. 174.
10. Everett Swinney, "Enforcing the Fifteenth Amendment, 1870–1877."
11. *Statutes at Large of the United States,* 16 (1871): 140–46, 433–40.
12. Ibid., 18 (1873): 13–15.
13. Ralph L. Peek, "Curbing of Voter Intimidation in Florida, 1871," p. 335; Tallahassee *Weekly Floridian,* 13, 27 February 1872.

14. Peek, "Voter Intimidation," pp. 333–48.
15. Rendig Fels, "American Business Cycles, 1867–79," p. 349.
16. Constitution of the State of Florida, Framed at A Convention of the People, Begun and Held at the City of Tallahassee on the 20th Day of January, A.D. 1868, Together with the Ordinances Adopted by the Said Convention (Jacksonville, 1868).
17. Florida *Acts and Resolutions*, 1869, p. 12.
18. Ibid., pp. 7–11.
19. See Correspondence and Reports, American Missionary Association Archives.
20. Richardson, *Negro in the Reconstruction of Florida*, pp. 114–15.
21. Florida Superintendent of Public Instruction, *Reports*, 1869–80.
22. Richardson, *Negro in the Reconstruction of Florida*, p. 118.
23. This law did not allocate funds for the institution immediately; both the Cookman Institute of Jacksonville, under the auspices of the Freedmen's Aid Society, and the Brown Theological Institute of Tallahassee, organized by the African Methodist Episcopal Church, preceded it.
24. Bureau of Census, *Negro Population 1790–1915*, p. 415.
25. Tallahassee *Sentinel*, 12 August 1870, 4 September 1875.
26. *Congressional Globe*, 42d Cong., 3d sess., index.
27. Ibid., 43d Cong., 1st sess., index.
28. Ibid., 42d Cong., 2d sess., p. 3939; Jacksonville *Florida Union*, 12 March 1874.
29. Alrutheus A. Taylor, "Negro Congressmen a Generation After," p. 159.
30. Tallahassee *Sentinel*, 8 October 1870.
31. Commissioner of Lands and Immigration, *Sixth Annual Report*, p. 70.
32. *Tenth Census of the United States*, 1880, 1:378.
33. George E. Pozzetta, "Florida's Minorities, 1870–1910: A Comparative Approach."
34. *Tenth Census of the United States*, 1880.
35. Richardson, *Negro in the Reconstruction of Florida*, pp. 205–6.
36. Florida *House Journal* 1869, appendix, pp. 2–3; ibid., 1875, appendix, pp. 37–38.
37. Jacksonville *Daily Florida Union*, 3 October 1876; Florida *House Journal* 1877, appendix, p. 33.
38. Richardson, *Negro in the Reconstruction of Florida*, pp. 207–8.
39. Ibid., p. 208.
40. Florida *House Journal* 1877, appendix, p. 7.
41. R. H. Gamble to B. E. Tucker, 23 July 1870, in Comptroller's Letter Book.
42. Richardson, *Negro in the Reconstruction of Florida*, p. 212.
43. Florida *House Journal* 1874, appendix, p. 100; Jacksonville *Daily Florida Union*, 24 January 1876.
44. Florida *House Journal* 1877, appendix, p. 6.
45. Horace Mann Bond, "Social and Economic Forces in Alabama Reconstruction," reprinted in *Reconstruction: An Anthology of Revisionist Writings*, ed. Stampp and Litwack, pp. 370–404; Vernon L. Wharton, *The Negro in Mississippi*, passim.

Chapter 5. Southern Strategy Begins

1. See, for example, Henry, "Radical Republican Race Policy Toward the Negro During Reconstruction," passim; Patrick Riddleberger, "The Radicals' Abandonment of the Negro during Reconstruction."
2. Thomas B. Alexander, "Persistent Whiggery in the Confederate South, 1860–1877."
3. Ralph A. Wooster, "An Analysis of the Membership of the Secession Conventions in the Lower South"; Wooster, "The Florida Secession Convention."
4. T. Harry Williams, ed., *Hayes: Diary of a President, 1875–1881*, p. 164.
5. C. Vann Woodward, in *Reunion and Reaction: The Compromise of 1877 and the End of Reconstruction*, indicates his view that an underlying series of economic and social issues were involved, especially federal support for building the Texas and Pacific Railroad.
6. Shofner, *Nor Is It Over Yet*, p. 339.
7. Ibid., pp. 310–11.
8. Other important Republicans watching Florida's role during the dispute besides Chandler were Francis Barlow of New York, Gen. Lew Wallace of Indiana, John Kasson of Iowa, and former Gov. Edward F. Noyes of Ohio.
9. New York *Herald*, 20 November 1876.
10. Marcellus Stearns to William E. Chandler, 24 December 1876, Chandler Papers.
11. Samuel B. McLin to Chandler, 24 December 1876, ibid.
12. Stearns to Thomas Osborn, 21 February 1877, ibid.
13. Tallahassee *Weekly Floridian*, 2 January, 3 April 1877.
14. Jacksonville *Florida Times Union*, 4 January 1877.
15. Clayton Cowgill to Chandler, 11 January 1877, Chandler Papers.
16. Jacksonville *Florida Sun*, 4 January 1877.
17. Alexander Crummell to J. W. Cromwell, 25 April 1877, Crummell Papers.
18. Tallahassee *Weekly Floridian*, 10 July 1877.
19. Jacksonville *Daily Sun and Press*, 30 June 1877.
20. Tallahassee *Weekly Floridian*, 10 July 1877.
21. See Florida *Senate Journal* (1877), pp. 7–9; Florida *Assembly Journal* (1877), pp. 4–5.
22. Florida *Assembly Journal* (1877), pp. 70–72, 94–95.
23. Ibid., p. 6; Florida *Senate Journal* (1877), pp. 9–10.
24. Shofner, *Nor Is It Over Yet*, p. 57.
25. Klingman, *Josiah Walls*.
26. Florida *Senate Journal* (1879), pp. 75–76; Florida *Assembly Journal* (1879), pp. 51–52.
27. Florida *Assembly Journal* (1877), p. 123.
28. Florida *Senate Journal* (1877), pp. 124–25.
29. Ibid.
30. Charles E. Dyke, Jr., to R. B. Ballard, 12 February 1877, Drew Letter Book.

Chapter 6. Shaping Dissent and the Search for Order

1. William E. Chandler to James G. Blaine, 2 October 1882, Chandler Papers.
2. New York *World*, 29 May 1884, quoted in John M. Dobson, *Politics in the Gilded Age: A New Perspective on Reform*, p. 87.
3. E. E. Schattschneider, *Party Government*, passim.
4. John Tyler, Jr., to John Sherman, 26 December 1878, Sherman Papers; Wallace, *Carpetbag Rule*, pp. 329–34, claimed that Conover accepted Stearns's bribe and pulled out of the 1876 governor's race only when he failed to receive a bribe from the Democrats to stay in.
5. F. E. Humphreys to Chandler, 20 July 1877, Chandler Papers.
6. Jerrell H. Shofner, "Fraud and Intimidation in the Florida Election of 1876."
7. Thomas Settle to Chandler, 11 February 1878, Chandler Papers.
8. Leonard Dennis to Chandler, 17 May, 1 October 1879, ibid.
9. W. G. Stewart to Chandler, 10 March 1879, ibid.
10. J. Willis Menard to Chandler, 14 March 1883, 27 November 1882, ibid.
11. Clayton Cowgill to Chandler, 11 February 1879, ibid.
12. The term "half breed" refers to those partisan Republicans opposed to the "stalwarts," who backed Grant. The half breeds turned to Blaine for leadership. They hoped that by electing their candidate president, they could enjoy a full share of the spoils that Grant's supporters had had during his previous two terms in the White House.
13. Martin to Chandler, 4 February 1880, Chandler Papers.
14. Dennis to Chandler, 18 March 1880, ibid.
15. Martin to Chandler, 4 April 1880, ibid.
16. Dennis to Chandler, 8 April 1880, ibid.
17. Jacksonville *Florida Times Union*, 10 May 1880; R. W. Rute to Lee Crandall, 18 May 1880, Chandler Papers. Crandall was the secretary of the National Greenback Labor Party.
18. *Minutes of the Republican National Nominating Convention* (1880), passim.
19. See Tallahassee *Weekly Floridian*, 27 July 1878, for the first district's nominating convention at Monticello.
20. Samuel Cox, *Three Decades of Federal Legislation*.
21. Arthur wanted, however, to reverse Hayes's policy, somewhat. Though Hayes applauded the collapse of southern Republicanism, Arthur attempted to rebuild it. He continually urged southern Republicans to cooperate in their campaigns, but in Florida the party seemed unable to foster true conciliation among its factions.
22. James Bell to Chandler, 5 October 1880, Chandler Papers.
23. Rute (citing Humphreys) to Crandall, 18 May 1880, ibid.
24. Gainesville *Weekly Bee*, 18, 25 August 1882; Cowgill to Chandler, 24 October 1882, Chandler Papers.
25. Rute to Crandall, 18 May 1880, Chandler Papers.
26. Menard to Chandler, 10 October, 27 November 1882, ibid.
27. C. Vann Woodward, *Origins of the New South, 1877–1913*, pp. 76–81.
28. Timothy Thomas Fortune, *Black and White: Land, Labor, and Politics in the Old South*, p. 132.

29. Jacksonville *Florida Times-Union*, 6 February 1884; Fernandina *Mirror*, 9 February 1884.
30. See J. Morgan Kousser, *The Shaping of Southern Politics: Suffrage Restriction and the Establishment of the One-Party South, 1880–1910*, pp. 139–81, for disfranchising conventions held throughout the South.
31. Jacksonville *Florida Times-Union*, 6 February 1884.
32. R. W. Rute to Lee Crandall, 27 February 1884, Sanford Papers.
33. Edward C. Williamson, "Independentism: A Challenge to the Florida Democracy of 1884."
34. Eldridge R. Collins, "The Florida Constitution of 1885," p. 15.
35. Tallahassee *Weekly Floridian*, 5 April 1881.
36. Palatka *Daily News*, 6 June 1884.
37. "Independent Platform and Record of the Candidates," Charles Lewis Papers, MSS Box 15.
38. Williamson, "Independentism," p. 138.
39. Jacksonville *Florida Journal*, 16, 19 June 1884.
40. Fernandina *Mirror*, 12 July 1884.
41. Tallahassee *Land of Flowers*, 29 July 1884.
42. Jacksonville *Florida Journal*, 14 July 1884.
43. Williamson, "Independentism," p. 141.
44. Jacksonville *Florida Times-Union*, 4 November 1884.
45. Tallahassee *Economist*, n.d., quoted in Jacksonville *Florida Times-Union*, 2 July 1884.
46. Tallahassee *Weekly Floridian*, 29 July 1884.
47. W. D. Bloxham, "The Disston Sale and the State Finances," P. K. Yonge Library of Florida History.
48. Williamson, "Independentism," pp. 151, 153.
49. Supposedly, Frank Pope killed a former schoolteacher, who had whipped him; ibid., p. 154.
50. Ibid., p. 153.
51. Jacksonville *Florida Times-Union*, 4 September 1884; Jacksonville *Florida Journal*, 28 August 1884.
52. Jacksonville *Florida Times-Union*, 2 September 1884.
53. Ibid., 10 September 1884.
54. S. H. Adams to Sanford, 16 September 1884, Sanford Papers.
55. Jacksonville *Florida Times-Union*, 19 September 1884.
56. Fernandina *Mirror*, 18 October 1884.
57. Tallahassee *Land of Flowers*, 20 September 1884.
58. Williamson, "Independentism," p. 148.
59. Both Williamson ("Independentism") and Kousser (*The Shaping of Southern Politics*) suggest that Perry's victory over Pope was close. Given the census data of 1885 showing more than 250,000 people in the state, it was. On the other hand, compared with most previous elections in Florida, Pope lost by a substantial margin.
60. Williamson, "Independentism," p. 156.

Chapter 7. Republicanism in the Solid South

1. Cleveland's entry into the White House did not produce a wholesale turnover in political power or appointments, although the president had more than 100,000 patronage positions at his disposal. Indeed, Democrats were angered by Cleveland's reluctance to turn out competent Republicans in federal jobs. On the other hand, Republicans threatened Cleveland with a revival of the Tenure of Office Act, which had brought down Andrew Johnson. Few expected the threats of impeachment to be carried out. See Mayer, *The Republican Party, 1854–1966,* pp. 209–13.

2. Ibid., p. 210.
3. Ibid., pp. 210–11.
4. Kousser, *The Shaping of Southern Politics,* p. 93.
5. Edward N. Akin, "When a Minority Becomes the Majority: Blacks in Jacksonville Politics, 1887–1907."
6. Kousser, *The Shaping of Southern Politics,* p. 94, demonstrates statistically that most Negro Republicans and white Independents did oppose the constitutional convention issue. Pope, however, was an anti-Bourbon Democrat; as the Independent candidate for governor he supported a revised constitution.
7. Collins, "The Florida Constitution of 1885," appendix.
8. Tallahassee *Weekly Floridian,* 4 July 1882.
9. Letter by "Leon," Jacksonville *Florida Times-Union,* 5 February 1882.
10. Ibid., 25 July 1885.
11. *Journal of the Proceedings of the Constitutional Convention of the State of Florida Which Convened at the Capitol, at Tallahassee, on Tuesday, June 9, 1885* (Tallahassee, 1885), pp. 346, 348–49, 361–62.
12. Ibid., pp. 402–4, 361–62.
13. See Kousser, *The Shaping of Southern Politics,* table 4.6, p. 97.
14. *1885 Convention Journal,* pp. 409–12.
15. Ibid., pp. 108, 228, 311–12.
16. Florida *Senate Journal* (1887), p. 943.
17. Florida *Acts and Resolutions,* pp. 52–66.
18. Florida *House Journal,* pp. 910–11.
19. Kousser, *The Shaping of Southern Politics,* p. 99.
20. Ibid., pp. 99–100.
21. Akin, "When a Minority Becomes the Majority," passim.
22. Florida *House Journal* (1889), pp. 591, 832–85, 995–1000; Florida *Senate Journal* (1889), pp. 766–67.
23. Jacksonville *Florida Times-Union,* 5, 6, 23 November 1889.
24. See Kathryn T. Abby, "Florida Versus the Principles of Populism, 1896–1911"; Samuel Proctor, "The National Farmers' Alliance of 1890 and Its 'Ocala Demands,'"; Wayne Flynt, *Duncan Upshaw Fletcher: Dixie's Reluctant Progressive,* pp. 10–23.
25. V. J. Shipman to Joseph E. Lee, 18 April 1882, Lee Papers; Tallahassee *Weekly Floridian,* 18 September 1888.
26. Jacksonville *Florida Times-Union,* 3, 6 August 1888.

27. Tallahassee *Weekly Floridian,* 23 October 1888; Jacksonville *Florida Times-Union,* 27 July 1888.
28. Jacksonville *Florida Times-Union,* 9 July, 27 April 1888.
29. Ibid., 10 May 1889.
30. Ibid., 26 June, 7 August 1888. See also Edward C. Williamson, *Florida Politics in the Gilded Age, 1877–1893,* pp. 154–55.
31. Juno *Tropical Sun,* (day not cited) 1892, quoted in James A. Mead, "The Populist Party in Florida," p. 13.
32. Ocala *Banner,* 2 May 1890.
33. Orange City *Times,* 6 September 1890. This paper was still pro-Republican at the time.
34. Woodward, *Origins of the New South,* pp. 254–55; George B. Tindall, *The Disruption of the Solid South,* p. 14.
35. Williamson, *Florida Politics in the Gilded Age,* p. 171.
36. Orange City *Times,* 23 April 1892.
37. Akin, "When a Minority Becomes the Majority," p. 127.
38. Jacksonville *Florida Times-Union,* 5 April 1887.
39. Akin, "When a Minority Beomes a Majority," p. 127.
40. Ibid., p. 130; T. Frederick Davis, *History of Jacksonville, Florida and Vicinity, 1513 to 1924,* p. 299.
41. Davis, *History of Jacksonville,* pp. 299–300.
42. Jacksonville, *Florida Times-Union,* 15 November 1888.
43. Ibid., 10 April 1889.
44. Akin, "When a Minority Becomes the Majority," pp. 138–39.
45. *Senate Documents,* 62d Cong., 2d sess., no. 876, "Extracts from the Journal of the United States Senate in all cases of Impeachment Presented by the House of Representatives, 1798–1904," p. 451; hereafter cited as *Senate Document 876.*
46. Arthur Odlin to William Eaton Chandler, 9 December 1893, Chandler Papers.
47. *Senate Document 876.*
48. Odlin to Chandler, 27 December 1893, Chandler Papers.
49. Eagan to Chandler, 1 March 1894, ibid.
50. Jonathan Stripling to Chandler, 6 April 1894, ibid.
51. Stripling to Chandler, 17 April 1894, ibid.
52. John H. Flagg to Chandler, 9 April 1894, ibid.
53. Jacksonville *Florida Times-Union,* 28 May, 9 July 1896.
54. Biographical sketches of George Allen and Edward Gunby in Rowland H. Rerick, *Memoirs of Florida,* 2: 410–11, 539–50.
55. Jacksonville *Florida Times-Union,* 16 January 1896.
56. Ibid., 28 May 1896.
57. Ibid., 3 September 1896.
58. Tindall, *Disruption of the Solid South,* pp. 16–17.
59. Jacksonville *Florida Times-Union,* 3, 6 September 1896.

Chapter 8. Presidential Republicanism in Florida

1. Robert Marcus, *The Grand Old Party: Political Structure in the Gilded Age, 1880–1896*, p. 251.
2. Richard Hofstadter, *The Age of Reform*, p. 234.
3. Marcus, *The Grand Old Party*, p. 253.
4. See E. E. Morrison, ed., *The Letters of Theodore Roosevelt*, 7: 421n.
5. Theodore Roosevelt to Robert G. Rhett, 10 November 1902, ibid., p. 321. For a fuller explanation of Roosevelt's policy as president, see Richard B. Sherman, *The Republican Party and Black America: From McKinley to Hoover, 1896–1933*, pp. 23–51.
6. Isaiah Williams, "Biographical Sketch of Joseph E. Lee."
7. George M. Green, "Florida Politics and Socialism at the Crossroads of the Progressive Era," pp. 49–50; see also Green, "Republicans, Bull Moose, and Negroes in Florida, 1912."
8. Jacksonville *Florida Times-Union*, 7 February 1912.
9. Green, "Republicans, Bull Moose, and Negroes," p. 157.
10. Ibid.
11. Ibid., pp. 157, 159.
12. Tampa *Morning Tribune*, 9 June 1912.
13. A survey of the Miami newspapers during the time that Roosevelt visited on vacation indicates no reaction to the Palatka meeting.
14. Roosevelt eventually was forced to send a letter, widely circulated, to Julien Harris, son of author Joel Chandler Harris, explaining that southern blacks were less capable than northern blacks. The full text of the letter appears in Morrison, ed., *Letters of Theodore Roosevelt*, 7: 584–90. For a fuller explanation of Anderson's activity, see George Mowry, "The South and the Progressive Lily White Party of 1912"; Anderson to Roosevelt, 30 July 1912, Roosevelt Papers.
15. New York *Times*, 4 August 1912.
16. Green, "Republicans, Bull Moose, and Negroes," p. 162.
17. It is impossible to tell how many Florida Negroes voted for Taft, Roosevelt, or Wilson in 1912, though there were some 89,000 blacks of voting age in the state. The state did not begin canvassing primary campaigns until 1913. See *13th Census of the United States (1910)*, Statistics for Florida, p. 591; Allen Morris, *Florida Handbook, 1977–1978*, p. 468. As late as 1923, state party chairman Daniel Gerow claimed that Negroes were welcome in the Republican party. See Gerow to James G. Gavin, 19 December 1923, Gavin Papers.
18. *The Regular Recognized Republican Party of Florida*, pp. 8–13.
19. Wayne Flynt, *Cracker Messiah: Governor Sidney J. Catts of Florida*, pp. 40–61.
20. C. Vann Woodward, *Tom Watson: Agrarian Rebel*, passim.
21. Charlton W. Tebeau, *A History of Florida*, p. 364.
22. *The Regular Recognized Republican Party of Florida*, p. 12.
23. Ibid., p. 13.

24. *State ex rel Merrill v. Gerow* (85 So), pp. 144–46, Case 1,211, Division of Archives, History, and Records Management, Tallahassee.
25. Ibid. The opinion was rendered on 13 May 1920.
26. George Bean to members, state central committee, 15 March 1924, ibid.
27. Bean to Gavin, 19 March 1924, ibid.
28. Interviews with Elvey Callaway and R. E. Burchard.
29. Ibid.; Glenn B. Skipper to Gavin, 9 April 1928, Gavin Papers.
30. Callaway and Burchard interviews.
31. Callaway insists that Skipper appealed directly to the Ku Klux Klan for financial support. While it cannot be documented, it would not have been unlikely, considering the Klan's anti-Catholic position.
32. Bean to Republicans of Florida, 18 April 1928, Gavin Papers.
33. Interview with Callaway; Daytona Beach *Weekly Journal,* 9 May 1928.
34. Bean to Republicans of Florida, 18 April 1928, Gavin Papers.
35. Ibid.
36. Neither Callaway nor Burchard remembers Negroes at the 1928 state convention, nor are there references to Negroes participating in Howey's campaign. For a general discussion of blacks in the 1928 presidential campaign, see Sherman, *The Republican Party and Black America,* pp. 224–51.
37. Daytona Beach *Morning Journal,* 9 May 1928.
38. Ibid., 9, 10 May 1928.
39. Daytona Beach *Morning Journal,* 9 May 1928.
40. Ibid.
41. Ibid.; interview with Callaway.
42. Ibid.
43. Platform adopted by the Republican State Convention, 10 May 1928, Howey file.
44. Interview with Callaway; A. F. Knotts diary.
45. Interview with Callaway; Daytona Beach *Times,* 5 May 1928, in Howey file; Tampa *Southern Highways* (October 1928): 6. A careful reading of the extant Florida newspapers for 1928 indicates no recorded instance in which Howey attacked Smith's religion or supported John Roach Stratton's anti-Catholic fulminations.
46. Personal platform of W. J. Howey, Howey file; Miami *Herald,* 2 November 1928.
47. Herbert J. Doherty, "Florida and the Presidential Election of 1928."
48. Suwannee *Democrat,* 21, 28 September 1928, in Samuel Stubbs Talbert, "Treatment of the Presidential Campaign of 1928 by the Florida Press," p. 127.
49. *Report of the Secretary of the State of Florida, 1 January 1927–31 December 1928.*
50. Robert Bentley to Bert Dosh, 10 October 1928, Dosh Papers.
51. Miami *Herald,* 2 November 1928.
52. Tampa *Tribune,* n.d., in Bradford County *Telegraph,* 5 October 1928.
53. Miami *Herald,* 2 November 1928; Jacksonville *Florida Times-Union,* n.d., Howey file; *Report of the Secretary of State, 1928.*
54. St. Petersburg *Times,* 9 November 1928.

55. *Report of the Secretary of State, 1928.*
56. Ibid.; St. Petersburg *Times,* 9 November 1928.
57. Winter Haven, Auburndale, and Lake Alfred Tri-City *Times,* 11 November 1928, reported that Howey's success would mean "a thorough and complete Republican organization, from the precinct up, and will also mean complete county tickets and a state ticket in the field in 1930."

Chapter 9. Two-Party Vision, One-Party Reality

1. Tebeau, *A History of Florida,* pp. 377–92.
2. Stuart Mandel, "The Republican Party in Florida," p. 12. Mandel identifies Howey as an amateur politician because he never held a federal position in Florida.
3. Tampa *Tribune,* 13 April 1930, Jacksonville *Florida Times-Union,* 13 April 1930, Miami *Florida State Republican,* 9 April 1930, in Howey file. The Howey group included Peter Miller, Jacksonville collector of internal revenue, George Wentworth of Pensacola, John Shares of Daytona Beach, Charles Hildreth of Live Oak, Charles Pearce of Miami, Terrell Smith of Lakeland, S. P. Peacock of Tampa, R. E. Lee Pryor of Tampa, and A. F. Knotts of Yankeetown.
4. Interview with Elvey E. Callaway, 29 December 1973; Knotts diary.
5. Both Knotts and Skipper announced prior to the state GOP convention in Orlando in 1932, and announcements in their behalf appeared before April in the Jacksonville *Florida Beacon.*
6. Jacksonville *Florida Beacon,* 29 April 1932.
7. Ibid., 8 July 1932.
8. The Democratic state committee adopted its platform on 22 July 1932. The Republicans claimed that it was mainly Howey's 1928 platform, slightly revised; ibid., 29 July 1932.
9. Ibid., 29 April 1932.
10. Ibid.
11. Ibid. Although none, including Howey, was elected in North Florida, the gubernatorial candidate polled more votes there in 1932 than in 1928.
12. Gainesville *Sun,* n.d. See Jacksonville *Florida Beacon,* 29 July 1932.
13. Jacksonville *Florida Beacon,* 9 September 1932.
14. A one-week itinerary exemplifies Howey's commitment to campaigning in North Florida: August 17, Perry and Pensacola; August 18, Perry; August 19, Milton, Crestview, Pensacola; August 20, DeFuniak Springs, Careyville, Bonifay and Chipley; August 21, Panama City; August 22, Port St. Joe, Appalachicola, Wewahitchka, Bristol, Blountstown, and Marianna; August 23, Campbelltown, Graceville, and Marianna; August 24, Chattahoochee, Quincy, Havana, and Tallahassee; ibid., 12 August 1932.
15. Ibid., 12 August 1932.
16. Merlin G. Cox, "David Sholtz: New Deal Governor of Florida."
17. Jacksonville *Florida Beacon,* 9 September 1932. The charges were never substantiated by Howey, nor is there any record of Sholtz's alleged financial difficulties in any Volusia County court.

18. Ibid.
19. Ibid., 1 July 1932.
20. Cox, "David Sholtz," p. 143.
21. Jacksonville *Florida Beacon,* 19 August 1932.
22. Ernest Amos to James Hodges, 17 October 1932, Hodges to J. P. Newell, 18 October 1932, Box 154, Hodges Papers.
23. Edward Ball was an active supporter of Herbert Hoover and continued to support Republican candidates. Ball was a major stockholder in the *Florida Beacon.* See Hodges to George B. Hilles, 4 November 1935, ibid.
24. Jacksonville *Florida Beacon,* 12 August 1932.
25. Ibid.
26. Allen Morris, *The Florida Handbook, 1963–1964,* pp. 198–206.
27. See biographical sketch, Umatilla *Times,* 8 June 1932, in Howey file. Howey's businesses in Florida included the W. J. Howey Co., Ridge Holding Co., Orange Belt Securities, and Howey Hotel Co. He served as president and chairman of the board, or director, of Tavares and Gulf Rail Road, Bankers National Life Insurance Co., Howey Building and Loan Exchange, and Florida Citrus Exchange.
28. Jacksonville *Florida Beacon,* 27 January 1933.

Chapter 10. Primaries and Patronage, 1932–1952

1. Jacksonville *Florida Beacon* October 1935. Following the 1928 campaign, contributions to the *Florida Beacon* fell and publication dates varied. On several occasions throughout the 1930s the pro-GOP newspaper appeared only once a month.
2. William C. Havard, ed., *The Changing Politics of the South,* p. 708.
3. Ibid., table 10, p. 111.
4. Jacksonville *Florida Beacon,* November 1935.
5. Harry Wells to Fred M. Vause, 28 April 1938, Box 98, Hodges Papers.
6. James B. Hodges to Wells, 29 April 1938, ibid.
7. Jacksonville *Florida Beacon,* October 1935.
8. Ibid., July 1935.
9. Ibid., August 1935.
10. Ibid.
11. Ibid., May 1936.
12. Ibid., June 1933.
13. Ibid., October 1935.
14. Interview with Elvey Callaway, Bristol, Florida, 29 December 1973.
15. Tallahassee *Daily Democrat,* 27 May 1937.
16. Mandel, "The Republican Party in Florida," p. 29.
17. Ibid., p. 35.
18. Ibid., p. 32.
19. Republican Party 1952 file, Mrs. William G. ("Bobbie") James Papers. Mrs. James was appointed party historian by Governor Claude R. Kirk in 1966.
20. Tampa *Morning Tribune,* 3 December 1952.
21. Gainesville *Daily Sun,* 25 February 1952.

22. "Minutes of the Grass Roots Republican Committee of Florida," Republican Party 1952 file, Mrs. William G. (Bobbie) James Papers.
23. Quoted in open letter to members, State Committee, 19 April 1952, ibid.
24. Ibid.
25. Ibid.
26. W. R. Briggs to Pearl Yeager, 26 April 1952, Republican Party 1952 file, ibid.
27. Quoted in open letter to members, State Committee, 13 May 1952; "Fellow Republicans of Florida," 21 May 1952; both in Republican Party 1952 file, ibid.

Chapter 11. The New Breed and the Old Problem

1. There have been several studies outlining the emergence of southern Republicanism in the twentieth century. Among the more useful are Monroe Lee Billington, *The Political South in the Twentieth Century;* Alan F. Westin, ed., *The Uses of Power: Seven Cases in American Politics;* and John G. Topping, Jr., et al., *Southern Republicanism and the New South.*
2. *U.S. News and World Report,* 22 October 1962, p. 61; quoted in Tindall, *The Disruption of the Solid South,* p. 57.
3. Billington, *The Political South,* pp. 145–46.
4. Palm Beach County *Sun-Sentinel,* 30 December 1965.
5. Ibid., 27 December 1965.
6. Ibid.
7. Interviews with William G. James and Harold Stayman. Because of the fact that the Young Republican Trust Fund's early activity took place in relative secrecy, there are no written records available for much of the group's history. I am indebted to William and Bobbie James and to Hal Stayman for filling in so many of the details of the early group's activity.
8. Interview with Stayman, 27 May 1975. The lunch was held at the Robin Hood Inn, Miami Beach. Stayman claims that no one in the Trust Fund conceived of Kirk's success prior to the 1966 nomination of Robert King High by Florida Democrats.
9. The conspiracy idea was Hal Stayman's. None of the members of the Republican state committee prior to Bill Murfin's nomination for party chairman realized what Nerguard or Stayman was doing. One member of the committee, R. E. Burchard of LaBelle, remembers only that Stayman wanted him to oppose Tom Fairfield Brown during their first meetings. Only before the Tampa meeting did Burchard know that Charles Holley was not going to be the only anti-Brown candidate for party chairman. Interview with R. E. Burchard.
10. Bill James, Bobbie James, and Hal Stayman were all reluctant to suggest that Tom Brown personally stole money from Florida Republicans. Helene Morris was more open in her charges of corruption. See Tom Fairfield Brown file, James Papers.
11. Tom Fairfield Brown to Members of the Republican state executive commit-

tee, county chairmen, and vice-chairmen, 4 May 1966, Tom Fairfield Brown file, James Papers.

12. Ibid. The audit was prepared by the St. Petersburg accounting firm of Tornwall, Lang, and Lee. Brown noted that the report was filed late with the Florida attorney general's office because Mrs. Morris was unwilling "to furnish requested information to accountants for the state executive committee" (ibid.).

13. This issue was an important one in helping to create lasting dissension between Congressman Cramer's Pinellas County organization and the other factions in the Republican Party. None of the members of the Young Republican Trust Fund came from Pinellas County.

14. Interviews with Stayman. This meeting between the trust fund representatives and Alexander was so secret that other members of the fund never knew it took place. See interviews with William G. and Bobbie James.

15. William Murfin file, James Papers.

16. Tallahassee *Democrat,* 19 June 1966.

17. Ibid., 26 May 1966.

18. Few Republicans have argued that Claude R. Kirk could have beaten Haydon Burns if the incumbent governor had won the nomination instead of High.

19. Kirk had left American Heritage Life Insurance Company of Jacksonville in 1964, the same year he ran against Holland for the U.S. Senate seat. Even his closest friends at the time refused to support him. Ashley Verlander, president of American Heritage Life, sponsored the press conference in Jacksonville during which Kirk first announced his campaign against Holland. Nonetheless, Verlander contributed to the Democratic senior senator's campaign. Interview with Ashley T. Verlander.

20. After the election, ex-Governor Burns stated that though he did not campaign actively for Kirk against High, he permitted his own staff members to do so. Tallahassee *Democrat,* 9 November 1966.

21. Ibid., 27 May, 23 July, 14 August 1966; Miami *News,* 6 November 1966.

22. The 1966 state elections were the first under the new state election law requiring that state executive committees return filing fees to candidates. The result was that an extra $200,000 to $300,000 was made available to GOP candidates, including Kirk.

23. During the years that Governor Kirk was in office, Republican party leaders often felt that he refused to cooperate with them because he owed his election to Democrats who crossed over to vote for him. See interviews with Pat Dodson, Stayman, and Bill and Bobbie James. See also Galen A. Irwin, "Florida Gubernatorial Election of 1966: A Look at Transitions"; he concluded that Democrats "decided the election" and that the most remarkable fact was High's poor showing, even in Florida's larger counties. Malcolm Johnson, political analyst for the Tallahassee *Democrat,* reported that High's campaign was damaged by the light voter turnout and the fact that he could not make Kirk into the same kind of political villain that he had been able to do with Haydon Burns. See Tallahassee *Democrat,* 10 November 1966.

24. Tallahassee *Democrat,* 6 November 1966.

25. Ibid., 7 November 1966.

Chapter 12. The Kirk Years

1. Palm Beach County *Sun-Sentinel*, 4 January 1967; Tallahassee *Democrat*, 3 January 1967.
2. Palm Beach County *Sun-Sentinel*, 4 January 1967.
3. The full text of Governor Kirk's inaugural speech was carried in many of the state's newspapers. The following references to the speech come from the Palm Beach *Post*, 4 January 1967.
4. Ibid.
5. Palm Beach County *Sun-Sentinel*, 4 January 1967.
6. Palm Beach *Post*, 4 January 1967. George Wackenhut was qualified to head the new state crime commission. He had been with the FBI in Atlanta and Indianapolis investigating criminal and political security matters before resigning to head his own firm in 1954. He also served on several crime-related advisory boards under previous Democratic administrations in Florida. See Tallahassee *Democrat*, 3 January 1967.
7. See materials on the Governor's Club, especially "The Governor's Club Articles of Association," and "Report to the House Elections Committee by Special Staff Assistant," James Papers.
8. Jacksonville *Florida Times-Union*, 8 October 1967.
9. Quoted in Neal R. Pierce, *The Megastates of America: People, Politics and Power in the Ten Great States*, p. 465.
10. Florida *House Journal* (1967).
11. Interview with William G. James. James pointed out that Fred Schultz, speaker of the house, had refused to push for the salary increases until the Republican members had guaranteed Governor Kirk's support.
12. Florida *House Journal* (1969), pp. 176–77; Florida *Senate Journal* (1969), p. 117.
13. Florida *House Journal* (1969), p. 218.
14. Ibid., p. 255.
15. Ibid.
16. Interview with William James. James described one instance in which Senator Gurney approached him to urge that GOP state legislators oppose salary increases. James told Gurney that legislative salaries would be reduced when congressional salaries would also be reduced.
17. Pierce, *The Megastates of America*, p. 465. Kirk's travel expenses were a special burden on the Florida GOP. The expense ledgers of the state executive committee indicate that in 1968 rental for the governor's Lear jet alone ran to more than $90,000. See Republican state executive committee financial statement file, James Papers.
18. Tampa *Tribune*, 27 April 1969; Florida *House Journal* (1969), p. 256.
19. Florida *Senate Journal* (1969), p. 117; Florida *House Journal* (1969), p. 256.
20. Interview with Pat Dodson.
21. Ibid.
22. Appointments, Executive Orders, Proclamations, Speeches, 1968–71, Kirk Files.
23. *Time*, 16 February 1968.

24. Interview with Pat Dodson.
25. Interview with William James; Fort Lauderdale *News and Sun-Sentinel,* 2 June 1968. See also letter of apology, Nathaniel Reed to William James, 4 June 1968, and a letter of thanks, William C. Cramer to James, 28 June 1968, Republican executive committee file, James Papers.
26. Interview with William James.
27. Ibid.
28. Miami *Herald,* 26 March 1968.
29. Robert C. DeYoung to Republican legislators, 26 March 1968, Republican state executive committee, 1968 file, James Papers.
30. R. E. Burchard to all members of the Republican state executive committee of Florida, n.d., ibid.
31. Palm Beach *Post,* 27 March 1968.
32. Interview with William James; Fort Lauderdale *News,* 28 March 1968.
33. News releases, 5 April 1968, Republican state executive committee 1968 file, James Papers.
34. *Florida Republican Challenger,* 15 September 1968.
35. David R. Colburn and Richard K. Scher, "Florida Gubernatorial Politics since the Brown Decision." Colburn and Scher point out that Collins blocked more drastic anti-integration measures, including interposition, creation of a private school system, and prosecution of teachers who worked in integrated schools, desired by the Florida legislature. In 1959 he opposed thirty-three such anti-integration bills alone.
36. Miami *Herald,* 5 May 1968.
37. Palm Beach *Post-Times,* 5 May 1968.
38. *Florida Republican Challenger,* June 1968.
39. Press release, 8 April 1968, MSS Box 10B 3, Collins Papers.
40. Miami *Herald,* 17 December 1967.
41. Interviews with William James and Pat Dodson.
42. Arthur O. White, *Florida's Crisis in Public Education: Changing Patterns of Leadership,* pp. 1–24.
43. Ibid., p. 31.
44. See chronology of the entire school crisis, Miami *Herald,* 19 October 1967.
45. Orlando *Sentinel,* 4 June 1967.
46. White, *Florida's Crisis in Public Education,* p. 35. All levels of public education were affected by the veto, including plans for Florida International University in Miami and the University of North Florida at Jacksonville, a million-dollar program for industrial training, and junior college expansion. Only the Democrats, opposing Kirk in the legislature by extending their session, prevented financial ruin.
47. Pensacola *News-Journal,* 20 August 1967.
48. White, *Florida's Crisis in Public Education,* p. 41.
49. Claude R. Kirk, Jr., to William James, 11 October 1967, Republican Party 1967 file, James Papers.
50. "Toward Excellence: Changing Concepts for Education in Florida," *A Report by the Governor's Commission for Quality Education to Governor Claude R. Kirk, Jr.*
51. White, *Florida's Crisis in Public Education,* p. 58.

52. Ibid., pp. 67, 69.
53. Ibid., p. 64.
54. Interview with Pat Dodson.
55. Interview with Harold Stayman, Palm Beach, 27 May 1975.

References

Contemporaneous Sources

Letters and papers

American Missionary Association. Correspondence and Reports. Dilliard University, New Orleans. Microfilm copy, P. K. Yonge Library of Florida History, University of Florida, Gainesville.
Attorney General's Appointments Papers. Diplomatic, Legal, Fiscal Branch. National Archives, Washington.
Bloxham, W. D. "The Disston Sale and the State Finances." P. K. Yonge Library of Florida History, University of Florida, Gainesville.
Chandler, William Eaton. Papers. Library of Congress, Washington.
Collins, LeRoy. Papers. University of South Florida Library, Tampa.
Comptroller's Letterbook, April 21, 1870–May 5, 1871. Florida State Library, Tallahassee.
Cory, J., Jr. Letter. P. K. Yonge Library of Florida History, University of Florida, Gainesville.
Crummell, Alexander. Papers. Microfilm copy, University of Florida, Gainesville.
Davidson, Robert M. Letter. P. K. Yonge Library of Florida History, University of Florida, Gainesville.
Dosh, Bert. Papers. P. K. Yonge Library of Florida History, University of Florida, Gainesville.
Drew, George F. Letterbook. Florida State Library, Tallahassee.
Fleming, Francis P. Papers. Florida Historical Society, University of South Florida, Tampa.
Gavin, James. Papers. Florida State Library, Tallahassee.
Governor's Letterbook. Florida State Library, Tallahassee.
Hart, A. B. Papers. P. K. Yonge Library of Florida History, University of Florida, Gainesville.
Hart, Ossian B. Biographical sketch. Florida Historical Society, University of South Florida, Tampa.
Hodges, James B. Papers. P. K. Yonge Library of Florida History, University of Florida, Gainesville.
Howey, William J. File. Microfilm, P. K. Yonge Library of Florida History, University of Florida, Gainesville.

James, Garth. Papers. In possession of William Childers, Gainesville, Florida.
James, Mrs. William G. (Bobbie). Papers. In possession of Mrs. William G. James, Delray Beach, Florida.
Johnson, Andrew. Papers. Library of Congress, Washington. Microfilm copy, University of Florida Library, Gainesville.
Kirk, Claude R., Jr. Files. University of South Florida Library, Tampa.
Knotts, A. F. Diary. 1928. In possession of Eugene Knotts, Yankeetown, Florida.
Lee, Joseph E. Papers. Joseph E. Lee Community Center, Jacksonville, Florida.
L'Engle, E. M. Papers. Southern Historical Collection, University of North Carolina, Chapel Hill. Microfilm copy, P. K. Yonge Library of Florida History, University of Florida, Gainesville.
Lewis, Charles. Papers. P. K. Yonge Library of Florida History, University of Florida, Gainesville.
Lincoln, Abraham. Papers. Library of Congress, Washington.
Minutes of the Republican Nominating Convention (1880). University of Florida, Gainesville.
Roosevelt, Theodore. Papers. Library of Congress, Washington.
Ruffin-Roulhac-Hamilton. Papers. Southern Historical Collection, University of North Carolina, Chapel Hill.
Sanford, Henry Shelton. Papers. Sanford. Microfilm copy, P. K. Yonge Library of Florida History, University of Florida, Gainesville.
Sherman, John G. Papers. Library of Congress, Washington.
Union-Republican Club of Jacksonville. Proceedings. Florida. Florida Historical Society, University of South Florida, Tampa.
Yulee, David L. Papers. P. K. Yonge Library of Florida History, University of Florida, Gainesville.

United States documents

U.S. Bureau of the Census. *Eighth Census of the United States.* 1860.
U.S. Bureau of the Census. *Tenth Census of the United States.* 1880.
U.S. Bureau of Census. *Negro Population, 1790–1915.* Washington, 1918.
U.S. Congress. *Congressional Globe.* 38th Cong., 1st sess.; 42d Cong., 2d sess.; 43d Cong., 1st sess.
U.S. Congress, House of Representatives. *House Executive Documents,* 38th Cong., 2d sess., no. 18; *House Miscellaneous Documents,* 42d Cong., 2d sess., no. 34, 45th Cong., 3d sess., pt. iv, 46th Cong., 1st sess., no. 26.
U.S. Congress, Senate. *Senate Reports.* 38th Cong., 1st sess., no. 876.
United States. *Statutes at Large of the United States.* 1870, 1871.

State of Florida documents

Acts and Resolutions, 1869, 1887.
Commissioner of Lands and Immigration. *Sixth Annual Report.* Tallahassee, 1874.
House Journals, 1869–1969.
Journal of the Proceedings of the Constitutional Convention of the State of Florida

References

Begun and Held at the Capitol, at Tallahassee on Monday, January 20th, 1868. Tallahassee: Edward M. Cheney, 1868.

Journal of the Proceedings of the Constitutional Convention of the State of Florida Which Convened at the Capitol, at Tallahassee, on Tuesday, June 9, 1885. Tallahassee: N. N. Bowen, 1885.

Report of the Secretary of State of Florida, January 1, 1905–December 31, 1905, and *January 1, 1927– December 31, 1928.*

Senate Journals, 1872–1969.

State ex rel Merrill v. Gerow (85 So), Case no. 1,211. Division of Archives, History, and Records Management, Tallahassee.

Superintendent of Public Instruction. *Reports, 1869–80.*

"Toward Excellence: Changing Concepts for Education in Florida." *A Report by the Governor's Commission for Quality Education to Governor Claude R. Kirk, Jr.* Tallahassee: State of Florida, 1967.

Newspapers

Bradford County *Telegraph*.
Chicago *Tribune*.
Daytona Beach *Morning Journal*.
Daytona Beach *Times*.
Daytona Beach *Weekly Journal*.
Fernandina *Mirror*.
The Florida Republican Challenger.
Fort Lauderdale *News*.
Fort Lauderdale *News and Sun-Sentinel*.
Gainesville *Daily Sun*.
Gainesville *New Era*.
Gainesville *Weekly Bee*.
Jacksonville *Daily Sun and Press*.
Jacksonville *Florida Beacon*.
Jacksonville *The Florida Journal*.
Jacksonville *Florida Sun*.
Jacksonville *Florida Times-Union*.
Jacksonville *Daily Florida Union*.
Miami *Florida State Republican*.
Miami *Herald*.
Miami *News*.
Ocala *Banner*.
New York *Times*.
New York *Tribune*.
New York *Herald*.
Orange City *Times*.
Orlando *Sentinel*.
Palatka *Daily News*.
Palm Beach *Post*.
Palm Beach *Post-Times*.
Palm Beach County *Sun-Sentinel*.
Pensacola *News-Journal*.
St. Petersburg *Times*.
Tallahassee *Democrat*.
Tallahassee *Land of Flowers*.
Tallahassee *Sentinel*.
Tallahassee *Weekly Floridian*.
Tampa *Morning Tribune*.
Umatilla *Times*.
Winter Haven, Auburndale, and Lake Alfred *Tri-City Times*.

Interviews

R. E. Burchard, LaBelle, May 26, 1975.
Elvey E. Callaway, Bristol, December 29, 1973.
Pat Dodson, Pensacola, August 19, 1973.
Mr. and Mrs. William G. James, Delray Beach, January 4, 1974.
Mr. and Mrs. Euguene T. Knotts, Yankeetown, December 27, 1973.

Harold Stayman, Tampa, April 19, 1974; Palm Beach, May 27, 1975.
Ashley T. Verlander, Jacksonville, March 4, 1974.

Secondary Works

Abbey, Kathryn T. *Florida, Land of Change*. Chapel Hill: University of North Carolina Press, 1941.

———. "Florida Versus the Principles of Populism, 1896–1911." *Journal of Southern History* 4 (November 1938): 462–75.

Ackerman, Philip D. "Florida Reconstruction from Walker through Reed." Master's thesis, University of Florida, 1948.

Akin, Edward N. "When a Minority Becomes the Majority: Blacks in Jacksonville Politics, 1887–1907." *Florida Historical Quarterly* 53 (October 1974): 123–45.

Alexander, Thomas B. "Persistent Whiggery in the Confederate South, 1860–1877." *Journal of Southern History* 27 (August 1961): 305–29.

The American Annual Cyclopedia and Register of Important Events, 1861–1874. New York: D. Appleton and Company, 1862–1875.

Basler, Roy P., ed. *The Collected Works of Abraham Lincoln*. 9 vols. New Brunswick, N.J.: Rutgers University Press, 1955.

Billington, Monroe Lee. *The Political South in the Twentieth Century*. New York: Charles Scribner's Sons, 1975.

Bond, Horace Mann. "Social and Economic Forces in Alabama Reconstruction." *Journal of Negro History* 23 (July 1938).

Colburn, David R., and Richard K. Scher. "Florida Gubernatorial Politics since the Brown Decision." Paper, annual meeting, Florida College Teachers of History, Daytona Beach, 1974.

Collins, Eldridge R. "The Florida Constitution of 1885." Master's thesis, University of Florida, 1939.

Conkling, Alfred R. *The Life and Letters of Roscoe Conkling, Orator, Statesman, Advocate*. New York: C. L. Webster and Company, 1889.

Cox, Merlin G. "David Sholtz: New Deal Governor of Florida." *Florida Historical Quarterly* 42 (October 1964): 142–52.

Cox, Samuel S. *Three Decades of Federal Legislation*. Providence: J. A. & R. A. Reid, 1894.

Crandall, Andrew Wallace. *The Early History of the Republican Party, 1854–1856*. Boston: R. G. Badger, 1930.

Davis, T. Frederick. *History of Jacksonville, Florida and Vicinity, 1513 to 1924*. St. Augustine: The Record Company, 1924. Facsimile edition, Gainesville: University of Florida Press, 1964.

Davis, William Watson. *Civil War and Reconstruction in Florida*. New York: Columbia University Press, 1913. Facsimile edition, Gainesville, University of Florida Press, 1964.

Dobson, John M. *Politics in the Gilded Age: A New Perspective on Reform*. New York: Praeger Publishers, 1972.

References

Doherty, Herbert J. "Florida and the Presidential Election of 1928." *Florida Historical Quarterly* 26 (October 1947): 174–86.
Eckenrode, Hamilton J. *The Political History of Virginia During Reconstruction.* Boston: Peter Smith, 1964.
Ewing, Cortez A. M. "Florida Reconstruction Impeachments." *Florida Historical Quarterly* 36 (April 1958): 299–318.
Fels, Rendig. "American Business Cycles, 1867–79." *American Economic Review* 61 (June 1951): 325–49.
Fenlon, Paul E. "The Notorious Swepson-Littlefield Fraud: Railroad Financing in Florida, 1868–1871." *Florida Historical Quarterly* 32 (April 1954): 231–61.
Foner, Eric. *Free Soil, Free Labor, Free Men: The Ideology of the Republican Party Before the Civil War.* New York: Oxford University Press, 1970.
Fortune, Timothy Thomas. *Black and White: Land, Labor, and Politics in the Old South.* New York: Fords, Howard, and Hulbert, 1884.
Flynt, Wayne. *Cracker Messiah: Governor Sidney J. Catts of Florida.* Baton Rouge: Louisiana State University Press, 1977.
———. *Duncan Upshaw Fletcher: Dixie's Reluctant Progressive.* Tallahassee: Florida State University Press, 1971.
Garner, James W. *Reconstruction in Mississippi.* Boston: Peter Smith, 1964.
Green, George M. "Florida Politics and Socialism at the Crossroads of the Progressive Era." Master's thesis, Florida State University, 1962.
———. "Republicans, Bull Moose, and Negroes in Florida, 1912." *Florida Historical Quarterly* 42 (October 1964): 153–62.
Havard, William C., ed. *The Changing Politics of the South.* Baton Rouge: Louisiana State University Press, 1972.
Henry, G. Selden. "Radical Republican Race Policy Toward the Negro During Reconstruction, 1864–1872," Ph.D. dissertation, Yale University, 1963.
Hofstadter, Richard. *The Age of Reform.* New York: Random House, 1955.
Hume, Richard L. "Membership of the Florida Constitutional Convention of 1868: A Case Study of Republican Factionalism in the Reconstruction South." *Florida Historical Quarterly* 51 (July 1972): 1–21.
Irwin, Galen A. "Florida Gubernatorial Election of 1966: A Look at Transitions." *Governmental Research Bulletin* 5 (January 1968): 1–6.
Johns, John E. *Florida During the Civil War.* Gainesville: University of Florida Press, 1963.
Key, V. O., Jr. *Southern Politics in State and Nation.* New York: Alfred A. Knopf, 1949.
Klingman, Peter D. *Josiah T. Walls: Florida's Black Congressman of Reconstruction.* Gainesville: University Presses of Florida, 1976.
———. "Ring Versus Anti-Ring: Jacksonville Republican Politics, 1870–1875." Paper, Conference on Jacksonville History, Jacksonville, Florida, 1977.
Kousser, J. Morgan. *The Shaping of Southern Politics: Suffrage Restriction and the Establishment of the One-Party South, 1880–1910.* New Haven: Yale University Press, 1974.

Lewis, Elsie M. "The Political Mind of the Negro, 1865–1900." *Journal of Southern History* 21 (May 1955): 189–202.

Litwack, Leon F., and Kenneth M. Stampp, eds. *Reconstruction: An Anthology of Revisionist Writings*. Baton Rouge: Louisiana State University Press, 1969.

Lonn, Ella. *Desertion During the Civil War*. New York: Peter Smith, 1928.

Loving, Rush, Jr. "Ed Ball's Marvelous Old-Style Money Machine." *Fortune* (December 1974): 170–85.

McCormick, Richard P. *The Second American Party System: Party Formation in the Jacksonian Era*. Chapel Hill: University of North Carolina Press, 1966.

Maddex, Jack P., Jr. *Virginia Conservatives, 1867–1879: A Study in Reconstruction Politics*. Chapel Hill: University of North Carolina Press, 1970.

Mandel, Stuart G. "The Republican Party in Florida." Master's thesis, Florida State University, 1968.

Marcus, Robert. *The Grand Old Party: Political Structure in the Gilded Age, 1880–1896*. New York: Oxford University Press, 1971.

Mayer, George H. *The Republican Party, 1854–1966*. 2d ed. New York: Oxford University Press, 1967.

Mead, James A. "The Populist Party in Florida." Master's thesis, Florida Atlantic University, 1971.

Meador, John A. "Florida Political Parties, 1865–1877." Ph.D. dissertation, University of Florida, 1964.

Morris, Allen. *The Florida Handbook, 1963–1964*. Tallahassee: Peninsular Publishing, 1964.

———. *The Florida Handbook, 1977–1978*. Tallahassee, 1978.

Morrison, E. E., ed. *The Letters of Theodore Roosevelt*. 8 vols. Cambridge: Harvard University Press, 1954.

Mowry, George. "The South and the Progressive Lily White Party of 1912." *Journal of Southern History* 6 (May 1940): 237–47.

Nathans, Elizabeth S. *Losing the Peace: Georgia Republicans and Reconstruction, 1865–1871*. Baton Rouge: Louisiana State University Press, 1968.

Owsley, Frank L. *King Cotton Diplomacy*. Chicago: University of Chicago Press, 1931.

Parrish, William E. *Missouri under Radical Rule, 1865–1870*. Columbia: University of Missouri Press, 1965.

Peek, Ralph. "Curbing of Voter Intimidation in Florida, 1871." *Florida Historical Quarterly* 43 (April 1965): 333–48.

Pierce, Neal R. *The Megastates of America: People, Politics, and Power in the Ten Great States*. New York: W. W. Norton Company, 1972.

Polakoff, Keith Ian. *The Politics of Inertia: The Election of 1876 and the End of Reconstruction*. Baton Rouge: Louisiana State University Press, 1973.

Pozzetta, George E. "Florida's Minorities, 1870–1910: A Comparative Approach." Paper, annual meeting, Florida Historical Society, Tallahassee, May 1974.

Proctor, Samuel. "The National Farmers' Alliance of 1890 and Its 'Ocala Demands.'" *Florida Historical Quarterly* 28 (January 1950): 161–81.

Ramsdell, Charles W. *Reconstruction in Texas*. Boston: Peter Smith, 1964.

The Regular Recognized Republican Party of Florida. Pensacola: n.p., 1927.
Reiger, John F. "Deprivation, Disaffection, and Desertion in Confederate Florida." *Florida Historical Quarterly* 48 (January 1970): 279–98.
Rerick, Rowland H. *Memoirs of Florida*. 2 vols. Atlanta: Southern Historical Association, 1902.
Richardson, Joe M. *The Negro in the Reconstruction of Florida, 1865–1877*. Tallahassee: The Florida State University Press, 1965.
Riddleberger, Patrick. "The Radicals' Abandonment of the Negro during Reconstruction." *Journal of Negro History* 65 (April 1960): 88–102.
Schattschneider, E. E. *Party Government*. New York: Farrar and Rinehart, Inc., 1942.
Scher, Richard K., and David Colburn. "Florida Gubernatorial Politics since the Brown Decision." Paper, Florida College Teachers of History, Daytona Beach, 1974.
Sherman, Richard B. *The Republican Party and Black America: From McKinley to Hoover, 1896–1933*. Charlottesville: University Press of Virginia, 1973.
Shofner, Jerrell H. "The Constitution of 1868." *Florida Historical Quarterly* 41 (April 1963): 356–74.
———. "Florida in the Balance: The Electoral Count of 1876." *Florida Historical Quarterly* 46 (October 1968): 122–50.
———. "Fraud and Intimidation in the Florida Election of 1876." *Florida Historical Quarterly* 42 (April 1964): 321–30.
———. *Nor Is It Over Yet: Florida in the Era of Reconstruction, 1863–1877*. Gainesville: University Presses of Florida, 1974.
Smith, George Winston. "Carpetbag Imperialism in Florida, 1862–1868." *Florida Historical Quarterly* 27 (January 1949): 260–99.
Stampp, Kenneth M. and Leon F. Litwack, eds. *Reconstruction: An Anthology of Revisionist Writings*. Baton Rouge: Louisiana State University Press, 1969.
Stover, John F. *The Railroads of the South*. Chapel Hill: University of North Carolina Press, 1955.
Sumner, Charles. "Clemency and Common Sense: A Curiosity of Literature; With a Moral." *Atlantic Monthly* (December 1865).
Swinney, Everett. "Enforcing the Fifteenth Amendment, 1870–1877." *Journal of Southern History* 28 (May 1962): 202–18.
Talbert, Samuel Stubbs. "Treatment of the Presidential Campaign of 1928 by the Florida Press," Master's thesis, University of Florida, 1947.
Tampa Southern Highways 1 (October 1928).
Taylor, Alrutheus A. "Negro Congressmen a Generation After." *Journal of Negro History* 7 (April 1922): 127–171.
Tebeau, Charlton W. *A History of Florida*. Miami: University of Miami Press, 1971.
Thompson, C. Mildred. *Reconstruction in Georgia: Economic, Social and Political, 1865–1872*. Boston: Peter Smith, 1964.
Time, February 16, 1968.
Tindall, George B. *The Disruption of the Solid South*. Athens: University of Georgia Press, 1972.
Topping, John G., Jr., et al. *Southern Republicanism and the New South*. Cambridge:

Republicans for Progress and the Ripon Society, 1966.
Trelease, Allen W. *White Terror: The Ku Klux Klan Conspiracy and Southern Reconstruction.* New York: Harper and Row, 1971.
U.S. News and World Report, October 22, 1968.
Wallace, John. *Carpetbag Rule in Florida.* Jacksonville: Da Costa Printing and Publishing Company, 1888. Facsimile edition, Gainesville: University of Florida Press, 1964.
Wesley, Charles. *Negro Labor in the United States.* New York: Vanguard Press, 1927.
Westin, Alan F., ed. *The Uses of Power: Seven Cases in American Politics.* New York: Harcourt Brace Jovanovich, 1962.
Wharton, Vernon L. *The Negro in Mississippi.* Chapel Hill: University of North Carolina Press, 1947.
White, Arthur O. *Florida's Crisis in Public Education: Changing Patterns of Leadership.* Gainesville: University Presses of Florida, 1975.
Williams, Isaiah, III. "Biographical Sketch of Joseph E. Lee." Manuscript, Joseph E. Lee Community Center, Jacksonville, Florida.
Williams, T. Harry, ed. *Hayes: Diary of a President, 1875–1881.* New York: D. McKay Company, 1964.
Williamson, Edward C. *Florida Politics in the Gilded Age, 1877–1893.* Gainesville: University Presses of Florida, 1976.
———. "Independentism: A Challenge to the Florida Democracy of 1884." *Florida Historical Quarterly* 27 (October 1949):131–56.
Woodward, C. Vann. *Origins of the New South, 1877–1913.* Baton Rouge: Louisiana State University Press, 1951.
———. *Reunion and Reaction: The Compromise of 1877 and the End of Reconstruction.* Boston: Little, Brown, and Company, 1951.
———. *Tom Watson: Agrarian Rebel.* New York: Oxford University Press, 1963.
Wooster, Ralph A. "An Analysis of the Membership of the Secession Conventions in the Lower South." *Journal of Southern History* 24 (November 1958): 360–68.
———. "The Florida Secession Convention." *Florida Historical Quarterly* 36 (1957): 373–85.

Index

Adams, S. H., on Bisbee-Walls debate, 92
Agnew, Spiro T., 176
Akerman, Emory, 145
Alden, George, 31
Alexander, G. Harrold: and political patronage, 147–48; as state Republican party chairman, 164
Allen, George, 91, 109–10, 116–17
Allison, Abraham K., 6; indicted for electoral fraud (1870), 53
Alston, Charles, as black Progressive Republican leader, 115–16
American Independent party, 194
American Missionary Society, 55
Amos, Ernest, 137
Anderson, Herbert L., as state Progressive party chairman, 114–15
Arthur, Chester A., 94; as vice-presidential nominee (1880), 82
Askew, Reubin, 188

Bafalis, L. A., 169
Bainum, Noah, 123
Baker, Henry, and 1885 constitutional convention, 96
Baker v. Carr, 172
Ball, Edward, 138, 145, 166
Balmer, George, 191
Barnes, William, 90; and 1868 congressional campaign, 32–33
Battle of Olustee (1864), 5, 14
Bean, George, 131, 141; and defense of political patronage, 118–20; as national Republican committeeman (1918), 117
Bell, James, 83
Bent, James, 148
Biggers, C. Garland, 148
Billings, Liberty, 19, 21–22, 37
Bisbee, Horatio, Jr., 29–30, 79, 102; as congressional candidate, 83–93; debate with Josiah Walls (1884), 91–92; and Union-Republican Club, 18
"Black and Tans," 101, 108–11
Blackburn, Edward, 174
Blaine, James G.: and 1880 presidential campaign, 80; and 1884 presidential campaign, 94
Bloxham, William, 77, 84–85; and 1870 gubernatorial election, 35–37, 44, 68, 110; and Florida Liberal-Republican party, 42; as governor, 79
Booth, John, 149
Booth, John Wilkes, 28
Boutwell, George, 20
Bovay, Alvin, 4
Boylston, Gray, 180
Bradford, Clarence, 125
Bremer, Arthur, 191
Britten, Fred, 123
Brown, B. Gratz, 42
Brown, Sidney, 121
Brown, Tom Fairfield, as state Republican Party chairman, 155, 157–61, 163
Browne, Jefferson B., 118

225

Brown v. Board of Education, 181
Bryan, William Jennings, 112
Bryant, Farris, 184
Burbridge, John, 104–5
Burchard, R. E., 121, 179
Burke, Herbert, 147, 179
Burns, Haydon, 182, 184, 189, 192; farewell address of, 168; and 1966 gubernatorial campaign, 165–67

Call, Wilkinson, 73, 77, 107
Callaway, Elvey E.: and 1936 gubernatorial campaign, 145; and political patronage, 121, 131–32, 143, 146
Carleton, Doyle, 120, 126, 137
Carswell, G. Harrold, 191–93
Carter, Jimmy, 191, 194
Catts, Sidney, 116–17, 120
Challen, James, and 1885 constitutional convention, 96
Chandler, H. W., and 1885 constitutional convention, 96
Chandler, William E., 46, 69, 76, 94
Chase, Salmon P., 12–13
Cheney, Edward, and Union-Republican Club, 18, 29, 88, 91
Chiles, Lawton, 183, 194
Chipley, WIlliam, 90
Christian, Floyd, 186
Chubb, Henry S., 116
"Citizens' Ticket" (1887), 104
Civil Rights Act of 1964, 158
Clarendon Hotel (Daytona Beach), 123–24
Cleveland, Grover, and 1884 presidential campaign, 94
Cobb, S. C., 90
Coker, J. P., 51–52
Collins, LeRoy, and 1968 senatorial campaign, 181–82
Commission on Marine Science and Technology. *See* Florida Commission on Marine Science and Technology

"Compromise of 1877," 68
Conant, Sherman, 29, 30
Cone, Fred, 145
Conkling, Roscoe, 10
Conover, Simon B., 72, 77–78, 81; and 1872 senatorial election, 40; and 1876 gubernatorial campaign, 45; and 1878 congressional campaign, 82; and 1885 constitutional convention, 96
Constans, Phil, 186
Constitutional conventions: of 1868, 20–25; of 1885, 95–98
Cooke and Company, J., 30–31
Coolidge, Calvin, 118
Coombs, James, 116
Cooper, C. M., 106
Corselius, Robert, 160–61
Cowgill, Clayton, and Union-Republican Club, 18, 80, 84
Cox, James, 117
Cox, Minnie, 113
Cramer, William, 176; and 1970 senatorial campaign, 147, 157, 163, 178–79, 182, 191–93
Crawford, John, indicted for electoral fraud (1870), 53
Crist, Robert C., 113
Crittenden, Duke, 189
Crum, William, 113
Crummel, Alexander, 71
Cubberly, Fred, 123

Dancy, William, 104–5
Daniel, J. J., 105
Davidson, Robert, 82, 84
Day, Samuel, 41; and 1870 gubernatorial election, 35–39
Democratic Party: factions within, 100; 1932 presidential platform, 134
"DemoKirks," 167, 174
Dennis, Leonard, 73, 83, 88–89, 91; and 1880 presidential campaign, 81
Denny, Gage, 125

Index

Department of Natural Resources. *See* Florida Department of Natural Resources
Department of Transportation. *See* Florida Department of Transportation
DeYoung, Robert, 178
Dickinson, John Q., 51
"Dixiecrats," 142, 156
Dodson, Pat, 175
Doughtery, Charles, 88
Douglas, Stephen A., 3
Douglass, Frederick, 72
Dover, J. Williard, 160
Drew, George F.: and 1876 gubernatorial campaign, 45–46, 68–69; as governor, 70, 72–73; and political patronage, 74–75
Dyke, Charles, 37, 39, 74

Eagan, Dennis, 79, 88, 91, 110
Eckerd, Jack: and 1970 gubernatorial campaign, 187–88; and 1974 senatorial campaign, 193–94
Eisenhower, Dwight D., 148–49
Elections bill, federal (1890), 103–4
Enforcement Acts of 1871, 50, 52–53

Faircloth, Earl, and 1968 senatorial campaign, 182
Farmers' Alliance, 100
Ferguson, Thomas, 175, 178
Finlayson, John, 51
Finley, Jesse J., and 1882 congressional election, 83
Fischer, Thelma, 160
Flagler, Henry, 100
Fleming, Francis, as governor, 105–6
Fletcher, Duncan, 132
Florida Board of Canvassers, and 1876 presidential election, 47
Florida Board of Law Enforcement, 171
Florida Commission on Marine Science and Technology, 187

Florida Constitutional Revision Commission (1966), 168–70
Florida Department of Natural Resources, 187
Florida Department of Transportation, 187
Florida Development Commission, 178
Florida Direct Tax Commission, 12
Florida Dispatch Company, 87
Florida Education Association (FEA), 184, 186–87
Florida Federation of Women Republicans, 148
Florida Federation of Young Republican Clubs, 160–61
Florida Highway Commission, 145
Florida International University, 187
Florida Public Service Commission, 193
Florida Railroad Company, 85
Florida Republican Party. *See* Republican Party, in Florida
Florida Securities and Exchange Commission, 137
Florida State Agricultural College for Negroes, 56
Foor, Samuel, 182
Ford, Gerald R., 191
Fortune, Emanuel, 32, 52
Fortune, Timothy T., on black Independent movement, 84–85
Fowler, C. Lewis, 149
Freedmen's Bureau. *See* U.S. Bureau of Refugees, Freedmen, and Abandoned Lands
Frey, Lou, 147, 160–61, 163

Gamble, Robert, 28, 31
Garfield, James A., and 1880 presidential campaign, 68, 82
Garrison, Florence, 148
Gavin, James, 119
Gerow, Daniel T., 117. *See also Merrill v. Gerow*

Gibbs, Jonathan C., 41; and 1885 constitutional convention, 96–97; as superintendent of public instruction, 27, 33, 55–56; and Union-Republican Club, 18
Gilbert, Abijah, 39, 45, 77; and political patronage, 29
Gleason, William, 30–32, 34, 43
Gober, William, 145
Goldner, Herman, and 1968 senatorial campaign, 181–82
Goldwater, Barry, and 1964 presidential campaign, 155, 157–58
"Governor's Club," and political fundraising, 171
Grady, John, 194
Graham, Robert, 194
Grange movement, in Florida, 85–86, 160
Grant, Ulysses S.: and 1872 presidential campaign, 44; and 1880 presidential campaign, 30, 65, 80, 94; and Liberal-Republicans, 42
Grass Roots Republican Committee (1952), 148–50
Greeley, Horace, and 1872 presidential campaign, 42–44, 66
Greeley, Jonathan C.: and 1885 constitutional convention, 96–97; and Independent Party, 88; and Union-Republican Club, 18, 88
Grizzle, Mary, 177
Gunby, Edward, and 1896 gubernatorial election, 109–11
Gurney, Edward J., 147, 157, 163, 181–82; decline of political career, 193

Hagen, Fred, 160
Hamilton, Charles, and 1868 congressional campaign, 32–33; and 1870 congressional campaign, 30, 41
Hammond, Mary Lou, 164

Hanley, Glenn, 125
Hanley, Joseph, 77
Hanna, Mark, and 1896 presidential election, 94, 112
Hardee, Cary, and 1932 senatorial campaign, 136, 138
Harding, Warren G., 117–18
Harmon, Henry, 41
Harris, E. J., 32
Harris, John, 142–43; and political patronage, 132, 136, 139, 141, 144–45
Harrison, Benjamin, and federal elections legislation, 103
Hart, Ossian B.: and 1872 gubernatorial campaign, 19, 21–22, 24, 29–30, 39, 43–44, 58; and Union-Republican Club, 17–18
Hathaway, Fons, 120
Hawkins, Paula, 177; and 1974 senatorial campaign, 193–94; and 1980 senatorial election, 195
Hay, John, and Florida Unionists, 13
Hayes, Rutherford B., 65; and 1876 presidential election, 46, 66, 69; and political patronage, 71
Haynesworth, Clement, 192
Hessee, Charles, 166
Hewitt, Abram, as Tilden's campaign manager (1876), 46–47
High, Robert King, and 1966 gubernatorial campaign, 165–67, 171, 182, 189
Hines, F. G., 89
Hodges, James B., 134, 137, 143
Holland, J. J., 102
Holland, Rush, 123
Holland, Spessard, 149, 183, 191
Holley, Charles, 160–64
Hoover, Herbert: and 1932 presidential campaign, 120, 126–27, 133, 138; and Reconstruction Finance Corporation, 133
"Hoovervilles," 138

Index

Hostleter, Dorie, 164
Howey, William J., 120, 125–26, 131–32, 138, 141–43; and 1932 gubernatorial campaign, 126, 134–39
Hull, Noble, 79
Humphrey, Hubert, and 1968 presidential election, 181, 190
Humphreys, F. E., 78, 83

Independent Party, in Florida, 87–93
International Hotel (Tampa), 164
Irwin, Auburn, 32

"Jackson County War" (1869), 51
Jacksonville, Pensacola, and Mobile Railroad, 33–35
James, Garth, 31–32
James, William, 160, 177
Jenkins, Horatio, 22, 31, 41
Johnson, Andrew: and Proclamation of Amnesty and Pardon, 9; and Reconstruction Acts of 1867, 14–15, 27; Reconstruction policies of, 8–10
Johnson, Beth, 173–74
Johnson, Lyndon B., 156, 165, 176, 182
John's Restaurant (Bartow), 160
Jones, Charles, and 1884 presidential campaign, 78, 89–90, 99, 101
Jones, Charles W., 45
Jones, Clarence, 171

Kansas-Nebraska Act of 1854, 3, 4
Kendrick, William, indictment for electoral fraud, 53
Kennedy, John F., 156
Key, David M., 68
Key West, First National Bank of, 109
King, Martin Luther, Jr., 181
Kirk, Claude R., 165, 172–80, 189, 192, 195; on education, 183–87; inaugural address (1967), 168–71; and 1966 gubernatorial campaign, 166–67; and 1970 gubernatorial campaign, 187–88; and political patronage, 175; and "war on crime," 170–71
Knight, Alva A., 43, 79
Knights of Labor, 102, 104
Knott, William, 116–17
Knotts, A. F., 121, 131–32, 140
Kolby, Thelma, 148
Ku Klux Klan, and 1928 elections, 121; in Florida, 50–53

Lafferty, Richard, 182
"Lafferty's Fables," 182
Lane, David, 173
Lawless, J. J., 125
Lawson, W. C., 124
League of Nations, 111
Lee, Joseph, 48, 110, 114–15; and 1884 Republican national convention, 88
Lewey, Mathew, 109
Lewis, Charles, and 1885 constitutional convention, 96
Liberal-Republican Party (1872), 42–44
Lieb, Helen, 148
"Lily Whites," 101, 108–11
Lincoln, Abraham: early relations with Republican Party, 4–5; on Harriet Beecher Stowe, 71
Lincoln Brotherhood, 19
Littlefield, Milton, 34
Locke, E. O., 90, 106
Lodge, Henry Cabot, and "force bill" of 1890, 103
Loeb, William, 175–76
Logan, John, 94
Long, Huey, 141
Long, T. W., 74
Lowry, Sumter, 181
Loyal League of America, 19, 21

MacArthur, Douglas, 142, 148–49

McCaskill, Alexander, indicted for electoral fraud, 53
McClellan, George, and 1864 presidential election, 12
McCook, Edward, 6
McHarg, Ormsby, 115
McKinnon, A. D., and 1882 congressional campaign, 84
McKinnon, D. L., and 1882 congressional campaign, 90
McLin, Samuel, 70
Mann, Austin S., 96–97
Mansfield, Bill, 183
Marble, Manton, 69
Martin, John, 136; and 1932 gubernatorial campaign, 138
Martin, Malachi, 90; and 1880 presidential campaign, 80–81
Marvin, William, Jr., 8, 99
Matfield, Erika, 185
Mathews, John, 169, 173
Maytag, Marquita, 161
Meacham, Robert, 41, 43, 74, 82
Meade, George, 22
Menard, J. Willis: and black Independents, 85; and 1882 congressional campaign, 84; and political patronage, 79–80
Merrill, J. Eugene, 117–18. *See also* Merrill v. Gerow
Merrill v. Gerow, 118–21
Meyers, Paul, 165
Military Reconstruction Acts of 1867, 8
Miller, Frank, 127
Miller, H. E., 97
Miller, Peter, 121, 143
Milton, John, 6, 11
Missouri Compromise (1820), 3
Mitchell, Henry, 107, 108
Mitchell, John, 190
Mixon, Wayne, 194
Montgomery, David, 31
Morris, Helene, 162, 177

Muldrew, Richard, 165, 171
"Mule team." *See* Loyal League of America
Murfin, William L., 164, 176, 178–80, 189; and defense of George Wackenhut, 171; and Florida Young Republican Trust Fund, 163; and 1968 presidential campaign, 180–81

National Community Relations Board, 181
National Education Association, 184; in Florida, 55–56
National Federation of Young Republicans, 160
National League of Cities, 182
Nerguard, Charles, 161, 163
"New Deal," 141
Nixon, Richard M., 176, 180, 191; at Gov. Claude Kirk's inauguration, 175; and 1968 presidential election, 181, 190

Odlin, Arthur, 106
O'Neal, Michael, 176
Osborn, Thomas, 19, 21–22, 27, 29, 32, 39–41; and Florida Freedmen's Bureau, 17
Osgood, A. B., 74

Pasco, Samuel, 107, 108; and 1885 constitutional convention, 96
Peabody Fund, 59; and education in Florida, 55
Pearce, Charles, 27, 33, 54, 72; and 1870 congressional campaign, 41
Pensacola and Atlantic Railroad, 90
Perry, Charles, 187
Perry, Edward A., and 1884 gubernatorial campaign, 89–93
Petty, Samuel, and 1885 constitutional convention, 96
Phillips, Kevin, and the "southern strategy," 190–95

Index

Pinchback, P. B. S., 72
Pitts, Bayard, 144
Pitts, Clarence, 121
Pomeroy Circular (1864), 13
Pope, Frank, and 1884 gubernatorial campaign, 88
Pope, Verle, 169, 174
Popular sovereignty, 3
Populism, in Florida, 100
Progressive Party (1912), 114
Purcell, J. W., 109
Purman, William, 25, 29; and 1870 congressional campaign, 41; and 1872 congressional campaign, 43; and "Jackson County War," 51

Quay, Mathew, 94

Randall, Edwin, 37, 69; and 1876 elections, 70; and 1885 constitutional convention, 96, 97
Reagan, Ronald, 195
Reconstruction: historical interpretation of, 15–17; myths of, 7–10; as national issue, 8–10
Reconstruction Acts of 1867, 14–15, 17
Reconstruction Finance Corporation, 133
Reed, Don, 169, 173, 176–77, 179
Reed, Harrison, 13, 24, 26, 30–31, 37, 39–40, 57–59, 70; attempted impeachments of, 31–38; and Florida Direct Tax Commission, 12; political style of, 27–28; and Union-Republican Club, 18
Reed, Nathaniel, 177
Reed, Opie, 127
Replogle, J. Leonard, 122, 131–32, 144–45
Republican party, 3–10, 39–42; attacks on Bourbon Democrats, 45–46; congressional representation of, 10; and decentralization, 26; and Democratic racial policies (1932), 138–39; demographic changes in, 157; and electoral fraud, 47–48, 103; establishment of (1854), 3–4; and exclusionary legislation (1885), 98–99; factionalism in, 27, 45, 73–75, 83–93, 108–11; in Florida, and "Come Across" drive (1968), 180–81; and Grass Roots Committee (1952), 148–51; impact of frontier on, 7; impact of 1929 depression on, 130; in Jacksonville (1887–89), 104–6; and leadership changes, 191–95; and League of Nations, 117; and *Merrill v. Gerow*, 118–20; organizational meeting of (1869), 29; political dominance by, 76–77; and political patronage, 78–80; racial attitudes of, 9–10; and Roosevelt-Taft factionalism (1912), 114–16; and state committee, 44; and state legislative elections, 49–50; and state primary issue, 145–51; strategy after 1876, 65–68; strategy after 1932, 141–42; and Watergate, 191; and Young Republicans, 160–66. *See also* "Black and Tans"; "Lily Whites"
—and conventions and meetings: black independent meeting of 1884, 85; constitutional convention of 1885, 95; Tallahassee meeting of 1877, 71–72; state convention of 1928 (Daytona Beach), 120–25
—and elections: of 1872, 42; of 1880, 81–82; of 1884, 88–89; of 1888, 102–3; of 1890, 104; of 1928, 128–29; of 1930, 131; of 1966, 166–67
—platforms: of 1867, 19–20; of 1928, 125; of 1932, 133–34
—and presidential elections: of 1876, 46–47, 70; of 1880, 82; of 1964, 155–58

—during Reconstruction: and economic development, 56–57; and education, 54–56; and financial planning, 58–59; and myths, 7–10; reactions to terrorism, 50–53; and state debt, 60–61; and taxation, 60
Republican Party National Committee, 26
Richards, Daniel, 19, 21–22
Robinson, Solon, 21
Rockefeller, Nelson, 176, 180
Roosevelt, Theodore, 114; and southern Republican policy, 113
Rowe, Hannibal, and 1885 constitutional convention, 96
Rupert, H. G., 150
Rute, R. W., and 1880 congressional campaign, 84

Safire, William, 175–76
Sammis, John, 13; and Florida Direct Tax Commission, 12
San Juan Hotel (Orlando), 132
Saunders, William U., 19, 21; and 1868 congressional campaign, 32–33
Scott, John R., 48, 110
Settle, Thomas, 78
Seymour, Truman, 5, 14
Shaw, George Bernard, 190
Sherman, John, and 1880 presidential campaign, 80
Sherman, Laurence, 123
Sherman, William Tecumseh, 5
Shevin, Robert, 194
Shields, Bill, 164
Shipman, V. J., and 1888 gubernatorial campaign, 101–2
Sholtz, David, and 1932 gubernatorial campaign, 136–38
Shulte, A. W., 148
Skinner, E. F., and 1882 congressional campaign, 84
Skipper, Glenn B., 131, 132; and 1928 elections, 120

Slade, Tom, 179, 185
Smith, Alfred E., 120, 126–27
Smith, C. B., 105
Smith, O. B., 104
Southern Association of Republican Chairmen, 147
Spades, C. C., 148
Stayman, Harold, 160–61, 164, 188
Stearns, Marcellus, 24, 29–30, 36, 58, 71, 73, 77; and Arkansas Commission, 78; and 1872 gubernatorial campaign, 43; and 1876 gubernatorial campaign, 45; and 1876 presidential election, 68–70
Stephens, Ray, 148
Stewart, William J., and political patronage, 79
Stickney, Lyman, 12–13; and Florida Direct Tax Commission, 12
Stillman, John, 110
Stone, Richard, and 1974 senatorial campaign, 194
Stout, F. A., 125
Stowe, Harriet Beecher, 71
"Straightout" Democrats, 104
Stratton, John Roach, 127
Stripling, Jonathan, 108
Sumner, Charles, and radical Reconstruction, 9
Swan, Harry, 148–49
Swayne, Charles, 106–7
Swepson, George, 33–34
Swepson-Littlefield fraud case, 56, 60–61

Taft, Robert A., 148–49
Taft, William Howard, 114
Taylor, Bill, 160
Teapot Dome affair, 118
Thomas, L. E., 189
Thomas, Pat, 167
Thompson, William, 98
Thurmond, J. Strom, 142; and Dixiecrats (1948), 156

Index

Tilden, Samuel J., and 1876 presidential election, 46, 69, 74
Turlington, Ralph, 169
Turnbull, Samuel, 97
Tyler, John, 77–78

Unionist sentiment, in Florida, 11–12
Union party, 27
Union-Republican Club, 17, 19, 29; charter of, 18
U.S. Bureau of Refugees, Freedmen, and Abandoned Lands, 17, 29, 59
U.S. Congress, Joint Committee on Reconstruction, 22

Varn, Wilfred, 161–62, 164
Varnum, John, 32

Wackenhut, George, 170–71
Walker, David S., 8, 25, 36, 57; gubernatorial administration of, 15
Walker, Samuel, 32
Wallace, George C., 158, 175, 176, 182; and 1968 presidential election, 181, 190
Wallace, John, 21, 72, 109
Walls, Josiah T., 16, 27, 33, 41, 48, 57, 73, 89, 111; and 1872 congressional campaign, 43–44; and 1874 congressional election, 44–45; and Independent Party, 88; and Republican factionalism, 83
Walter, Philip, and 1888 elections, 98
Warbritton, Barclay, 124–25
Washington, Booker T., 113
Watergate affair, 191, 193
Watson, J. Thomas, on Florida primary system, 146–47
Weeks, Edmund C., 82, 103, 111
Welch, Adonijah, 30, 39
Wells, David, 160–61, 163
Wentworth, George, 34, 37, 59, 78, 121, 132
Westcott, James, 28
Whig Party, 66–68
White, Pleasant Woodson, indicted for electoral fraud, 53
Williams Hotel (Daytona Beach), 123–24
Wilson, George, 107–8
Wolf, Jim, 175, 178
Wood, Leonard, 117
"Wormley House bargain," 65, 67, 69

Yeager, Pearl, 148
Young, Bill, 147, 177, 179
Young Men's Democratic Clubs, 50
Young Republicans, 145
Young Republicans Trust Fund, 160–64
Yulee, David Levy, 6, 11, 36